YOUNG GIRLS

GISELA KONOPKA is Director of the Center for Youth Development and Research, and Professor of Social Work at the University of Minnesota. She is an international consultant and teacher and the author of 10 books, including *The Adolescent Girl in Conflict* and *Social Group Work: A Helping Process*. Among her special honors are the Distinguished Teacher Award, University of Minnesota, and the highest Merit Award of the Federal Republic of Germany. She is a past president of the American Association of Orthopsychiatry, has been on the Board of Directors of the National Association of Social Workers, and is a member of the Joint Commission on Juvenile Justice Standards, American Bar Association.

YOUNG GIRLS

A PORTRAIT

OF

ADOLESCENCE

GISELA KONOPKA

A SPECTRUM BOOK

PRENTICE-HALL, INC., Englewood Cliffs, New Jersey

Library of Congress Cataloging in Publication Data

Konopka, Gisela.
   Young girls.

   (A Spectrum Book)
   Includes bibliographies and index.
    1. Adolescent girls. 2. Adolescence.
I. Title.
HQ798.K65   301.43'15   75–33014
ISBN 0–13–977215–4
ISBN 0–13–977207–3 pbk.

This book is based on a research project financed by the Lilly Endowment, Inc., of Indianapolis, Indiana.

10 9 8 7 6 5 4 3 2 1

Prentice-Hall International, Inc., *London*
Prentice-Hall of Australia, Pty. Limited, *Sydney*
Prentice-Hall of Canada, Ltd., *Toronto*
Prentice-Hall of India Private Limited, *New Delhi*
Prentice-Hall of Japan, Inc., *Tokyo*
Prentice-Hall of Southeast Asia Private Limited, *Singapore*

*To Young Women
and
to all people with vision,
compassion,
and courage*

CONTENTS

ACKNOWLEDGMENTS

This book represents a small concentration of a monumental effort. Many people participated, and each one put thought and concern into it. My very first thanks go to all the girls, almost 1,000 of them, who allowed us to interview them. They were open and outspoken and many opened up to us their private writings, poems, or diaries. I cannot name each one, but I want them to know that if this book improves services to girls and understanding of girls, it is they who deserve the credit.

My next thanks go to the twenty-six interviewers, all young women, who helped the girls to respond and who also helped me by letting me know how much this experience meant to them. They were ably supported by the nine coordinators in the twelve states in which we interviewed. They are my colleagues and friends and they did a superb job.

Twelve graduate and undergraduate students labored over this rich and vast material, excerpting and analyzing it. Many warm thanks to them.

My very special thanks go to my closest co-researchers, Marion Freeman, who carried the responsibility for organization and did it in a gentle, competent way; Thomas Wick, who used his creative mind to think and rethink the research design, worked on the material, and gave me personal encouragement when I needed it; and Michael Baizerman, who showed deep respect for various approaches to research and contributed generously from his great store of knowledge.

My special thanks go as well to the experts who carried out library research and helped translate Spanish interviews, and to two outstanding researchers, Professor Joseph Eaton and Dr. Rhetta Arter, for their competent consultation.

Many also helped with typing and filing. My thanks go to all of them, especially to Faye Hayes, who combined work in the office with some very sensitive interviewing of girls in rural Minnesota; and to Patricia Noer who worked on this manuscript.

My close friend Dorothy Sheldon read this manuscript carefully and did some editing.

All this work would have been impossible if I had not had extraordinary support from two major organizations:

The *Lilly Endowment, Inc., of Indiana* gave generous financial support, and the three representatives who worked closely with this effort, Richard

Ristine, James Morris, and Susan Wisely, showed such genuine concern and interest in the subject that I felt more than financially supported.

I also want to thank the *University of Minnesota* whose representatives encouraged the study.

Last, but not least, very special thanks go to my husband. He had suffered previously through several of my books, but this time my long hours, writing, thinking, and worrying were particularly burdensome. But his patience endured.

The girls are right: All of us need to be listened to, supported, and loved. Thank you, all of you, who did just this.

PREFACE

*A writer should employ a language
that can pierce the heart
or awaken the mind.*[1]

How I hope I can achieve in this book not only what Edward Dahlberg asks for but something more: the impetus to *act* on the awakened mind *and* the increased sensitivity and compassion. Years ago, with the earnest intensiveness with which only the young can look at us, one of them asked me, "And now that you got older and achieved much, what will you do?" It took me aback—*she* asked me about *my* future hopes. I reflected. My answer: "Just continue, continue learning about and working for and with those whose voices are not heard enough or heard distorted, confused. . . ."

The serious young face nodded and—in my mind—it becomes another one: the gentle, stern, quiet face of the old Kathe Kollwitz, the great artist, whose work constantly called for justice and understanding. I had stood before her when I was only 17 years old, shyly trying to tell her how much her painting had influenced me. Her dark eyes seemed to penetrate my thoughts—no adult had ever listened so deeply to me—and she said "You are young now—so you are full of ideals. Keep those when you get older—most people forget." I heard this warning—it seems to me—all my life. It has accompanied me through a year of work in factories during which I did monotonous labor on machines and saw women struggle to make a living and raise their children; through the then following years at the university when one meal a day had to satisfy physical hunger, but where libraries and thinking were so much more important and exhilarating that hunger could be forgotten; and later again during the desperate struggle against fascist oppression—the horror of defeat, of separation from loved ones, degradation in concentration camps, degradation of a life as refugee. . . . For years I myself was part of the "voiceless" ones, learning constantly the great lesson of "realistic idealism," which means to see the world and human beings as nearly as possible as they really are: good, bad, mean, capable of such great generosity, loving and hating—finding all this in all of them, whether young or old, rich or poor, man or woman,

[1] Letter from Edward Dahlberg to Robert Hutchins in E. Seaver, ed., *Epitaphs of Our Times: The Letters of Edward Dahlberg.* New York: Braziller, 1966.

from whatever nationality, race, creed; yes, and finding all this in myself too. I continued learning about the importance, no, necessity, to keep and have ideals, to know what to strive for, always. The "what is," the reality, had to be as hard and conscious in me as the "what should be," the goal to strive for: justice for all—human understanding and affection.

I have to let the reader know about this personal philosophy, the "screen" through which all my perceptions pass because no one who says anything about other human beings is without such a screen. In trying to look at others and to let them speak so that all of us enhance our understanding, I must be aware of my own "screen." Otherwise I may distort too much of what I hear. I must know that I would *wish* all young people to be idealistic, honest, concerned with justice, but I must try to see them as realistically as possible. Whatever I find may please me or the reader, but it also may not. It is important that we do see the reality. Then—only then—can we, from the goals we cherish, think through what we want and how we want to change ourselves in working with others. This is why I will present the girls' feelings and thoughts without too much interpretation. The last chapter will contain my own conclusions.

This is an inquiry into the reality of young women—adolescent girls, ages 12 through 18, in our time in the United States. This is an attempt to learn how they experience this world, and to learn about their hopes, concerns, and aspirations. The reader may say "You said you are concerned with the voiceless ones. Young people make a lot of noise." Noise does not mean voices. It is a din that frequently hides feelings and thoughts, and it is a din that the adult world often shuts out by closing two opposite doors: One is marked "Dangerous, Nuisance," the other "Marvelous, Ideal, Hope of the Future." Both doors spell "Keep Out." Both keep us from listening. I—with the help of a sensitive staff—tried to listen and to hear individual voices.

It is my hope that this book will help girls themselves, boys, and the adults who come close to them—parents, teachers, youth workers, judges, probation officers—actually all of us to understand better and learn to live and work together with deep respect for the infinite and rich variety in all human beings.

YOUNG GIRLS

PURPOSE, POPULATION, AND METHOD OF THE STUDY

The scientist has no other method than doing his damnedest.[1]

Approximately ten years ago, I did a research project to understand adolescent girls in delinquency institutions. The book resulting from it, *The Adolescent Girl in Conflict*[2] was an attempt to understand girls better who had come into serious conflict with the existing society. In that study, I found, among other characteristics, that the changing cultural position of women had a great impact on the girls, that they were resentful of the "double standard" but saw little hope that anything would change for them. I also learned of the special plight of girls from rejected minorities, Black and American Indian (the study included only Minnesota girls who were in delinquency institutions). There was much self-disapproval among these young women. Far too frequently they had internalized the negative image that others had of them. When I had finished the study, I felt very strongly that I was not only looking at problems all girls have in common in a changing society but also that I would like to have studied a cross section of all adolescent girls.

Ten years have passed since that study and more changes have occurred. It is customary to say that the major changes are technical ones but I do not see it this way. Many major technical changes occurred long ago and had much more impact on the older generation, which moved from the scratchy sounds of a crystal radio to color television and from the simple airplane to jumbo jets. Changes that have occurred within recent years are not that dramatic, and young people today expect technical changes. In fact, it is my contention that nobody is really "shocked" by such changes. The changes that make a strong impact on everyone, young and old alike, are changes in human relations. To me the most significant major change in the last ten years is the worldwide active *self-assertion* of whole groups who previously had accepted comparatively quietly an

[1] P.W. Bridgman, quoted in Abraham Kaplan, *The Conduct of Inquiry*. Scranton, Pa.: Chandler, 1964, p. 27.

[2] Gisela Konopka, *The Adolescent Girl in Conflict*. Englewood Cliffs, N.J.: Prentice-Hall, 1966.

1

inferior status for long periods: various racial groups, women, the poor, youth. It is with this concept of major change that I looked into attitudes, feelings, actions, hopes, and concerns of girls.

> *I am a bottle sealed with feeling*
> *too deep for anyone else.*
> *I am a bottle floating in an eternal ocean*
> *of people trying to help.*
> *I am a bottle keeping my fragile contents inside.*
> *Always afraid of breaking and exposing me.*
> *I am a bottle frail and afraid of the rock.*
> *And afraid of the storm.*
> *For if the storm or rocks burst or cracked me,*
> *I would sink and become part of the ocean.*
> *I am a person in the people of the world.*[3]
>
> JOANNE RHIGER (16, *White, urban*)

The cry to be a person—it is *the* cry of all mankind for centuries for self-assertion, for self-respect. To be *somebody*, not a thing to be used, not just a drop of water unrecognized in the vast sea, not a worm to die unseen—to be a *person!* From ancient times to the present, whole groups of people deprived others of this "personhood" through active and deliberate subjugation, through neglect, through early instillment into the victim that he or she was innately incapable, through ignoring the other's capacities, through disregard for their total being. Whatever the reason for the denial, both the oppressor and the oppressed lost the beauty of their capacity to be a "Mensch," a human being who can be creative, responsive, can work and play, think and feel, be gentle and considerate, in spite of making mistakes and occasionally hurting himself and others. Both sides lost the opportunity to be a "person *in* the people of the world."

Why start an inquiry into the needs, concerns, and aspirations of adolescent girls (they sometimes prefer to be called young women)? Because this struggle for "personhood" is the touchstone of our time. It is not new, but it is spoken about louder than ever, it is worldwide, probably influenced by the enormous spread of communications, and it involves the young who themselves begin to see that they cannot be always just a "pre," a "pre-adult," a preparation, but must take on the specific responsibilities of their age. What are those responsibilities? What do the young women themselves think, feel, want? And what is the responsibility of the adult generation at this time in the history of the "new" continent with a

---

[3] Throughout this book I will quote the girls anonymously. Names are given for poems, with special permission of each girl. Age, ethnic background, and urban, rural, or small town designation is given to emphasize the variety of the population.

democratic intent, 200 years old ("All men are created equal"), that needs more than ever to erase the disastrous dilemma[4] between the ideal of equal acceptance of all and the inhuman heritage of superiority of one group over another, ignorance and greed? There is always fear and puzzlement and conflict between generations. Conflict—if it is worked through—is helpful to progress. A totally static society dies. But a "gap"—the much discussed "generation gap," if it really exists—would also destroy it. There needs to be continuity, communication.

Much of what I looked for in this study probably applies to all young people, men and women alike. Yet, adolescent girls need special understanding because of the newly reawakened awareness by women of their personhood and rapidly changing expectations made of them set against a world of adults that is very ambivalent about this change. Also, most books on adolescence consider girls not at all or only as an afterthought.[5] And teachers, parents and youth workers have expressed to me frequently their confusion and helplessness in working with girls.

How does one gain an understanding of such a varied population? My staff and I struggled to find out what approach to use. Methods of investigation vary among disciplines. In the study of *The Adolescent Girl in Conflict*, I approximated the method of the anthropologists by living with the girls, interacting with them in everyday life. This was possible at the time because I had chosen a very limited population. It was my intent this time to acquire knowledge about as *wide a variety* of girls as possible. I did not want to follow the many authors who had written about youth populations that were limited to one cultural, ethnic, racial, or economic group, yet pretended to talk about the total population.[6]

In sociological research, one often finds information through the use of standardized questionnaires given to a "stratified sample" of a population. This is an efficient method; it saves money; it saves time; it saves staff. It claims to yield accurate information from a few that can be generalized into many. But I cannot see this method as furnishing real insight into needs and aspirations of a vast variety of people. People's opinions and feelings are too different one from the other and they cannot be sampled as one can sample soup by tasting a spoonful. I thought it was necessary to allow the girls to choose what they had to say and to listen to their own reasoning. Imitating the methods of physical scientists in social investigation may sometimes impede understanding. A researcher, Valerius

[4] Gunnar Myrdahl, *The American Dilemma*. New York: Harper, 1944.

[5] This applies even to one of the finest books on adolescents, Erik Erikson's *Childhood and Society*. New York: Norton, 1950.

[6] An example of such is Charles A. Reich, *The Greening of America*. New York: Random House, 1970. Our population included approximately one-half white girls and one-half from minority populations: Black, Chicana, Inuit (Eskimo), American Indian, Oriental, and Puerto Rican.

Michelson, in another applied field, architecture, who used observation as his research tool once wrote:

> If this seems rather unscientific, one has only to be reminded of the disastrous consequences of much of our scientific social planning—with its continuous reliance on statistical data as the sole means of predicting future events. Intuitive paradigms, when applied to the phenomena of life and mind (without question the base of human society), at least respect the essential non-randomness of these phenomena.[7]

I wanted this study to retain the integrity of what the young people were saying, to preserve, as my co-worker, Michael Baizerman said, "The music and the lyrics of what they are talking about." I therefore had to rely on open-ended interviews and the creation of a coding system based on the distribution of actual responses. The advantages of open-ended interviews is that they allow the informant's own frame of reference to shine through rather than imposing one upon her *a priori*. Thus the confidence that I have in my data will not lie upon strict claim of statistical significance. It will rest on my ability to present views of experiences, opinions, and hopes that the girls themselves expressed about issues relevant to them. Since I could not myself interview approximately 1,000 girls, I enlisted the help of additional interviewers. The first interviews, though, were conducted by myself and my co-worker, Marion Freeman. From those initial interviews, we learned about some content areas that seemed especially significant in understanding adolescent girls. In addition, in discussions with people concerned with this subject and based also on published material and my own experience, we added some other themes that we wanted to find out about. We decided that interviewers should bring up those specific areas if they were not introduced spontaneously as part of the interview and if the interviewers thought them appropriate to a particular interview. This left the interviewer room for judgment. It must therefore be understood that not all girls talked about all the themes that I will discuss.

Other data beyond the interviews that influenced the content of the results of my study follow.

1. Group discussions with girls. These discussions were less frequent than the individual interviews, but enabled the girls to argue out opinions with some of their peers, something that was not possible in the individual interview wherein the interviewer was supposed only to be a good listener.

2. Written communications by girls (diaries, poetry, stories) given voluntarily to interviewers by the girls. Because they were spontaneous expressions, these communications provided an intimate insight into the girls' feelings. I have to say that at times I felt I should not write about anything that the girls said and

---

[7] Valerius Michelson, "Towns on the Threshold of Change." Mimeographed paper describing an exhibit and audio-visual presentation in the court of the Architecture Building, University of Minnesota, December 1973.

just let them speak through their poetry. I am aware, though, that their writings are mostly expressions of *feelings* whereas the interviews also included *thinking* through concepts and ideas.

3. Professional writing regarding adolescent girls over the last decade. This search helped us test and enrich our own findings and provided a necessary service to future research, teaching, and practice regarding adolescent girls. The bibliographies following each chapter give a small sample of this material.

4. A survey of popular or "trade" books written over the last decade for adolescent girls and read by them. This survey provided a feeling for the kind of models presented to them in popular publications compared with what had been available in previous decades.

5. A questionnaire to test some of our data was administered to a randomly selected sample of 10 percent of 6,000 4-H young people attending a one-week summer workshop in Washington, D.C., in June–August, 1974. All respondents were female, between 15 and 18 years old, mostly from rural areas. Questions were based on preliminary analysis of our interview data.[8]

6. My own experiences in working for years with adolescent girls. I can neither deny this knowledge nor pretend that all insights yielded were brand new. I will try, though, to indicate where a new dimension is added.

These methods were used to gain information. How was the population chosen? As I said earlier, we could not and I cannot make the claim of a "representative sample." There exists in the literature the term "purposive sample" or "non-probability quota sample." [9] Our selection fits better into this concept. I wanted to get as wide a variety as possible of different population groups existing in the United States. Obviously, to include the total variety would require a much larger study. It is my hope that other researchers will take my findings as a base, raise new questions, and study specific populations. To gain the variety, I first of all tried to find geographical areas in the United States that would provide a variety of populations.

Interviews were held in *Alaska, California, Georgia, Indiana, Kentucky, Massachusetts, Minnesota, Oklahoma, Oregon, Puerto Rico,* and *Texas.* As part of the research design in each geographic area, one central coordinator was asked to find the appropriate girl population and to employ two young women interviewers to do the interviewing. The coordinator was asked to emphasize the ethnic or racial population dominant in her area. She was also instructed to be sure to include the following variety:

Age: The population must include girls 12 through 18 years.

Socio-economic status: The population had to include various economic strata.

Locale: The population must also include urban, suburban, small town, and rural areas.

[8] "Personal Development Opportunities," *Staff Development Newsletter,* University of Minnesota, St. Paul Campus, December 1974.

[9] Pertti Pelto, *Anthropological Research: The Structure of Inquiry.* New York: Harper and Row, 1970, pp. 166–167.

And finally, in each area, about one-third of the girls should be

1. Adjudicated delinquent, institutionalized girls.
2. Girls presently affiliated with youth organizations.
3. Girls not presently affiliated with youth organizations, but not delinquent.

We tried to eliminate the effects of variation in interviewing as much as we could. Although we are sure that male interviewers could have done the work, too, to diminish the variation we used only female interviewers. Interviewers were primarily skilled graduate students, predominantly from social work and psychology. They comprised a variety of racial and ethnic backgrounds. Approximately 100 interviews were conducted in each location, with the exception of Alaska and Puerto Rico. There—because of scarce funds—we could interview only fifty girls each. To insure reasonable standardization of interviewing technique, the central staff prepared and distributed to each location a package of materials that provided complete administrative and procedural instructions. Also Marion Freeman or myself visited each site prior to the interviewing and conducted a two-day interview training session. During that training session, a videotape produced for training interviewers especially for this research was shown and discussed. Interviewers and the coordinator/organizer were asked to keep the interview open-ended, to use their own judgments about whether they wanted to raise questions concerning specific themes, but especially to raise questions framed in general terms so as to ascertain *opinions.*

We knew that girls would spontaneously bring in information of a personal nature, but interviewers were asked to avoid direct personal and private questions. We wanted no invasion of a girl's sense of privacy. It must be said that these suggestions were not always followed. Some interviewers who forgot those instructions did ask personal questions. Others were so anxious to cover as many subjects as possible that they became quite directive and rigid in their approach. If we caught this attitude early enough in the central office by reading the transcribed tapes, we telephoned the organizer to try to correct such approaches in the future. We were not always successful. In general, though, we can say that the interviewers did an unusually sensitive and skilled job.

With the permission of the girl, every interview was tape recorded and ran from 45 to 90 minutes in length. Recorded interviews were transcribed in each of the regional headquarters with the exception of Puerto Rico. The Puerto Rican interviews had been conducted in Spanish and had to be translated through the central office and then transcribed. All transcripts were collected in the general office.

Every interviewer was asked to stress confidentiality with the interviewees and such confidentiality had to be strictly adhered to. Each informant was promised that her identity would not be revealed, except in the case of poetry where special permission was given.

After the interview, comprising usually thirty double-spaced pages, was typed, staff in the central office read each interview carefully, using a coding sheet organized according to the themes that we had developed and adding themes if new ones appeared. This material was then transcribed to McBee cards that identified demographic data without any name at the bottom of each card. It was important that transcription on McBee cards included the girl's exact words, not any summary or interpretation by a reader. In all, we had approximately 15,000 McBee cards, derived from 920 usable interviews, and 20 individuals in group discussions. (Some interviews could not be used because of faulty taping.) After this filing was done, staff again read each McBee card and punched it according to questions I had raised about the content. They then tabulated responses according to frequency. This procedure gave us an organized way of listening to the interviews. During the whole period of the project I myself interviewed girls and read interviews. Yet I could not trust my memory to be sure that I did not remember only what I wanted to hear. For example, perhaps I might be so impressed by the antiwar feelings expressed by girls that I might conclude that the majority considered this theme important. I needed a more objective check whether this response really was as frequently expressed as I thought. My account of the range of ideas will therefore be based on accurate tabulations.

Just as many interviewers stressed, we cannot present a composite picture of *the* American girl. The young women's thoughts and feelings convey to us the *enormous variety of all human beings*. We hear the cries of despair, the expressions of gentle contentment, of pride and humiliation, of glowing hope, of cynicism, of love, hate, of philosophy, and other attitudes. Although no one person is exactly the same as any other, we find some similarities among many of them as well as small subgroups. Perhaps the greatest insight we gained was that this range of opinions and values not only exists but must be accepted. This may be reassuring to those who think they are confronted with a monolithic "new generation"; it may be frightening to those who want everyone to think and be the same. Some similarities, some like emphases could be found. Yet *no generalization will ever apply to any specific girl.* One says it better than I can.

> *I used to be . . .*
> *a grape in a bunch*
> *and all the other*
> *grapes were the same.*
> *But now . . .*
> *I'm an apple, crisp*
> *and fresh, and every*
> *one is different.*
> *My, how life has changed!*
>
> ELAINE CARTER (15, *White, small town*)

To share my insights, to make them useful by presenting ranges of responses, while at the same time preserving the individuality of the girls and the trust they placed in me and my co-workers, is the aim, hope, and concern of this writing. Ideas, opinions, and thoughts are carried by persons, by people of flesh and blood.

> *A poet is someone*
> *Who can feel*
> *A summer evening*
> *When it's winter outside.*
> *Who feels 65 years old*
> *When she's only 16.*
> *Who cries without shedding*
> *a single tear.*
> *Who sees beauty*
> *in hail storms.*
> *And can find more value in a sunset*
> *Than within herself.*
>
> PEARL NESTOR (16, *Inuit, urban*)

Pearl, who wrote this, is slender, dark-haired, of Inuit (Eskimo) parentage. I am not violating any confidence by telling more about her than the others because she wants people to know about her feelings. She is young but she has behind her a life full of hurt, anger, and at times, degradation. She has spent some time in a mental hospital even though she obviously did not belong there. Listen to her about that experience:

> *"You aren't normal, you know,"*
> *The fat nurse said accusing me.*
> *"No, I don't know,"*
> *I said heavily under my breath.*
> *She heard me though, as her neck stretched out*
> *Straining to hear more.*
> *"What is your goal in life?"*
> *"To castrate all the boys in town, and marry the women."*
> *(Not really, just playing a little game.)*
> *She changed the subject because of her uncomfortable position*
> *And fixed her gaze steadily upon my poetry book.*
> *"What's your favorite poem?"*
> *"I Hear America Sighing."*
> *"Isn't it 'I Hear America Singing'?"*
> *"Not the way things are going nowadays,"*
> *Said I in a flat tone.*

The psychos got up for lunch,
    And she stood there directing the line.
I think she felt safer with them.

PEARL NESTOR

What a deep insight Pearl shows into the feelings of others. How she recognizes the fear of the adult, how old she is in spite of her real age. And yet, look at her poem. She can see "beauty in a hail storm," she can "find value in a sunset"—but unfortunately, more value in the sunset than she finds in herself. That is one side of Pearl. There is another one, a wish to become an architect, her new hopes for her life. And she is concerned with others, too.

Somehow Pearl does represent many girls of many backgrounds. Almost all of them respond to the world around them with *personal* statements. All human beings do, but many pretend to be "objective." There is an extraordinary, refreshing honesty in the admission that one sees the world through one's own eyes, colored by whatever one has gone through. There is a tremendous resiliency—although certainly with exceptions—in spite of life experiences which to the outsider often seem totally disastrous.

A 13-year-old, when asked what she would like to shout into the world if she could really do so, said, "To give young people a chance. All of them. Don't be so pessimistic about them."

And a 17-year-old says with quiet insight, "We don't know why we are—I guess sentimental. We don't know why, but we do. We just can't help it. You just have to be patient with us. We go through a lot of changes, and we don't understand ourselves."

BIBLIOGRAPHY

BLUMER, HERBERT, "What is Wrong with Social Theory?" *American Sociological Review*, Vol. 19, August 1953, pp. 3–10.

ERIKSON, ERIK, *Childhood and Society*. New York: Norton, 1950.

FILSTEAD, WILLIAM J., *Qualitative Methodology: First Hand Involvement with the Social World*. Chicago: Markham, 1970.

GLOCK, C. Y., "Survey Analysis in Socio-Cultural Investigations," *Survey Research in the Social Sciences*. New York: Russell Sage Foundation, 1967.

KAPLAN, ABRAHAM, *The Conduct of Inquiry*. Scranton, Pa.: Chandler, 1964, p. 27.

KONOPKA, GISELA, *The Adolescent Girl in Conflict*. Englewood Cliffs, N.J.: Prentice-Hall, 1966.

MARKOFF, JOHN, *et al.*, "Toward the Integration of Content Analysis and General Methodology," in David R. Heise, ed., *Sociological Methodology*, publication of the American Sociological Association. San Francisco: Jossey-Bass, 1975.

MICHELSON, VALERIUS, "Towns on the Threshold of Change." Mimeographed paper describing an exhibit and audio-visual presentation in the court of the Architecture Building, University of Minnesota, December 1973.

PELTO, PERTTI, *Anthropological Research: The Structure of Inquiry.* New York: Harper and Row, 1970, pp. 166–67.

REICH, CHARLES A., *The Greening of America.* New York: Random House, 1970.

THE THEMES

*Now I shall be that bell, sounding: Life, Life, I will not exalt
death but life . . .*[1]

It seems comparatively easy to understand one person—but is it really? When so many voices are raised, so many subjects touched, such a variety of opinions offered, how can we arrive at true meaning? How do we bridge time and often totally different experiences? How does one order this vast universe?

It is the nature of the human being that we see ourselves as the center of the universe—even the most unselfish of us. Each one of us experiences, remembers, reacts, interacts, feels, and thinks always through our own personality. The most divergent philosophies accept this fact of man's self-boundedness. Hume[2] described it in the extreme, hardly recognizing any reality outside of human perception. Kant[3] added the concept of an *a priori* value system, popularly called the "Golden Rule"; but it, too, is based on human judgment and personal insight. All religious systems assume an inner, personal religious experience.

The earlier in the individual's development, the more self-bounded he or she is. A small child explores only his or her closest environment: its mother's breast, the bottle, his or her own fist or thumb. When it grows a little older, it begins to see, take possession of, defend, or possibly share other things. Its world widens. If this world around the child provides comfort, love, and affection, the whole world may be perceived as a good one or at least a potentially good one that one can trust. If this small world includes hunger, violence, and cold anger, the perception of the whole world is one of danger and is to be feared. And so our ideas, our values, our whole being continues to develop in ever-widening circles all through life. Our experiences change, our "I" changes.

In adolescence, this "I" experiences a dramatic change within itself, biologically the onset of sexual maturity, never to be experienced again in the same way. It is one experience all adolescents have in common and has

---

[1] Joanne Greenberg, *The King's Persons*. New York: Avon, 1972, p. 318.

[2] David Hume, *Philosophical Works*, Vols. 1–4. Edinburgh, 1826.

[3] Immanuel Kant, *Kritik der Praktischen Vernunft*. Leipzig: Philipp Reclam, Jr., 1788, 1792, 1797.

deep significance for their whole view of themselves, and of others. Yet even this common experience is not the same for everyone. It is enmeshed with many other cultural, environmental factors. When I use the word "culture," it means to me the sum total of all the *experiences* and *expectations* with which a person grows up—not a stereotype of some national, ethnic, racial, sexist phantom into which this world has been divided and twisted. There are many varieties within such groupings. The cultural and maturing experience of each girl may be quite different from the one in which a girl of the so-called same culture grew up. Yet they have *some* experiences in common. The spread of public communication, especially T.V., has made them highly conscious of the wider world around them. They know about the struggles of depressed peoples, of wars, and political scandals, and depressions even if they are not involved themselves. They know about those events—surely, not all the facts, but they know something about them and they hear varying opinions.

Although the parent generation has lived practically a lifetime in a prosperous economy—which does not mean that all of them participated in prosperity—and the grandparent generation had lived through depression, therefore cherishing hard work and "material goods"—again not all of them—these twelve to eighteen-year-olds were born into international and national strife with a beginning inflation and depression, with beginning realistic high hopes for better justice for all and harsh reaction against this.

Like all people, but more so because they are self-conscious adolescents and even more so because they are female, which includes in this time of transition a heightened self-consciousness, their own selves are at the center of their concern.

Our interviewees hardly ever talked spontaneously about an abstract "self-concept," but everything they said was permeated by it.

The order of importance and significance to them of the various themes that emerged from the interviews seemed to be:

1. The girl's present drives, her dreams for the future.
2. Her family as a supporting and limiting power to this expanding "I".
3. Friends as needed mirrors of the self.
4. Organizations they may join.
5. The school, again as a supporting and limiting power.
6. The political and social scene.

BIBLIOGRAPHY

HAMMARSKJOLD, DAG, *Markings* (translation). New York: Knopf, 1964.
HUME, DAVID, *Philosophical Works*, Vols. 1–4. Edinburgh, 1826.

KANT, IMMANUEL, *Kritik der Praktischen Vernunft*, Leipzig: Philipp Reclam, Jr., 1788, 1792, 1797.

KONOPKA, GISELA, "Formation of Values in the Developing Person," *American Journal of Orthopsychiatry*, Vol. 43, No. 1, January 1973, pp. 86–96.

――――, *Eduard C. Lindeman and Social Work Philosophy*. Minneapolis: University of Minnesota Press, 1958.

NELSON, LEONARD, *Socratic Method and Critical Philosophy* (translation). New Haven: Yale University Press, 1949.

――――, *System of Ethics* (translation). New Haven: Yale University Press, 1956.

PIRSIG, ROBERT M., *Zen and the Art of Motorcycle Maintenance*. New York: William Morrow, 1974.

SEAVER, E., ed., *Epitaphs of Our Times: The Letters of Edward Dahlberg*. New York: Braziller, 1966.

ONE

LIFE GOALS

I am growing world.
I am reaching and touching and stretching
and testing
And finding new things, new wonderful
Things.
New frightening things.
I'm just growing, world, just now.
I'm not tall, I'm not strong. I'm not
Right.
I'm just trying to be.
I'm a person, I'm me!
Let me test, let me try, let me reach,
Let me fly!
Push me out of my nest (but not too fast).
There is much I don't know.
There are things that I want—don't
Hide me from the sight of the world.
Give me room, give me time. There
are things I'm not frightened
To try.
Let me tumble and spring, let me go
Let me be. Wait and see. . . .
I am growing, world
Water me with the wisdom of
Your tears.

        CHERIE A. MILLARD (17, *White, urban*)

There are in the words of this 17-year-old girl the search and hope, the expectations, the fear, a sense of inner power combined with a distrust of herself, a wish to "go it alone" and yet a wish to be helped, but not too much. Those feelings were expressed by all the girls when they were thinking about their goals for the future. Among the older ones, thoughts were more crystallized than among the younger ones, but not totally so. I would not dare to make any predictions about what this generation of girls really will do when they are approximately 30 years old. But the response to our question of how they see themselves 15 years from now, how they dream their lives to be, gives us an insight into their struggles *now*. Though the girls rarely discussed spontaneously their plans for the future, most of them responded to the question with considerable animation. It gave them an opportunity to dream, to reveal themselves. And this theme was important to them.

As in any subject, we received a variety of responses. There was one opinion that stood out and showed an attitude different from what was prevalent about ten years ago: *Practically all girls contemplated some job or career after high school and accepted the fact that they should be prepared for some kind of gainful employment.* Only ten years ago, marriage was frequently regarded as an escape from work. This concept rarely surfaced in our interviews. Yet the girls struggled with two major questions:

1. How do I choose among the vast opportunities of work possibilities? Do I really have a choice? And,
2. How do I combine work with marriage and having children?

CAREER CHOICES

Very prevalent was the feeling of confusion about what the girls wanted to be, because they thought of employment as such an important and significant part of their lives. Often girls felt they could not weigh all the alternatives, but knew of some and wanted to be sure of making the correct choice.

Consonant with the general trend in the country, the majority of girls wanted to have white-collar jobs, and most of those who talked about future educational plans wanted to go to college. A very small number wanted blue-collar work and only two girls mentioned careers in farming. We found very little difference between girls of various racial or ethnic backgrounds or geographical areas. About three-fourths of the girls who wanted white-collar careers chose the professions. Professions chosen or talked about ranged from very traditional ones to those that seemed to be more accessible to girls. They talked about wanting to be nurses, teachers, social workers, entertainers, artists; but some wanted to be doctors, lawyers, veterinarians, politicians, architects, archeologists, and explorers. The non-traditional career choices were in the minority. Only one girl among all those we interviewed saw herself in a managerial position:

> I will own a corporation when I get out of Law School. I want to set up a big corporation and then I want to set up my own school, my own law schools all over the country. And then I want to have my own airport and I want to learn how to fly, so I can fly myself. (14, *Black, urban*)

Next to professional careers, girls talked most often about entering clerical or sales work. Many wanted to stay home after they were married. Still, they wanted to be prepared for a job.

> Maybe be a secretary or something like that. Hopefully I will be married with some children. That's what I want to do, I guess that's the way I've been

brought up. I don't want to have any career. We started having career reports at school and I was at a loss of what to do because I don't want a career. I do want to have something that I can do and I do want to get married and have children. I do want to have something to fall back on if something happens or if I decide to go back to work.   (15, *White, suburban*)

Some, as mentioned, also had career ambitions:

Be a stenographer—I don't know what comes after stenographer, but one higher than that, not necessarily a higher paying job, but a higher position you know.   (16, *Black, urban*)

Reasons for career choices varied. Surely not all girls gave us reasons why they wanted to choose a certain career. The reason most often offered was the wish to help people.

I want to go into social work because it is one of the nicest jobs for me, because it tries to help people in all their problems whether it be at their homes, school or everywhere. I think that social work is very good for the commu-nity. . . .   (16, *Puerto Rican, urban*)

I'd like to be a nurse. I just like to work with people like in a nursing home.
                                                                  (16, *White, urban*)

I'd really like to be a, something that just involved kids, you know, something like having a club or something like that. It's just something I always wanted to do, to be Camp Fire leader, just any little thing that involves kids.
                                                                  (18, *Black, urban*)

To others, but a smaller number, the choice of career was mainly related to a strong personal interest: auto mechanics, painting, or veterinary medicine. Several girls, but actually the smallest number of those who commented on this subject, wanted to work purely for self-centered reasons.

To be on my own and to make my own decision.

I wanna be glamorous and have my own house, my own car and probably my own husband.

I want to travel a lot more than I have.

I'm afraid without work it will be hum drum.

I want to set my own hours . . . it has to be something terribly creative or I'll go bananas.

Mostly have plenty to eat.

I want to be free.

MARRIAGE AND CHILDREN

Overwhelmingly, girls today struggle with the question of how to combine a career or any outside work with marriage and having children.

Sometimes we forget that women have always worked; they have, in fact, worked very hard, inside as well as outside the home. In practically all societies, their task has not been exclusively one of raising children. They have worked in the fields, at the loom, have prepared the family soap and food; they were among the first factory workers. Since the extended family consisted of many people, even those things women prepared at home had to be made in large quantities. Women were expected to bear the children and do hard physical work, often immediately after giving birth. In many countries women are still "the beasts of burden," carrying heavy loads on their heads and on their hips, walking the difficult and dusty roads while the men ride the horses or donkeys or camels. The concept of women as frail creatures to be protected is really a nineteenth-century invention and applied only to the women of the upper-income class. They profited from the exhausting labor of other women. Women of the upper classes frequently did not raise their own children, but turned this task over to their less affluent sisters.

In the United States the performance of equal tasks by husbands and wives was actually more prevalent than in most of the countries from which the immigrants came. Even after World War II, I remember how surprised visitors from middle Europe and Asia were to see American men helping diaper an infant or clean a house. The concept that such activities are not appropriate for men existed mostly in those families that kept strictly to their older traditions. Yet American literature and education, the socialization of young people, was shaped in the traditional way, and this increased after World War II. I remember vividly a film, *The Red Shoes*, being shown in the 1940s. It dealt with the question whether a woman could have a career and be married. At the time I saw it, it seemed to me totally ridiculous. My own middle European pre-Hitler Youth Movement background stressed cooperative and equal work in all areas between men and women, and most American families I had met adhered to this same value system. I learned only later that my experiences at that time had been far too limited. Actually, for many Americans of all socio-economic strata, but especially the large middle class, femininity was equated with "being cared for," making oneself beautiful, and staying at home. In many lower-income families, women resented having to go out and do boring work. The minority of women fought for better wages and working conditions; a majority hoped to leave the labor market as soon as possible.

When I did the study of *The Adolescent Girl in Conflict* in the 1950s, I saw the influence of this "traditional" concept of "femininity." Staff in delinquency institutions for girls deliberately fostered a picture of the "sweet girl," forced the girls to wear skirts, taking it as a sign of "deviant personality" when they wanted to wear jeans or slacks. They gave the girls no help in choosing any future careers outside of very traditional ones. Marriage was presented as the only legitimate goal for them.

In this present study we found this same influence evidenced in the responses of many adjudicated girls in institutions. Not only was their choice of careers more traditional than that of the non-adjudicated girls, but so was their concept of marriage and its relationship to work. Staff in many delinquency institutions seem to continue to be insensitive to changing needs of adolescent girls.

To all those who think that marriage as a value and goal is disappearing, it may be startling to hear that *we found the majority of girls wanting to be married,* but they also contemplated seriously the *possibility of combining marriage with a career.* Only 3 percent of all the girls who talked about careers and marriage volunteered the idea that *maybe* they would stay single, a very small number indeed. They expressed their concern about combining career and marriage in many ways. Some had thoughts about the time they hoped to get married:

> I won't get married until I'm twenty-four. I just think that people should do as much as they can before they get married. Marriage is for a lifetime.
> (15, *White, urban*)

The specific age mentioned in this quote is not so significant as the wish to have done something, experienced something, before getting married. "Doing" meant to them traveling, finishing school or college, establishing a career.

Only about fifteen years ago adults in this country worried about teenage marriages. In talking with the girls today, no girl expressed the wish to be married while she was in high school. A small number wanted to get married shortly after high school and the largest number, later. About half of them talked about getting married after they were 25, and the other half before that time. One should not want to "settle down" too early. The world was just opening up, beckoning; the girls thirsted for adventure, for experiences.

> I want to go to India, I wish that I could travel all over the world and see everything because I like to know what's happening all over. And I just like to travel. I just wish I could travel all over. (14, *American Indian, small town*)

The wish to be married was expressed by almost all girls across geographical, economic, racial, ethnic lines.

It is important to understand what the girls saw as an ideal marriage. They seldom meant a form of marriage that was traditionally considered "the right one"; namely, a marriage dominated by the male. Most girls, even those who thought in traditional terms of the man taking care of the family finances, expected husbands to share household chores and be concerned with the raising of children. They thought of *marriage as a partnership.* This kind of relationship does become the ideal. Here's how a girl who carried the comparatively traditional image of a family expressed it.

Oh, I want to get married. The biggest thing in the whole world I'm looking forward to is having a baby. That's just one thing that tickles me to death just thinking about having a baby. Just to think that you're bringing somebody into the world and that they're coming in through you and you're making them grow and you're keeping them and I just love that. That's the only thing I'm looking forward to. After I got married I would want to wait maybe a year or two or three or even five years because I want to get to know my husband before I have a kid. I think that if you just have a kid when you get married that you never get a chance to really know your husband cause it's you and him and the kid all the time.   (16, *White, small town*)

The conscious wish to postpone having a child indicates the concept of husband and wife as partners. This concept is also reflected in the comments of the younger girl in the following:

But I've been thinking a lot about it lately and I almost feel lucky these days that I'm a girl, because if I have a husband that is really understanding, I can do almost anything that *I* want. He *has* to make money the way things are today. He can't do anything he wants to; he can't go hide in the mountains. He has to make money. If he has a family, he has to support it.

But if I want to stay home and take care of my kids for the rest of my life, I can do that. And if he understands, I can do just about anything else, whether it makes money or not. I can be a teacher, or social worker, or work in the theater, anything I want to do, if he understands and if he makes enough money.   (15, *White, urban*)

Their thinking is really quite similar to the girl who exemplified the non-traditional view:

If I do get married . . . marriage seems like such a confining thing, but it would be an equal thing. I want to go out and work and then, if I had kids . . . I don't know right now if I will . . . I would want my husband to help raise them. . . .   (17, *White, suburban*)

The girls who were deeply interested in the quality of marriage saw as its main attribute equality of the spouses, in privileges, responsibility, and decision making. There were expressions like:

Well, my fiance is real nice and he thinks a lot of me. . . . He wants me to do what I want to do and I let him do what he wants to do. . . .

My future husband is also Indian and we feel equal to each other. I want to have a good home, work for a year or two, then have children—not more than four.   (17, *American Indian, small town*)

There were some very optimistic and some very pessimistic views of marriage. The ideal was a marriage relationship built on trust, respect, love and understanding of mutual needs. A 17-year-old, very active in youth organizations, said:

I want kids, two children. I would want to have a career though. I feel very strongly about this. . . . In marriage there should be happiness, fulfillment, someone that understands me; that is my friend.   (17, *White, urban*)

Similar ideas were expressed by a 15-year-old Black girl from a small town who also was active in youth groups. She wanted to study medicine, but she also wanted to be married:

> . . . with about five kids . . . somewhere I could raise my kids without worrying about getting knocked down for something.   (15, *Black, urban*)

She obviously, more than her white contemporaries, realizes obstacles in the way, but she is sure she wants to overcome them. When she talks about work and marriage, she says that they can be combined "with determination." She talks about all girls:

> There's got to be love and determination. They've got to be determined to be a mother that they want to be. They got to be determined to be that decent person in society that they want to be and be determined to maintain their right state of mind.

And another spoke up with real hope for such a marriage:

> I'd rather really be more like friends with my husband. You know, that comes first to me; and the romance, too, but I know that marriage isn't all romance and it shouldn't be because it wouldn't work that way; and I just want to marry someone that shares a lot of the same interests that I do and we can get along with each other.   (17, *American Indian, urban*)

The concept of husband and wife as *friends* is a most significant one. "Romance" was not rejected, but it was not the only theme. Sharing interests was the most important quality. The general hope was very simply expressed by the girl who said:

> I want a good marriage, a solid marriage—and some money put away.
> (14, *Black, urban*)

But along with the hope for a good marriage went a strong fear of it. One element of this fear was related to the possibility of divorce. The old picture of the happy ending when the bride walks down the aisle and the "I do" is said, seems frequently to have been replaced by a picture of children being left unhappy and lonely because of divorce. The concern was predominantly for the child but the girl's fear of the divorce for herself also was very real. It was something dreaded; it spelled terrifying hurt. Those who had experienced it as children saw divorce often as inevitable. In a group discussion, five girls expressed their wish to have children, but were not sure they wanted to be married because of this—as they expressed it—"awful ending—the children are just left alone." Their longing to hear about a marriage that worked was almost pathetic. To them, divorce meant insecurity and economic hardship. Their fear was increased by the statistics showing an increase in marriage failures. The girls seemed to be unaware of the fact that a large portion of this breakup occurs in the older age bracket. Their fragile sense of beginning independence made them especially fearful of being abandoned.

I just wouldn't want to get married. See, maybe, if we do, if we would get married and maybe our marriage wouldn't work out, then you have to go through the divorce suit, and I really wouldn't want to go through that.

(14, *Black, urban*)

Another 15-year-old:

I want to get married when the time comes and the time is right. But I don't want to rush it. Because I want to make sure when I get married. And in a way I don't want to get married. Because like if there was a problem you'd have to pay so much money to get a divorce. And I don't . . . I don't believe in money. And I don't think it's right if two people love each other they should be able to stay together without having those laws between them.   (15, *White, urban*)

An older girl:

I dream mostly about getting married, the wedding or something and not the afterward. I hope to get married. I think it's very serious. I don't just want to get married and get divorced. I want it to be permanent if I ever do it.

(18, *White, rural*)

I don't really plan on getting married. It's too much hassle, and too many divorces. That's about all.   (13, *White, suburban*)

In addition to the terror of being a child of divorced parents, the girls' pessimistic view of marriage was related to their fear of being dominated by a man.

I ain't gonna get married. I think if you get married you are always trapped. You always have to do everything. . . . Well, see, my mother . . . my father and her have disagreements about stuff, you know, and my mother thinks that my father owns her and so does my father. And so I . . . I want to be free. I don't want to be owned at all, "Do this and do that."   (13, *White, urban*)

During one of the interviews, the girl (16, *American Indian, rural*) turned suddenly to the interviewer and asked shyly and hesitantly, "Tell me, how is it really—being married? Does he beat you a lot?" She yearned to hear of a marriage in which husband and wife were on an equal footing—she hoped for it.

Another one angrily explained why she did not want marriage:

There's too many men jumping on their wives and stuff, beating 'em and making them do stuff and I'll have to kill them.   (15, *White, urban*)

A serious 14-year-old, in a delinquency institution, said wistfully:

Everyone gets married or wants to. But I never dream about those things at all. I don't want a husband who would beat me or fight with me all of the time—I just couldn't stand it. So it would be better to be single and take care of myself if I could. I really don't know. . . .   (14, *White, urban*)

The experiences of these young people had made them so distrustful of close relationships with a man that they even rejected the "living together" alternative to marriage that some girls occasionally choose. The girl who chose this form of relationship voluntarily often was optimistic about intimate relationships, but we found in our population few girls who chose it. I assume this is mostly because we talked to high school girls predominantly. It may be significant, though, that so few even talked about this possibility, even when they thought of the future.

We did find a few girls who talked about a less traditional pattern of marriage than all the others, as for instance:

> I will probably be a writer or an actress or a probation officer . . .
> [At thirty]: I would be married, but it wouldn't be a conventional type of marriage. I mean, I would have a husband who wouldn't get all uptight about being two-timed. As a matter of fact, it wouldn't be looked upon as being two-timed. I believe in extra-marital affairs on both parties' parts, provided if it is necessary to keep the marriage together.
>
> I will be employed, I might even be self-employed as a writer doing something I like on my own time limits and stuff. I like to set a lot of my own rules. I think I will be writing. I write, I think, pretty much serious stuff. And I would be financially comfortable.
>
> I am very unsure as to whether I would like to have children or not. I think I would be happy to have one child and adopt one.
>
> I think having young children poses a strain on the working woman but I think that the responsibility of bringing up children should rest on the husband partially too, and that he should be available to take care of the children too.
> (17, *White, urban*)

CHILDREN

Marriage for most of the girls meant *having children* and coming to terms with a wish not to be dominated and also a wish to participate in life beyond the "kitchen, church and children." Most of the girls wanted to bear their own children. We found a small number though—obviously a newer thought to young women—who planned to adopt children. They discuss this decision intelligently and with consideration. Usually the girl who was concerned about wider issues, as for instance overpopulation, considered adopting other children.

> When I am thirty . . . to have a good house, and have money, and have my job then, be good at my job, modeling and acting. Possibly, I don't plan on it, but I might have one child. I'm not going to *have* one, I'm going to adopt one. There's too many kids already. I'm going to adopt one. (13, *White, suburban*)

In contrast to this attitude we found a number of adopted girls who resented being adopted, either because they were told about their own adoption too late or only when they made "trouble." One of the girls described how her father had not told her she had been adopted until she was on her way to the delinquency institution, obviously implying that there was something "bad" in her heritage. In this particular conversation, which was a group discussion, two other girls who were also adopted spoke with deep anger about their feelings of never having lived up to the expectations of the parents who adopted them. Marietta Spencer, an outstanding social worker and writer, has based her post-adoption work with parents and their adopted children on the premise that during adolescence young people raise renewed questions about their biological origin.[1]

Though the desire for children was strong, only a few girls, actually only seven out of the many who talked about this subject, wanted children so much that they would have them whether they were married or not.

> I don't believe in marriage but want three children, boys and girls . . .
>
> (14, *American Indian, small town*)

She was one of the girls who, because of very unfortunate family experiences, was afraid of a relationship that might only hurt her and subjugate her.

Reflecting on my own experience as an adolescent in the 1920s, a far larger number of girls, active in the labor and women's movements, would have talked about having children purposely out of wedlock as a protest against degrading marriage laws. We found none of this attitude today.

We found in all the responses an unusual honesty among the young women. The "tell it like it is" response seemed to be far more prevalent than in other times and included an honest confrontation with their own feelings. Not so long ago, girls would have considered themselves abnormal if they did not want to have children and would have hidden such feelings. Now we found respondents admitting that they preferred to be childless. Those girls represented only a small minority, but they were open about it. Their reasons for not wanting children were mostly that they felt that the world was in bad shape and they did not want anybody to have to live in such a world. Extremely few, perhaps six or seven girls, said that they did not like children. One of them—she was the only one—said frankly:

> No, I can't hack kids; I mean, I can't hack them when they are little babies. I almost beat a kid when I babysat; he got on my nerves so much. I could be a child abuser, until I realized what I was doing. The poor kid was all black and blue and I couldn't help it. He just got to me and I hit him.   (16, *White, urban*)

The average number of children desired seemed to be two. This is less than Sylvia Lee[2] found in a study of 365 high school girls in 1968.

---

[1] See Marietta Spencer, *Post Adoption Workshop Support Materials*, Children's Home Society of Minnesota, revised 1975; and her "Sense, Safeguards and Service in Agency Adoption," *Child Welfare*, Vol. LIII, No. 10, December 1974, p. 632.

[2] Sylvia L. Lee, and others, *High School Senior Girls and the World of Work— Occupational Knowledge, Attitudes and Plans*, Research and Development Series #42, Office of Education (DHEW) Washington, D.C., June 1971, 56 pp.

Sixty-two percent of these girls wanted three or four children. These numbers were mentioned by some of the girls we interviewed and a few wanted five or more.

In general, the number of children was not discussed very much. Far more important and really the reason they talked about marriage and children involved the original question of whether one could combine work, marriage, and having children. There was a pervasive sense of responsibility for the care of children. Girls wanted to be sure that they "did right by them." They constantly asked how old a child should be before the mother could take on outside work without neglecting the child and also whether it was good for a child to be—even partially—raised by others than the mother. We found practically no trace of the upper-class European or Asian tradition of letting children be raised by outsiders such as the "English Nanny," "boarding schools," or "house servants." In the girls' minds the only question was how to combine their own needs for a certain independence and their interest in outside work with their equally intense wish to take care of their children. The most common theme to emerge was that women could not or should not work when children were small, but they did not know why they thought so. It simply was something they had heard, and they did not know what "small" really meant. What influenced them predominantly was the thought of a very dependent infant. Most of them knew very little about the developmental needs of children; in fact, they thought of children predominantly as babies and of pre-school age. Since so many wanted a career, they usually indicated that they would postpone careers until the children went to school and "I can be back home when the child gets home from school." Most of the girls said that one can combine work and marriage and children, and were quite determined about it. They know that this meant hard work and extra effort. Their ideas about how one could work this out were as varied as the girls themselves.

> I want to have a good career—in drama or in modeling cause I want to learn to be a model too. I don't want to get married in a long time. . . . They usually want younger women, so I'm just going to tell my husband I'm going to get a job. Umm, unless you've got some kids you have to baby. Then you stay home with the babies until they're older. (15, *Chicana, urban*)

> If I get married I probably will work for awhile anyway. If we decide to have kids then, probably, by the time I'm too far along to work, I'd have to quit work. But otherwise, I probably would because there isn't that much for a girl to do in the home, really. You can get that done and still work. A lot of people have the problem of having nothing to do. I'll probably need the money anyway. Even if you don't need the money I think you should go out and join a service organization. . . . If you have small children like up through second, third or fourth grade or so, you'd want to be home to take care of them, but after that I don't think there is that big a problem. (18, *Oriental, suburban*)

> I think women should work and be married at the same time and I don't

think it is too much of a hardship cause men work and they are married. Well, about when they are about one or two years old I think they should stay home, but when they get three or four I think they can put them in a nursery or something. (14, *Black, urban*)

I would like to be some type of supervisor in retail selling. I am majoring in marketing in college with French. I haven't really thought about marriage. I took a course and I just decided I am not ready to settle down. When I do get married, my husband is going to have to accept the fact that I will not stay at home. I am not going to be one of those soap opera housewives. When I am sick, I'll stay home to get rid of it, but I go nuts after one day. I've got to be doing something so I want to be a married career girl if I can. I hope to have maybe one or two children and while they are growing up, until five or so, I will stay home. After they are school age I want to go back to work or maybe work part-time. I've got to be doing something, I can't sit home. (17, *White, urban*)

These comments all show how much the girls wanted to combine marriage and career but how strongly they realized the responsibility of raising children and how much they felt that *they* were the *major* ones responsible for what would become of the children. This attitude cut across all economic and ethnic backgrounds. They understand the importance of the first years of life in the development of the human being. Most of them assumed that the mother's staying at home during the early childhood of her offspring was essential. Research[3] that refutes the harmful effects of mothers working outside the home and stresses the greater significance of quality of relationship between mother and child is quite unknown.

There were girls who did not want any combination of child rearing and career because they saw themselves as *the* marriage partner who was totally responsible for the children.

This lady, she lets her kids roam all over the place; she's so tired. She never wants to take 'em anywhere. She don't even talk with them. She goes straight to bed. (16, *Chicana, urban*)

These girls also considered themselves the person who must keep the house in order.

I don't want to work after I'm married. I want to stay home and keep a spotless house. (17, *White, small town*)

I think that if the house can't be maintained with the salary of only one person, she must work, but only until she has children. When she has children she should dedicate herself to her home even if the husband does not have enough. She should try to economize and in this way help him. (16, *Puerto Rican, urban*)

It's very hard. My mother does it and she finds it's very difficult to keep up with the housework and meals and all of that and her job. She gets real tired. I think if you're gonna work you need somebody at home to take care of the

[3] Alva Myrdal, and Viola Klein, *Women's Two Roles: Home and Work*, 2nd Ed. London: Routledge and Kegan Paul, 1968).

housework, at least once a week. Because otherwise it's too much of a strain on the person.   (17, *White, urban*)

In our general population, this traditional view was in the minority with one outstanding exception. *Twice as many adjudicated girls opposed rather than supported the idea that women can combine work and marriage and children.* This concept fits in with the observation that adjudicated girls almost exclusively chose traditional careers. They exhibited a strong tendency toward very traditional ideas of home and husband.

I would stay home and take care of the house. Cause somebody should be home and straighten up the house, in case somebody comes over. And you have the house clean.   (16, *White, adjudicated*)

Their ideas were expressed in sentences like:

You should stay home so the children would not run wild.

Children with babysitters and in day care centers are not being brought up the way they should.

Children might develop a sense of insecurity.

Children would be more attached to the babysitters than to their own mothers.

Again we can only speculate about why the adjudicated girl thought this way, but we can hear it partially from her own words.

She had particularly bad experiences and often felt rejected by home and community.

She was constantly exposed to teachers, judges, social workers, psychiatrists, and psychologists, who had a tendency to relate her problems to her home experiences and made her feel that her difficulties were her mother's fault.

Her own self-concept was intertwined with this concept of the "bad mother."

She also may have wanted to please those people on whom she was dependent and who, as I said earlier, expected from her certain "feminine" behavior.

It is striking that most of the girls saw themselves as good mothers and wives with a career. But unlike the preceding generation, they seemed less directed *against* men. They took a relaxed attitude:

Women manage work and marriage by having a husband who understands what they're doing. If you got a partner that encourages you and helps you with all this, well, then it automatically is going to work out.   (17, *Black, urban*)

But there were girls who added to this optimistic view a realistic appraisal of women in transition, their own anxious ambivalence, and the many blocks placed in their paths by economic or racial discrimination.

There is, for instance, a kind of resignation and despair in the response of one 15-year-old girl from a blue-collar background. She wants to be a nurse's aide, but when asked how she thinks her life would look at age 30, she says:

> Probably I'll be sitting in a room by myself in my old age, watching over a family. I won't have much of a career because this world won't be much of anything fifteen years from now. . . . (15, *White, urban*)

She does want marriage and children but thinks it is hard to work and have children. "They can, but they shouldn't. They shouldn't because they should be home with their children." She feels very defeated by her own ambivalence.

Others are advised by friends or counselors to give up specific ambitions because their choice of a career was not for girls, or because their race or ethnic background supposedly would make it impossible for them to advance. One 12-year-old girl from a lower economic background had her spirits crushed by such "advice" and simply accepted the fact that she could not choose a profession. Another girl who wanted to be a forester gave up partially because she was told this was no career for women. But this same girl seemed to rally her strength and said in the course of the interview:

> I really want to be a governor or mayor or something like that. But I really doubt if anybody would elect me. Why? Cause I'm a girl. Cause there are very few women congressmen and things like that. They just don't give us a ride at all. And I really think there ought to be a woman president if she knows how, and she's really got the knowledge. Cause lately the men presidents we've had, they could use some help. . . . I'll probably be a lawyer or teacher. Probably a lawyer. My mom doesn't want me to, but I'd rather. . . . I want a family, but I only want two children because I don't want to overpopulate the world.
> I like for people not to hurt other people, so that maybe I might be able to be in politics without somebody coming after me with a rifle. (12, *White, urban*)

Unfortunately, according to what we heard, it seems that *most* counselors or professional guidance people have made very little impact, or occasionally even a negative impact, in the area of career choices. Guidance or counseling was rarely mentioned in the context of discussing career aspirations. Occasionally, a girl would say that she could talk with the school counselor, but in general, counselors were regarded as adults who had no time for the girls, did not listen, and did not understand.

> I wonder if there are any good counselors for schools? Talking to those counselors is like talking to a brick wall. (14, *White, urban*)

In fact, choice of career was almost exclusively dependent on girls having had some contact with somebody in a certain job or profession.

> I was thinking about working with key-punch and get a job with the air lines. Cause I know this lady that did that, all she had to do was sit around and

pass these cards from one place to another. She was making like $400 a month, plus, they get to go to New York for $6.   (17, *White, small town*)

In view of the enormously increased variety of career possibilities, this situation means real deprivation of choice. This lack of choice was especially evident in girls from lower-income groups whose parents did not have a wide circle of acquaintances in various occupations. The world of many girls was thus locked in, not only in terms of present experience, but also in terms of any future opportunity to widen their horizon. If we really mean to provide "equality of opportunity," then conscious efforts must be made to let girls meet adults from a wide variety of careers and learn about their work. Young people learn best by meeting "models." Career options need to be presented to them by women of various careers, races, ethnic backgrounds. Often, in times of rising unemployment, women have been told to leave the labor market. Yet in view of the awakened self-esteem of girls and their almost general acceptance of being involved in gainful employment, this recourse will not be possible anymore.

SUMMARY

Our findings regarding life goals showed that:

1. Most girls wanted a career, marriage, and a family, and thought that women were able to combine them. A minority of the girls thought that such a combination was not possible and preferred exclusively either a career or a family.
2. Adjudicated girls adhered twice as often as other girls to the idea that such a combination was not possible.
3. Their ideal marriage was a partnership, with rejection of the domineering male and a sense of shared responsibility, including the upbringing of children.
4. Some feared marriage because of possible divorce and possible subjugation of the woman by the man.
5. A minority of girls wanted strictly separate roles in marriage, with the male taking on the responsibility of taking care of the financial support of the family and the female taking care of the home.
6. The majority of girls wanted children and felt responsible for them. Some wanted to adopt children. Only a very small minority did not want children.
7. Marriage should await some other experiences (career preparation, travel). No exact desirable age for marriage could be isolated, but in general it was considerably later than high-school age.
8. Occupational choices by the majority of girls fell in the white-collar area,

with increasing preference for the professions and some non-traditional occupations.

9. Adjudicated girls almost exclusively chose traditional occupations.
10. Choice of careers was mostly influenced by life experiences, by meeting adult models. There was very little conscious exposure of girls to the variety of careers possible.

BIBLIOGRAPHY

Center for Youth Development and Research, *Youth Encounters the World of Work*, Seminar Series No. 4, University of Minnesota, Minneapolis, Center for Youth Development and Research, 1973.

ENTWISLE, DORIS and ELLEN GREENBERGER, "Adolescents' Views of Women's Work Role," *American Journal of Orthopsychiatry*, Vol. XLII, No. 4, July 1972, pp. 648–656.

HERMAN, MICHELE and WILLIAM SEDLACEK, "Career Orientation of University and High School Women," University of Maryland: College Park Counseling Center, August 1973.

KUVLESKY, WILLIAM and MICHAEL LEVER, "Occupational Goals, Expectations and Anticipating Goal Deflection Experienced by Negro Girls Residing in Low-Income Rural and Urban Places." Paper presented at the Southwestern Sociological Society Meetings, Dallas, Texas, March 1967.

LEE, SYLVIA L., and others, *High School Senior Girls and the World of Work—Occupational Knowledge, Attitudes and Plans*. Research and Development Series #42, Office of Education (DHEW), Washington, D.C., June 1971, 56 pp.

MYRDAL, ALVA and VIOLA KLEIN, *Women's Two Roles—Home and Work*, 2nd Ed. London: Routledge and Kegan Paul, 1968.

National Board of the Y.W.C.A. of the U.S.A., *Summer Youth Demonstration Project*. Report to the United States Department of Labor, I, November 1967.

STOLZ, LOIS MEEK, "Effects of Maternal Employment on Children," *Child Development*, Vol. XXXI, 1960, pp. 749–782.

TWO

SEXUALITY

> Man/woman is so intricate
>   my God I have so many lines in my hand
> Man/woman is so fantastic
>   it built a building—I have to tilt my head back to see the top.
> Man/woman is always changing things
>   my God, look what it's done to my world.
> Man/woman is killing and being killed
>   has it noticed there's been a war?
> Man/woman is awake with its eyes closed
>   my God I never knew I had so many lines in my hand.
>   JEAN LEIBOWITZ (13, *White, suburban*)

"I had so many lines in my hand . . .", there are so many personal decisions to make—there are so many unknowns, today, and in the future. Much of this is inside her, a strong force, the sexual drive. We are sexual beings all through life in our need for emotional and physical closeness. Experience and research have shown the vital need of the infant for physical touch.[1]

I remember vividly after the Second World War visiting orphanages in which hundreds of babies were lying in separate sterile little cots, fed not too badly but hardly ever touched. They were listless babies, who hardly moved their eyes when you approached them and never reached for anything. I saw at the same time some 4-year-olds who had grown up under this regime and who still crawled on the floor like much younger children, who hardly spoke, and whose sad eyes looked dully at the world.

Touch—sexuality in its widest sense—was denied to those children, and so they deteriorated. The same kind of deprivation often has been experienced by the aged with the same sad results.

Now, as a society we finally admit to the fact that the sexual drive is continual and alive also in the aged, not to be ridiculed or denounced as lecherous. It is accepted as a fulfilling necessity for a rich life. And we certainly have always known the significance and strength of middle-age adult sexuality.

Adolescence marks the onset of one of the strongest of all human

[1] John Bowlby, "Maternal Care and Mental Health," *Bulletin of the World Health Organization*, No. 3, 1951, pp. 355–534.

physiological and psychological experiences, the maturation of the sex organs. The male can now produce sperm and the female can conceive. Adolescence includes vast glandular changes, which in turn influence physical growth and emotions. Unfortunately, adults often forget the enormous force, wonderment, and ache that adolescence entails. For the girl, there are two specific aspects to this new experience, different from boys:

1. The onset of maturation is sudden, dramatic, and may look to some like an injury (the menstrual flowing of blood).
2. She can now bear children.

All societies have established some rules in relation to sex activity because they are concerned with the development of offspring. Some rules also arose out of misinformation about female sexual development. There have been taboos against sexual intercourse during menstruation because the woman was considered "unclean" during that time. And in most societies male sexual activity was accepted more readily than female sexual activity because the consequences for the male were not the possible creation of another human being.

It is a misrepresentation of history to talk about the "good old times" when there was "morality" and sex was restricted to married couples. Anyone who knows history is aware of the fact that sex was certainly not only openly spoken about at the courts and in the aristocracy, but that "wife swapping" or extramarital relations were very common. Rulers and nobles left their "bastards" all over Europe and Asia and boasted of their physical powers. In a recent English television series, "Upstairs, Down-stairs," shown widely in Great Britain and in this country, class distinction in regard to "morality" was graphically depicted. While monogamy or abstinence before marriage was preached to the lower classes, the upper classes enjoyed sex with whomever they liked, inside or outside of marriage. The so-called "puritanical Anglo Saxon" attitude pertained neither to all ethnic or racial groups in this country, nor to any group totally. Steinbeck, who wrote about the concerns and life and problems of low-income groups, and Fitzgerald, who portrayed the manners and morals of the upper classes, reveal that in both groups there was much extramarital sexual activity. The Steinbeck characters simply were more frank about it.

In contrast to what was practiced, young girls were taught that sex was sin, that the child born out of wedlock was the child of sin. Boys expected premarital "purity" of girls, but not of themselves. Even as late as the beginning of the twentieth century, it was still common in some countries for fathers to take their sons to prostitutes so that they should become "true men" and learn what it was to be a male. These same fathers were most protective of their daughters' virtue. In central Europe, youth around 1900 not only questioned but actually broke with this tradition, not because they wanted indiscriminate sexual freedom but because they opposed hypocrisy. They also considered the underlying attitude demeaning to women. They sang a song that went something like this:

> Men and women and women and men
> are no more fire and water
> In their veins flows a new peace,
> they are becoming freer.
> Men and women, women and men
> Look at each other without fear.[2]

There was open discussion about sex and an idealistic and responsible attitude about the importance of human relations involving physical, mental, and emotional factors. In the United States, this period was followed by a rising fear of promiscuity and a return to especially restrictive attitudes toward young girls.

The basic change in attitudes toward sex today is partially the result of simpler and safer birth control methods. This change, combined with a general move toward individual decision making, has definitely led to greater frankness and openness in discussing sex. What did we find out about sexual attitudes from our girls?

Practically all girls discussed sexual issues because they were so very central to their lives. Some did it spontaneously; others answered questions easily and openly. They had done a great deal of thinking about their own attitudes and values. I was struck by the fact that we hardly ever heard a simple defiance of or compliance with so-called prevailing standards.

Perhaps the *most outstanding finding was that—whatever opinions the girls had regarding sex—they did accept themselves matter of factly as sexual human beings.* They were not ashamed of this, did not hide it, did not consider it unusual. One of my research assistants, a graduate student, was somehow disappointed because of what she considered a rather conservative attitude among the girls. I interpret the girls' attitudes less as conservative and more as a nonmilitant quality based on a healthy recognition of sex as part of their lives. Those are interpretations. The fact is that we heard a wide variety of opinions on several issues. We also found a few very conflicted and very angry girls.

OPINIONS REGARDING PREMARITAL SEX

In 1974, Daniel Yankelovich,[3] in an opinion survey of college youth between the ages of 16 and 25, reported that he found startling shifts in

---

[2] Free translation by the author of a German folk song.

[3] Daniel Yankelovich, "Startling Shifts Found in Youth's Views of Work, Morals," *Chronicle of Higher Education,* May 28, 1974.

views on premarital sex. The percentage of college students, male and female, who expressed moral disapproval of casual premarital sex had dropped from 34 percent in 1969 to 22 percent in 1973. Disapproval of extramarital sex dropped from 77 percent in 1969 to 66 percent in 1973.

Ira Reiss also found that, even though the prevalence of premarital sexual relationships has not increased, male and female student attitudes toward intercourse prior to marriage had become more liberal.[4] Our findings partially agree with their findings. We can add three additional insights:

1. Tolerance for the idea of premarital sex was also high among our young and exclusively female population. This point is new and not sufficiently appreciated.
2. The majority of girls did not talk about "casual" premarital sex; they placed conditions on their approval of premarital sex activity.
3. Tolerance was expressed even by girls who for religious reasons rejected premarital sex for themselves.

Practically all girls accepted *premarital sex if accompanied by love and caring.*

I think most parents don't understand it but I figure if you really love the guy it's not wrong, because I think you should share everything that you have with him. (14, *White, small town*)

Not with just anybody, but I believe if you care about him and he really cares about you, there's nothing wrong with it. (15, *Black, urban*)

The girls also felt that premarital relationships were right if they helped young people to decide whether or not they really belonged together, *to decide if they wanted to get married.*

If the people are sure they are going to get married and they are in love, you know, stuff like that, I think it's okay. But if they just do it for kicks, they just do it to hurt someone else. (18, *Chicana, urban*)

The wish to be respected was strong. They were fearful of being misused, "talked about," abandoned.

During one school summer vacation I interviewed a 15-year-old girl. She was babysitting every day for two small children, 2 and 3 years old. All during the interview the children were around her, sometimes sitting on her lap with her arm protective around the little boy or girl, sometimes playing close to her. When one of them cried, she scooped up the child and held it close. Every movement was calm, gentle. When she talked about her dreams for the future, she said:

I just want to get married and live on a farm because it's more calm there and you can be with your kids more often, and are doing things together. It's not

[4] Ira L. Reiss, "The Sexual Renaissance: A Summary and Analysis," *Journal of Social Issues,* Vol. XXII, April 1966, pp. 123–137.

money that brings love, it's love. That's what I want—and animals. When your kid grows up with animals when he is real young, he learns to be gentle. Like a kitten that is real soft, you learn to be gentle. You don't grow up to be sadistic or stuff like that.   (15, *Inuit, small town*)

When she talked about the kind of husband she wanted, she said:

I want him to be gentle, nice, a guy who does the work good and not half-way. I don't like things half-way done. If I did it half-way, then I might as well not have it done. I'd rather have it all done, finish it.

She has had sad experiences. She was separated from her family because, according to her, her mother died, her father was an invalid, and "they" (the authorities) would not let her take care of her younger brothers and sisters.

They don't listen to me. They just look at me and judge by my age. And they think I need the education. And I don't want my education as bad as I want my sisters and brothers.

From others in the group home where she lived, I heard that she had become mother and confidante to the other girls there, and a quiet helper of the young couple who worked with the girls.

She had had sex experiences, which she perceived as assaults on her self-respect, and she did not want boyfriends:

They think they can pick you up, and they treat you like you are stupid, like they can get something off you real easy. I don't like that.

When asked whether there was anything she would want most in life, the answer came unusually quickly for this quiet girl. "Respect," she said, and then:

I like to be respected. Not to go downtown and get picked up. I want to have respect for myself, but for other people too. I don't like it that they don't think nothing of themselves, and they act like nothing, like they are nothing.

It is this longing for respect that makes a girl hesitant about premarital relations. There are many girls who struggle.

Sex standards are fairly strict for myself. In other words, sex involves a commitment and without the commitment it really isn't anything. I don't much hold with the conventional idea of love: When you feel attracted to a person, therefore you are in love, therefore anything is legal. I feel that there is a lot more. For sex, I think that most people today are just too loose about it because they don't know any better. I can't say I disapprove but I can't say on the other hand that I think it's right. Sex involves all of this. You can't talk about it separately from commitment or from love or from tolerance, from anything.

My moral standards are pretty much Christian, I guess. I can't say I completely disapprove of sex before marriage, but it involves a certain commitment that you think that the person you're having sex with you're going to be with for awhile, possibly the rest of your life. That it's a deeper thing. A sexual relationship should be a commitment relationship saying "Well, okay, I love you enough that I'm going to have sex with you—therefore I love you enough that I'd like to stick around and not just leave.   (17, *White, urban*)

That depends on the people. I know a lot of girlfriends that have it now, you know, but they get so scared and everything, if they get pregnant or something. I don't know, I always skipped out and I always tell my boyfriend that, you know, I don't do that because I seen some people really scared.

(16, *Chicana, urban*)

Well, I feel really it's kind of a . . . like if a girl has sex the first time it kind of puts her under the dude's power. . . . She can kind of weaken herself and open herself up and get her feelings hurt because usually the dude doesn't care. Sometimes he does, but usually he doesn't, you know. I don't think it's all right to have sex . . . anytime you feel like it.

But I really can't say because right now I really don't know what I feel about that. I used to think, "Well, it's all right as long as you have feelings for everybody," but I don't know.   (17, *Black, urban*)

A small minority of the girls we talked to said that they were against premarital sex. Without adding any specific reason, the majority of those few who felt this way believed that intercourse should occur only after marriage. The next largest number of them did not approve of premarital sex because of the possibility of pregnancy. Approximately the same number considered it wrong and immoral because of religious reasons. Several also expressed fear of being deserted and ruining their reputations. The girls who did mention the possibility of pregnancy knew about birth control, but still saw pregnancy as a danger. Here are some examples of those various reasonings.

That's one thing I don't get into. I think a person should keep clean, and not go out and mess around. I think they should wait.   (14, *Chicana, urban*)

I don't think that you should have sex until you're married because it always seems like if a girl gets pregnant, the guy will leave her and she'll just be left there. She'll really be alone because her parents won't—they accept it but really not.   (14, *White, rural*)

I think that only when you're marrying someone. . . . And besides, it's by the Ten Commandments that you shouldn't do that in the Bible. And I just personally wouldn't because I guess the morals I've set for myself have been adopted from my mom. It's not the right thing to do, and I just wouldn't do it. So I think in marriage is better. When you're married to someone you're supposed to be sharing an experience, finding out more about the other person, not just having a fling.   (14, *Black, urban*)

Frequently, girls who said that they themselves would not have premarital intercourse were quite tolerant of others who might and would not look down on them:

Well, I don't know. If people want to do it, you know, that's their business but I think I'd wait till I was married. That's about all I can think; that's all I can see.   (13, *White, urban*)

> Like I say, for me I don't think it's good, but anybody else, if they want to do it I think that's their business and it don't bother me.   (17, *Black, urban*)

And there were those who saw sex simply as something natural and therefore did not consider the question as a great problem:

> Ain't nothing wrong with it, as long as you don't come up pregnant.
> (14, *Black, urban*)

> I don't see anything wrong with it at all and if you want to have a kid, that's your thing. If you don't want to have a kid, then there is a way you can prevent it. But other than that, I don't see anything wrong with sex.
> (15, *Inuit, small town*)

> I feel like sex is a very natural human desire, need, and I know a lot of feminines would disagree with me. They'd say, "You're out of your mind, you don't need sex, you don't need men at all," but I disagree. I think that it's natural and it makes me uptight when people criticize my moral character.
>
> When X and I were living together, that was the hardest time, it was really hard because I started back to school and it's just, you're immediately, especially by the generation before us, very frowned upon. I can see they were raised—to believe that it was wrong, you know. Even if you're married, the woman's place is to give to her husband, she should not feel she needs anything. Well, that's wrong.
>
> It's wrong to think that you have to have that license. You have to sign a piece of paper, you get a justice of [the] peace to sign it to do something that's natural. It's absurd. I also see that there is a big difference between the need for physical love and mental love, these are two different things. . . .
> (17, *White, urban*)

OPINIONS REGARDING SOLUTION TO PREGNANCY

We asked *what they thought a young girl should do if she were pregnant and unmarried.* Over half of the girls related to this question and responded to it. Sometimes girls phrased their opinions in terms of themselves, what they would do; sometimes they talked about others. It is significant that this is a subject they thought about a great deal, just as they thought about premarital sex. It is definitely not a "hidden" or unimportant subject. It is distressing that adult society gives girls so little opportunity to discuss it, except when they become pregnant.

We talked with a few girls who had experienced such pregnancies and they talked very freely about it. A girl who had her child at age 16 said:

> Well, me and my summer school teacher discussed it once. Her son is about the same age as mine, maybe about two or three weeks apart. Having a baby is really a beautiful experience, you know. . . . You go through pains, you go through agony, and all of that, but it is really beautiful to see that little head pop out, you know. And then you have something that you can call your own, and my first reaction was, "My God, you know he's beautiful." Maybe that's every mother's reaction, but childbirth is really a beautiful experience. . . .

I believe in people beginning to face reality about it and parents too.

(18, *Black, urban*)

Another young woman described her feelings as she went into labor:

I wasn't scared, but I didn't know what to do. My mother was with me, and my dad was with me, and I was happy, but I just didn't want it to hurt. I wanted it to stop and go home, and then when I really went into hard labor, I decided, "Well it's here so I might as well finish it." And then, it was kinda hard to believe after I had her. . . . Wow! She's really mine! She almost died something like three times and I guess that's why I appreciate her so much, cause I almost lost her.

They were all standing behind me, so that made it a lot easier.

(17, *American Indian, small town*)

This supportive experience obviously helped her and she can now help others.

I am now talking to my little sister, and keep her pretty well aware of things that can happen, because my mom's the type that gets embarrassed talking about things like that.

Another one could not talk to her parents, but had a good relationship with her boyfriend and his mother.

When I found out that I was pregnant I was so scared, scared, scared, and me and John sat and had so many talks. . . . We'd just sit and talk and talk. Like, we were both scared and kinda worried, you know, but we decided that we could work everything out. Abortion. . . . I wouldn't do it, though I thought about it. It would affect me forever. I would rather keep the baby. Giving it up would affect me forever too. I'll just keep it and stick it out . . . my fiance's mother said, "If you don't want the baby, or if you don't want it now and you want it later," she said, "I'll take it and keep it for you." (17, *White, small town*)

Another one was very realistic about her plans:

Well, I'm going to another group home and after I have it, I'm going to move to a foster home with the baby. And I'm going to finish school but I'm going to just take my main courses so, like it's half a day and I'm going to work the other half of the day.

Yes, the father is interested in the baby, but now that I found he was shooting up again, I told him that as soon as he got everything together and stopped, *then* he can call me. I would hate that after I have the baby and he's still shooting up and comes to see me and wants to take the baby out and something happens, you know. (16, *Black, urban*)

Even without personal experience as unwed mothers, girls talked freely about what one should do in such situations. They did not see simple solutions, nor did they stereotype. Girls did realize the complexity of the problem and also were aware of a variety of courses of action for the unwed mother. One of the "solutions" so prevalent in former centuries, suicide or the destruction of the newborn child, was hardly ever considered. Ten years ago when I talked with a woman physician about unmarried mothers, she said "People worry that we have more illegitimate children. I feel that this is great progress. In the early days of my practice I saw too many pregnant girls brought in on the 'slab.' They had committed suicide."

A small number, only fifty-two girls, said that the girl should get married regardless of whether she loved the man or not, just to give the child a father and a name.

> I think that she should marry the father and even if she doesn't love him, for the baby's sake and stuff like that. I'm old-fashioned.   (13, *White, urban*)

Seventeen percent of all live births in 1970 were to women 15 to 19 years old, and nearly three in ten were born to women out of wedlock.[5] Adoption agencies today have found that more girls want to *keep their children* than give them up for adoption. This tendency was borne out in the discussions we had with the girls. It is consistent with the high value they in general placed on having children and being a mother. The largest number suggested that an unwed mother should keep her child. Yet often the wish to keep the child was not a joyous affirmation of raising another human being, but more a rejection of other possibilities. Some, for instance, did not want an abortion:

> I think she should go ahead and have it. But . . . if she tells the boy who's the father and he don't love her, well, I don't think she should get married. I think she got herself into it and she should go ahead and have it instead of having an abortion. She should bring the child up. It's a lot of responsibility you know, if you're . . . to bring a kid up by yourself.   (16, *White, rural*)

Some hoped to marry the child's father at some time in the future. Sometimes the girl insisted that a pregnant young woman must keep her child as a punishment, much like wearing the symbol of the "scarlet letter."

> Have the baby cause it's her fault. She got that way. Keep it or get married.
> (15, *White, rural*)
> It takes two to tango with. The baby didn't ask to be born, see, so I think she should have it, cause you know, it's really not the baby's fault; it's your fault, you know.   (12, *Chicana, urban*)

And some just wanted the child. The girls who kept their children knew problems and yet were satisfied with their decision, but at the time we talked with them, the children were still babies.

> I wanted the baby but nobody was willing to help me and everybody was against me. All my girlfriends' parents wouldn't let them hang around with me

[5] M. Zelnick, and J. Kantner. "The Resolution of Teenage First Pregnancies," *Family Planning Perspectives*, Vol. 2, Spring 1974, pp. 74–80.

and I think that was what made me hold on to my boyfriend . . . he was like the only one left who would look at me or talk to me. I guess I smile now when I look back. It wasn't as hard as it seemed then. It was hard but I got over it. Like for awhile I held a grudge against my parents and I hated them and I wouldn't talk to them cause they threw me out and they wouldn't listen to my side. Now my mother realizes that she maybe made a few mistakes and she loves the baby and everything and she's trying to make up for it . . . it's not so bad now.

(17, *White, suburban*)

Beautiful! Really great. Like I wanted to get pregnant. I won't say I didn't. I really didn't think of a baby, if I had a baby, and I had a baby. It was great, 'cause now I got him and nobody can take him away from me. He's mine, I made him, he's great. Something real who can give me happiness. He can make me laugh and he can make me cry and he can make me mad. . . .

Some think to have a kid you have to have a father and you have to have a mother, and the father has to have a job from nine to five and the mother has to clean the house and cook the meals. . . . It's not like that. I mean, he gets up when he wants to get up. I get up and I do my things and I feed him and I don't have a husband and I'm getting along.

These old ladies like they see me at a bus stop and they say, "You have the baby yourself?" and I say, "He's fed, he's dressed and he's loved, what more could you ask for?" They look at me like I'm rude, but it's the truth.

(17, *White, suburban*)

The next largest number of girls would *place the child for adoption* because they thought that they were too young to be helpful to the child, felt that they had no resources for raising the child, or believed that it was important for a child to have two parents. They also resented forced marriages.

If I were to get pregnant I don't think I would be married. I would probably put the baby up for adoption because I think you are too young to marry at sixteen because you are kind of tied down. And if you have a child you can't finish your schooling really. And that's more important than being married.

(16, *White, suburban*)

It all depends on how mature she is and how much responsibility and if she's got things. When she first finds out she's pregnant, and she wants to keep the baby, she should have things like money for medical bills to go through with it, shelter. And if not, then I think the girl should give it up for adoption unless the parents are willing to take it.

(17, *White, urban*)

Abortion was discussed openly. Sixty-six percent of all the girls who talked about sex discussed it. Again, some talked from personal experience whereas others speculated. The girls who were against abortion were more outspoken. They usually advocated some other solution to pregnancy. About one-quarter of the girls who discussed abortion were for it and thought it preferable to bearing an unwanted child. Another 25 percent were either ambivalent about abortion, considered it an individual matter, or thought it was all right for others but not for themselves. In this group some girls considered abortion justified if the girl had become pregnant after being raped.

Here are some examples of opinions expressed *against* abortion.

I think abortion is wrong. You are killing a new life that is starting up. And you should think before you kill the baby because you wouldn't want to be killed if you were going to be born.

I think if they get pregnant, they should go ahead and have their baby and maybe give it away. I think it's [abortion] all wrong because there are a lot of people who would like to have that baby.   (17, *White, rural*)

I think abortion is terrible. Because it's killing, you aren't even giving the kid a chance. I think if you are going to fool around, you should get on the pill or something, because why kill it when you didn't really have to get pregnant.

And I would never have an abortion because I feel the baby is part of me. And I think having kids is just the greatest miracle in the whole world. So I'm against it.   (16, *White, suburban*)

I don't believe in abortion. I think that everyone has the right to life. And taking it away from them is, you know, something that shouldn't be done cause there were a lot of preventions that could have been made if they really didn't want the child.

I know about birth control pills and there are instruments that the male can use and foam that women can use.   (15, *Black, urban*)

And here are the voices *for* abortion.

Well, if she really loves the guy, she would put him through court. If not, she would have an abortion if she can afford it.

Well, I would force the guy to marry me. If not, I just wouldn't have a baby, I wouldn't feel right.   (17, *Chicana, urban*)

If it happens [pregnancy] and you think you have a man who loves you and will stay by you, keep it. But if you really think he is not—you still have a whole life ahead of you. Get an abortion.   (16, *Oriental, urban*)

I believe strongly that every woman, you know—it just seems so obvious to me that I can't imagine why people freak out over the thought of abortion. Of course, it should be the woman's decision. If she doesn't want to bear it, she shouldn't have to. And having somebody else control that choice just seems absolutely absurd to me; and people just freak out, and come at you with all this, "You're a murderer, murderer, you're killing." And they just, you know, just go practically berserk when the subject is mentioned. Now, if I didn't see people doing that around me it wouldn't even dawn on me that people would react like that. I really believe strongly in birth control, use a method of contraception other than abortion; I'll agree with anyone on that!
                    (16, *White, small town*)

And there were those who considered abortion all right but were not sure that they would want it for themselves.

I could never have an abortion myself, but I believe in it for other people at a very early stage. A lot of things I can really relate to other people but not to myself, I could never handle that.   (16, *Inuit, small town*)

> I accept the abortion and the birth controls because of the fact that sex really is the "in" thing and to other girls, it is a necessity, because sex is a very important part in life. And so, if the girl is really young, and she really don't want that child, and she knows that she can't take care of her child and stuff like that, then I can see where she could—but I would never do it.
>
> But if somebody else wants to do it, I wouldn't cut 'em down for it, because I'd figure that it's their and God's decision, not mine. And I'm not to judge anybody, and nobody's to judge me. I don't think that if I was in the situation of being pregnant now, I don't think I could do that. But if another girl wants to do that, it's her own business because it's her own body. So I think it's up to the person. I myself wouldn't do it.   (17, *American Indian, small town*)

There were those who felt that it was *up to the individual* to make decisions like that and they were very tolerant about it.

> I feel like it's . . . I would hate to take a child's life but if it's going to be better for the child, I'd do it. I just feel like whatever is best that you think. If you think you can afford to give your life to this child, work day and night and starve yourself, you know, like clothes and social activities and all that, go ahead, if you really want it. But if you really don't, if you really got something against it . . . I mean even if it's just the slightest doubt, don't keep it.
>
> I have a sister that got pregnant when she was 17, and I can see right now, you know, she's really had to sacrifice.   (17, *Black, suburban*)

And most girls, even those who were in general against abortion, were for it when rape was involved:

> I think abortions for the sake of having an abortion, getting pregnant, having another abortion is wrong. I think if someone does that, they don't deserve to have children. But abortions for the sake of saving a life, the mother's life or maybe . . . a lot of times you hear about rape and the mother just doesn't want the child. I think abortion is right then.   (17, *White, small town*)
>
> Abortion depends on the situation. If a girl just goes out and gets pregnant, I mean, if she has intercourse with a guy, it was just as much her fault, then I could really say abortion—forget it. But in a case of rape, or something unwillingly, I would consider an abortion, because then it's not . . . it's not really her fault.   (17, *Black, urban*)

DISCUSSION OF SEX EXPERIENCES

Opinions of the girls were not always related to actual experiences. Even though we did not ask the girls, many spontaneously talked about their own sex experiences. No girl advocated "casual" sex with several partners; in fact, we heard of comparatively few experiences of this kind. In the whole sample, only a small number were prostitutes. This fact does not mean that we can say that the number is not larger, nor that one should neglect this information even if only a few were prostitutes. By prostitution

I mean here only the sexual act performed for money. The few girls who talked about it were sometimes forced into it and some were very young. Here's a 13-year-old from a white-collar background:

> Prostitution . . . because I really needed the money. . . . Nobody ever discussed sex with me. My mom discussed the menstrual period with me before I had it, but that's about all. . . . Usually I didn't like prostitution because I was scared, so it made it unpleasant.
>
> I was molested once . . . So, I am watching TV, you know, watching TV on the floor right in front of the TV, and he [mother's boyfriend] was sitting on the couch, and he told me to come sit up next to him. So I did and I was sitting and I fell asleep on the couch . . . and I woke up . . . and so my pants were down and everything.   (13, *White, suburban*)

Here was a very young girl whose first sex experience was a forced and demeaning one and who had had practically no sex instruction.

Of the 756 girls who talked about sex, 30 percent volunteered that they had had intercourse. In no way does that mean that we therefore can conclude accurately that 25 percent of the total population had intercourse nor that this is a representative figure. We can only say that a quarter of the girls interviewed willingly talked about intercourse, reflected on it, and gave us some insight into their feelings about their experiences. And here we found some significant facts that should help parents, schools, and youth organizations to work with more sensitivity toward our adolescent girls. There emerged in the opinion of the girls—and based on their own experience—a watershed age at around 14 years. Girls felt that sexual intercourse before the age of 14 comes too early, is alarming. With the exception of one girl, all those who experienced sex before that age described it as unpleasant. Yet, girls with a variety of standards for themselves considered sexual activity after the age of 14 or 15 more usual, and more acceptable.

Adjudicated girls talked about earlier sex experiences more than girls in the rest of the population. One could conclude that they had matured earlier. I think though it is more related to the fact that the watershed concept is shared also by the adult population. Therefore, a girl who has early sex experiences and comes to the attention of authorities is considered more unusual and in danger. Unfortunately—as seen over and over again—the institutions supposedly created to help the girl instead aggravated her problem:

> 1. She was segregated from boys in girls' institutions and thus was unable to learn to establish a healthy, friendly relation with them.
>
> 2. She was exclusively with other girls, thus directing her awakening sexual instincts completely toward other females. It is known—or should be known—that affectionate relations both with other girls and boys are perfectly normal in adolescence. Yet the exposure to a one-sex living situation over a long period of time, such as in delinquency institutions, drives girls over into lesbianism.

And the frequently damaged self-respect that results from early, mostly forced, sex relations is further damaged by designating the girl as delinquent and exposing her to often humiliating practices, such as having to follow commands, join in mass activities, or make "forced confessions" before a group in so-called "therapeutic" positive peer culture sessions.

Although the older girl who talked about sex experiences usually described an ongoing, rather stable relationship, the younger girls talked of forced encounters, mostly (though not exclusively) by adults. Rape was done either by someone in their home (father, brother, cousin, stepfather, friends of mother)[6] or occurred while they were running away.

> I learned about sex when I was eleven from my cousin. He was thirty-four years old. He showed me. (14, *White, suburban*)

> My dad raped me when I was fourteen. The charges I pressed against him were for attempted rape, because my brother and sister were little and I couldn't see them being put into a home, like I was being put in and I hated to hurt my parents more than they had to be hurt. I was really hurt too, cause I was close to my dad and it kind of tore me up. (15, *White, urban*)

> One time I was raped on the run. This guy that gave me a lift . . . we started going out in these woods and I asked him where he was going and he said, he told me it was none of my business . . . he told me to take my clothes off, and I said "No!" He tore my clothes off of me and beat me and stuff. But I never did turn him in, cause I didn't want to turn myself in.
>
> (14, *White, small town*)

One girl described the terribly painful experience of being ostracized for a sex experience she had not wanted.

> Three men raped me. I had an infection after that. I didn't want to go to school. I didn't want to. . . . I didn't even want my brother to touch me. I didn't want nobody. And I hated my sister, cause she laughed. And then when she got mad at me she talked about that. She threw it up in my face and then it would make me feel bad. And she tells, "Don't touch her, kids," cause I had a disease and stuff like that. I couldn't sit down, I was bleeding all the time. I got over it, but I still was ashamed, and I felt bad. . . . (16, *Black, urban*)

What terribly insensitive treatment girls are exposed to after they feel already demeaned.

> I was raped when I was 12—it was when I ran away from home and this man picked me up. He took me to his house and he raped me. He was offering me a ride. I'd run away from home, and . . . well, he went around the house,

---

[6] Our findings are similar to those of C.R. Hayman, F.R. Lewis, W.F. Stewart, and M. Grant, "A Public Health Program for Sexually Assaulted Females," *Public Health Reports* 82, June 1967, pp. 497–504. In their study of sexually assaulted women in Washington, D.C., they found that the highest number was during ages ten to fourteen and that in seventy-five percent of cases the offender was known by the child.

and I went down the street and called my grandmother, and she came and picked me up. And then my mother took me to the doctor and the doctor told my mother something. When I got home I got a whipping. She said that I'd been bad. (16, *White, small town*)

We also found that girls experienced sex for the first time under the influence of drugs and alcohol (several reported that in such a case it was rather agreeable).

We wasn't in love for real, but we went out and we were smoking and stuff and the next thing I knew was . . . but I didn't want to. It was more high. I stayed in the house ashamed and I wouldn't go out. I was embarrassed. And then finally I just realized I'm going to have to go out sometime so I just went out, and you know, nobody put me down. (16, *White, rural*)

It takes girls a long time to overcome such early and destructive sex experiences.

When I did finally have sexual intercourse with my boyfriend it didn't mean nothing to me. I didn't like it. There was no feeling or anything. It didn't satisfy me.

. . . If I could, I would have saved myself till I was married to the right man. It's just that all you have to give to a man is your whole body, and love, and I feel you shouldn't give it out to every dude you go with. . . .

When I first had it, it hurt. I wasn't used to it . . . they say it's life, it's natural, so I know, I'm not going to hide from it. Once you get going, it's good. Which is the truth. Once you get going, it's good. You are relaxed and everything. (16, *Oriental, urban*)

In our population, we found comparatively few girls who expressed a preference for lesbianism. Those who did were mostly girls in institutions who had no other outlets for their sexual drives.

We got a perspective on the young women's attitude toward homosexuality when we raised questions about what kind of people they thought were "different." A comparatively large number, 34 percent of those who responded, saw homosexuals as different from themselves. Again, as with many other sexual attitudes, most girls were comparatively tolerant. They said that people had a right to choose their sex partners. They could accept homosexuality as long as it wasn't pushed on them. Although several felt uncomfortable around homosexuals, they did not consider them bad. Still, this is the only category of "difference" in which 100 young women expressed deep disapproval, considered it a disease or morally wrong. These attitudes apply across all racial groups, but with an especially high percentage of Chicanas expressing the most negative attitudes. Examples of the very few, only five young women, who expressed a positive attitude toward homosexuality are:

I'm for it. I could very easily be bisexual, if I could find a woman that I could love just as much as I can love a man. I could never be total . . . I could never be a Lesbian, because I don't, I guess I just can't give up men. (16, *White, rural*)

I think if guys can't associate with girls and they associate better with guys, it's great, you know? They have to have their sex somehow. They're pretty happy some of the time. They can't keep caging themselves up.

(14, *White, urban*)

Others who talked about the individual's right to decide either had known some homosexuals or were particularly opposed to any kind of prejudice.

. . . I suppose my attitude is a positive one as far as letting people live their own lives. My parents were once afraid that I was having an affair with an older woman. And, I think it scared them a lot. I wasn't having an affair with my friend. I was surprised at how much it scared them, and I don't know whether it would have scared them if this person had been a man. I think that people have to live their own lives, and to be down on somebody because of how they choose their life isn't fair.

(15, *White, urban*)

That is a matter of freedom. Nobody can oppose that. If one wants to do that, it is to oneself. I have always said when I was little, if I like women, that is my problem. If I like men, the same, because it is me who is going to be in the situation.

(17, *Puerto Rican, small town*)

And here are expressions from those who did not feel comfortable around homosexuals and considered them strange.

I don't know, I think they're pretty weird you know, but I guess they get a kick out of it. But I think it's better with a boy and a girl. (16, *Chicana, urban*)

. . . When I got over there, she told me that the two were Lesbians and wanted to share the room. It was a weird situation. It just does something to me to see two girls walking with their arms around each other. It just didn't seem natural to me. Maybe that's the way I was brought up. Maybe it's just hard for me to accept. But if that's what they want to do, I can't say anything.

(17, *White, rural*)

Well, I understand sometimes how they turn into one but if I . . . well I don't like them, and I couldn't really say I just don't like them. My uncle is one and I don't have anything to do with him. Just as long as he just says "Hi" and "Goodbye," well, that's okay. . . . If that's what they want to do, then fine.

(16, *Black, urban*)

Girls who felt this way were still tolerant. This was not the case, however, among those who felt strong animosity toward homosexuality.

I don't know really. I've never known nobody like that. But it seems like it's dirty. I don't know. I can't really picture anyone like that, but I just think it's dirty.

(14, *Chicana, urban*)

I think that it's not good at all because a man was not made for another man. They were made for the opposite sex. That's why there are two sexes. And I really feel sorry for homosexuals, cause they're losing a lot, you know. I think that something's really wrong with their minds, how they were brought up.

(17, *White, urban*)

I think that it is quite a heavy problem, because homosexuality, I think shouldn't be. God created a woman for a man and did not create men to make love among themselves. For this purpose he put Eve to accompany Adam . . . and homosexuality is not well seen by society or by anyone.

(16, *Puerto Rican, suburban*)

They're sick, send them to a sanitorium.   (14, *Chicana, urban*)

SEX EDUCATION

According to our information, *sex education* is more available today than twenty years ago, but it is still given too late, is poorly presented, and is insufficient:

My mother never told me about it, cuz at the time I was too young. I didn't learn about it until I had the experience.   (15, *Black, urban*)

When I first made sex, I didn't even know you could get pregnant. The first time I got pregnant. I was twelve. I do not think it is all right to have intercourse before you get married.

When I first found out I was pregnant and I didn't even know what pregnant meant and I went to the nurse and she told me, "That means you are going to have a little baby," and I said, "What?" and then I told my parents and I thought I had been really bad until I came up here. And when I came up here I didn't think I was bad.   (15, *Inuit, rural*)

My mother wouldn't ever talk or come right out and tell me about it. Even when I pick up a book, and read something that has just a little bit to do with boy and girl mush, she gets mad and asks me why I'm reading all those sex books, am I going to do it or what? But she wouldn't ever tell me anything about sex.   (16, *White, small town*)

I was in my home town, and it was a halfway house, see. My mother never told me about things like that, you know, she really didn't think too much about that. And they have this lady come out there once a week that would talk to all the girls.   (16, *Chicana, small town*)

And a most pathetic comment from a pregnant young woman:

I was about seven when my mom said . . . no I was about six when my mom said, "If you get kissed, you are going to get pregnant." So I kissed and I didn't get pregnant. And so she says, when I was about thirteen, "You screw around and you're going to get pregnant." So I screwed around and I got pregnant. That was about three years later.   (15, *White, urban*)

In a time when menstruation—because of our general good nutritional standards—is starting far earlier than about 100 years ago, and when general sex is discussed more openly, it is appalling to find how little girls know about biological facts in regard to sex and especially in regard to its influence as a life force and its relationship to a general philosophy of life. Girls frequently said that they received sex information, but there is much misinformation that goes along with the information.

Like one friend—one of my friends just, when I was about ten, came up to me and said, "You know what I found out?" And I said "What?" And she said, "I found out that babies come when daddy goes to the bathroom inside your mother." And I just went "Oh Jesus!" "God, how gross!"   (17, *White, urban*)

The school where I used to go didn't believe in sex education. My mother was too embarrassed to tell me anything. Everything I learned, I learned from other kids. Most of what they told me wasn't true. You know, they'd talk about birth control like they knew what they were talking about, but they really didn't. They wanted to be cool though.   (16, *White, suburban*)

The first time I heard about it, and I didn't believe it, but I was too scared to ask my mom, was in 5th grade. When this girl, I heard her talking to this other friend of mine, and they had this little book and she was just reading away and I told her that was a lie because I still believed in, I don't know, if it was the stork that I believed in or just. . . . I believed that if God saw that you got married, he just gave you a baby.   (15, *Chicana, urban*)

And girls are frightened by older women telling them about their awful lot in life and the terrors of suffering through the menopause.

Although mothers are usually the ones who explain menstruation to girls, they often do so only after it occurs. Sometimes it is not explained at all, or done in an embarrassing way. It is significant, for instance, that most mothers still hand girls pads at their first menstruation instead of telling them about the much more comfortable tampons—a sign of the mother's own discomfort with touching her body or misinformation about the use of those devices.

Oh, I knew what my period was all about but the thing that really bothered me was that I didn't know how to use a Tampax. That really bothered me because I hated using Kotex pads. Nobody taught me how either. I had to try to use them myself.   (14, *White, urban*)

The girls' descriptions of frightening and painful experiences at their first menstruation were touching and sad:

It was horrible. My twin sister had started about a month earlier and she told me about it and I said "Oh no, I'm just gonna die." I had never heard about it before and she had never heard about it until she started.
(14, *White, urban*)

I didn't tell my mother about it for about a year and a half 'cause I was too embarrassed. I didn't tell anybody. I was too embarrassed to tell anybody, and now I am really open about it. It doesn't seem to be wrong anymore. Boy, before I started—nobody else had it and I was just afraid it would spread around school or something. Now—it is something natural and you just have to accept it.   (16, *White, urban*)

I didn't know about it. She [mother] never told me anything like that. I was scared, I just started washing all my underclothing hoping that my mother won't find out but she came in and caught me, she caught me washing it, and she started laughing at me. I was in the 5th grade, maybe 4th grade. But she never did tell me what it was. You learn more of that from the Girl Scouts. I

mean she told me it wasn't anything to worry about, it's something that happens, you know, but she didn't tell me what it meant and stuff like that.
(18, *Chicana, urban*)

Ooh, I thought I was gonna die, I didn't know what was going on, cause my grandparents never told me nothing about it. My mother never . . . I've lived with my grandparents almost all my life. I started at a very young age. I said, "Mother, I'm bleeding." She looks down on me and she goes "oh-oh." She went and got me sanitary pads and everything else and started telling me about it. I was eight when I started.   (15, *Chicana, small town*)

It was weird. I don't know, 'cause see, my mother, like I said it happened when I was eleven years old. My mother never told me nothing about it, so one morning I woke up and then the bed was all full of blood and I was all freaked out and went to call my mother, "Look at it." I was so scared and didn't know what to do, and then she just told me what it was, but that's all I knew. I didn't even know where babies came from, or anything 'cause she never bothered to explain things to me. I was scared!   (15, *Chicana, urban*)

Yes, I remember, I was twelve years old when I first menstruated. I was outside riding my bike and I fell and when I got up I was just bloody all over. I thought I had hurt myself or something. So I went home and I was crying, and everything. My mom didn't know what was wrong with me till she couldn't stop the bleeding and then she found out where it was coming from. She said "Okay" and she sat me down and had my little talk.   (15, *Black, suburban*)

How can young women grow up to respect themselves and their being women if the first experience with their own sexual maturity is so disturbing, something to hide, to be afraid of? Though it was a minority of girls who told us that they had absolutely no preparation for menstruation, even those who said that they knew about it beforehand frequently talked about the fear that accompanied the actual occurrence. This only means that their preparation was not a positive one. How very different, and much more positive, does life look for the girls who are fortunate enough to have mothers or friends or teachers who not only prepare them but make them feel that it is wonderful to become a mature women.

I had my first period at twelve, knew about it before and wasn't scared. I thought I was feeling pretty good. Cause then I would know I was growing up to be a lady, you know. And I really had a nice feeling.   (17, *Black, urban*)

I had my first period at age twelve. I was visiting my mother and I went to work with her. She cleaned up offices and stuff like that for awhile, and I was helping her. I went to the restroom and I said, "Mother, I need a nickel." She said "What for?" and I said, "I think I started my period." I thought I'd already been grownup but I guess you could say I thought it was a real important day of my life.   (14, *Black, urban*)

I was in the seventh grade. All my friends had already started. I was at the end of seventh grade. And I remember so good, cause I couldn't wait. Cause we had a film in the sixth grade on it. And they gave us all these books and stuff, and they would say the ages between, I think, it was thirteen and sixteen. I was, I think, only thirteen. I don't know, it just came. I didn't have any feeling you know, I didn't feel any different.

I just knew when I went to the bathroom and I talked to a girlfriend. She told me that I was, you know, having a period, and I was so happy. I was waiting for it. My mother had already bought me all these things. I don't know, just felt like I was just growing up, you know. (16, *Chicana, urban*)

One cannot always blame parents for not having given early, accurate and thoughtful sex instruction, because many of them themselves know little about it and have been raised to be embarrassed about it. Frequently they do not know the right words to use with their children. Many probably would welcome it if someone in simple language and with respect for their own feelings would help them to know themselves better. Books are written but they are mostly directed toward a middle-class audience.

I remember decades ago, in the late 1920s, watching a gifted physician talking about sex with working men and women in the slum areas of Berlin. He never offended them by using fancy terms nor gave the slightest indication of his "superior" knowledge. He simply let them ask questions —which came hesitantly, slowly, sometimes in a whisper. He never made them ashamed of not speaking up. He totally respected their private being, but he helped them understand the workings of their own drives and thus enabled them to be happier with themselves and with their children. I learned much from him. I learned not to make sex something separate from the rest of life, to see the relationship between men and women as something ideally based on mutual respect, including their sexual activities. He talked as clearly and as openly with the parents as he did with young people. And he never separated the sexes so that they would not feel that they had something to hide from each other, but rather would realize that they had something to learn from and about each other.

Girls did tell us about sex information gained through the schools; in fact, schools were the major source named for such information. This surely is a step forward in informing our young people about this vital part of their being. Yet, unfortunately, it was often done as "this thing apart" or presented in a language totally foreign to the girls.

They had classes for us down there. It was really, really dumb. All the guys knew, you know. They handed out these little pamphlets for us girls, and they'd cart us off, supposedly, you know, discreetly from the room. And they'd cart us off at intervals, and they'd show us these films and everything.
(17, *White, urban*)

In fourth grade, it was a special presentation and the girls were separated from the boys. . . . I think it would have been better to have them both in the same room, because I never knew how a boy developed until about two years ago. I knew how girls developed and I thought it was something I should know. If you show it to them both at the same time, you won't get so embarrassed about it. (14, *White, urban*)

Sex education is okay but like in our school when we had it there, she used these words, I can't even understand them. They were so hard, they used such big words and everything and when we have a test or something, I get the words all mixed up. (16, *White, small town*)

Sex information in school is frequently given very hesitantly. Special permission slips are often necessary. There are, of course individual teachers who really help the girls, but they are still rare.

> I learned about sex in fourth grade, in school. . . . I thought it was good. My mother never talked to me about it and for her to have to explain it to me, I think it would have been embarrassing for both of us. I think it was good for me.   (16, *White, small town*)

> My mother never really talked to us. So, I was around fourteen, she was mentioning the word sex, you know, and she whispered it. I learned in school.
> (15, *Chicana, urban*)

> They keep it a big secret. Like you'd have to have permission slips to see a movie about your periods, you know, but I didn't. I learned a lot from my health teacher; she was a good teacher. She was one of my favorite teachers, she taught me a lot. She's the type of teacher that could talk to you easily about it, you know; a lot of teachers, they rush right through sex education; they don't really want to talk about it. But she didn't mind talking about it. I know she taught a lot of girls in that class something because they, I mean a lot of girls didn't know nothing when they went in there.   (16, *White, urban*)

> In biology, that's where I really learned about it. We learned about every kind of reproduction there is. The biology course was good. Like my freshman year I had biology, and we had some people, it was really weird. First we had people who were for contraceptions/contraceptives and abortions. And they came out, and they told us all about different kinds, like the pill and the IUD and everything. And then we had these two, three ladies. One of 'em was pregnant and they were from Birthright. And they showed us this hideous movie about the fetus after it's been aborted. And that just, oh, it was at about 9:00 o'clock in the morning they were showing us this, I thought it was just sick. And they were really, oh, they were so weird, they were so, they're such fanatics, you know. They got really upset if you asked them any questions about abortion, you know, while the other people were so calm about it.
> (17, *White, urban*)

Practically none of the girls discussed the possibility of venereal disease when they spoke about sex relations. As in so many other areas, they often seemed to have little information about it, though those who talked about sex information stated that it was one of the subjects discussed in school. One of the girls said:

> I feel we need to know more facts—I really do. We need to know more about VD and about getting pregnant and stuff like that. . . .   (17, *White, small town*)

And a 14-year-old said that all she had learned in school about sex was:

> You catch disease by doing that . . . sex before marriage is bad.
> (14, *Black, urban*)

Such poor information is available in too many areas in spite of the fact that venereal disease has taken on almost epidemic proportions.[7]

---

[7] *VD Statistical Letter*, U.S. Department of Health, Education and Welfare,

The intellectually inclined girl certainly finds information almost by herself.

The way I learned about it was in science I had this friend, it was this boy that I kind of liked and this other guy, and we had to do a term report in science. And so I chose people pollution. Went to Planned Parenthood, everywhere, adoption agencies, abortion, everything. I learned so much. I mean like every kind of device, the prices, everything possible to learn about it. I learned so much about the technical things about sex, you know, everything. And I really got a lot out of it. Because when we went to Planned Parenthood, we went through the classes, we went in there as if we were getting the pill. We got our blood tests, we had everything done, and we went to interview and everything. (15, *White, urban*)

Well, I shocked my mom because I learned mine from the encyclopedia. Like I'd be looking up different things, you know. This is probably when I was about first or second grade. You know a little bit then, but not too thorough. And, you know, it's all there in the encyclopedia. It just looked like an interesting article and then, little kids are always curious about sex anyway, so I would just read the article and I didn't think too much of it, and then all of a sudden I'd come up with these facts in conversation and mom would go "Where did you find that out? I never told you that yet." Mom's never made any distinctions about what we could and couldn't read. For some books she'd say "I wouldn't bother reading that. It doesn't have that good of a plot, and the rest of it's just kind of trash." But she wouldn't forbid us to read it, and so you just kind of pick up things.

I think I'm fairly well educated about sex. I haven't engaged in intercourse, but I don't think I'll be afraid of it when I'm married or anything like that. I think the biggest reasons against premarital sex is just because of all the legal hassle and difficulty you can wind up in. I'm not afraid of it emotionally. (17, *White, suburban*)

She can even get what she needs—like birth control pills—without her elders knowing about it. A girl openly told us her way of going about this.

You see, I have acne, and estrogen hormones are used to control acne. In fact, it's more broken out now because I am on my period now. I take twenty-one—you don't take it for a week. So what I did was, I got this article out of *Time* magazine, and I thought I would kill two birds with one stone. I'll clear up some of my acne and I won't get pregnant. So I would periodically say I wasn't going to go to school, and I would lock myself up in the bathroom and not go to school for up to a week at a time, if my face was broken out. I was very emphatic about it, and I told my parents that I was never going to go to school again because my face was so horrible unless they got, as I called them, hormone pills, birth control pills. They figured there was no way they were going to get me to school, so they took me to the doctor and got me the goddamned pills. I'm very good at manipulation. (17, *White, urban*)

August 1974, Issue No. 120, states that in 1973 the rate of syphilis per 100,000 population in females 15 to 19 years old was 19.7 percent and of gonorrhea was 1234.5.

Where there is a relaxed open information and discussion of sex, the girl has obviously more self-confidence, sees herself as a significant being, and sees any decision in regard to sex as part of a total value system, without being either defiant, or moralistic.

> When my mother was pregnant with my little brother, I used to ask her all the time how she got pregnant, so she had to tell me. She told me in detail, she took a lot of pain to tell me. And I was so proud because I was the only one in class who knew about it. I think sex education should be taught because most parents don't tell them. They try to put it off. Most people find it out in the back alleys.

> I wouldn't have sex before marriage. It depends on the individual but I don't want to. My mother has always told me "It's always up to you, but you've got to consider that you should never hurt a person. You might get pregnant with a child and you always have to consider that." A child needs the companionship of the father. It's different if he's dead. If he dies, the people in the community will know about it and the people will try to help him. But if he's illegitimate, they will look down on him. I think that's the attitude of people.   (17, *White, small town*)

> I learned about sex from my mother and my sisters, at a very early age. I was taught everything. I was at least eight or nine . . . when they started talking about it. Nothing was withheld. Everything was talked about even with my little brother and my little sister, and I benefited from it.   (17, *Black, urban*)

> I think I learned it at home. The open discussions I can carry on, especially with my mother. My father started working away from home about a year ago and so he doesn't get home until weekends. And being the oldest one at home now, my mother and I have grown on much more of a friend basis than we used to have. And we really get along good.

> Some kids think it's kind of crazy how I go home and tell mom about the party I went to or what X and I did that night. And they say, "You tell your mom that?" I just kind of laugh and my mother laughs too because we have such a close relationship. If it wasn't for that, I often wonder how some of these kids who have such a barrier with their parents get along, because there isn't any sort of education in our system that discusses sex. It's kind of frightening when you get out and find it's there.   (17, *White, rural*)

Basically the teenage woman, like all men and women over the ages, see sex as part of the emotion of love, with all its sorrow and its joy, and often as a deep commitment. Sometimes she cries out because she does not understand her own choice:

> *Dear God, who watches over me.*
> *Please help me solve this mystery*
> *I loved him and he broke my heart*
> *I love him still though we're apart.*
> *Please tell me why, why this must be*
> *that I love him, and he not loves me.*
> *To him, I'm dirt beneath his feet.*

And yet, I still believe he is sweet.
He lied and said he loved me more,
Than anyone he loved before.
A million tears, I know I've cried
since first I heard that he had lied.
He lied about the way he cared;
he lied about the things we shared.
All my dream or thought
all attribute to the love he brought.
So dear God, please try to see
why these problems bother me.
I tried so hard so I could see
why all these things should trouble me.

TERRI DURAN (15, *Chicana, urban*)

And also:

With you my love
We will walk on the sand of the beaches.
Hand in hand.
Through the darkness of the night.
Through the brightness of our love.
Together we will make it last
Our love is forever
Like the sand on the beaches.

ANONYMOUS (15, *Oriental, suburban*)

SUMMARY

1. There is no widespread "sex revolution" among the girls, but
2. Sex is spoken about very openly.
3. Premarital sex was not considered a sin by most girls, including those who did not want it for themselves.
4. Early sex experiences, especially before the age of 14, were usually disagreeable, often forced. They occurred mostly in the home or while girls were running away from home.
5. Sex experiences after the age of 14 were not considered unusual or frightening by many girls.
6. Premarital sex was accepted by most girls, conditional on love; casual sex was usually not accepted and was considered demeaning.
7. Illegitimate children were accepted as matter-of-fact, but girls still felt the pressure that illegitimate children would bring to them. Most girls would suggest keeping the child; others suggested giving the child up for adoption.

Abortion was talked about openly, with approximately half of the girls against it and half either for it or considering it an individual matter.

8. Sex information is more available than in earlier years, especially through the schools. It is, however, often given late, is inadequate, and—if received through friends—misleading.

BIBLIOGRAPHY

BOWLBY, JOHN, "Maternal Care and Mental Health," *Bulletin of the World Health Organization*, Vol. III, No. 3, 1951, pp. 355–534.

CARTER, LILLIAN and MARY OSTENDORF, "The Awakening of Adolescent Femininity," *Journal of the School of Health*, Vol. XL, No. 4, April 1970, pp. 203–205.

CARTWRIGHT, P., "The Teenage Sexual Revolution and the Myth of an Abstinent Past," *Family Planning Perspectives*, Vol. IV, No. 1, 1972, p. 24.

Center for Youth Development and Research, *Dialogue on Youth*, Seminar Series No. 1, University of Minnesota, Minneapolis, Center for Youth Development and Research 1970.

CONGER, JOHN JANEWAY, *Adolescence and Youth*. New York: Harper and Row, 1973.

FURSTENBERG, FRANK, JR., LEON GORDIS, and MILTON MARKOWITZ, "Birth Control Knowledge and Attitudes Among Unmarried Pregnant Adolescents—A Preliminary Report," *Journal of Marriage and the Family*, Vol. XXXI, No. 1, 1969, pp. 34–42.

"Girls Under Eighteen Can Consent to Birth Control Services in Two-Fifths of the States," *Family Planning Digest*, Vol. I, No. 6, November 1972.

HAYMAN, C.R., "Sexual Assaults on Women and Girls," *Annals of Internal Medicine*, Vol. LXXII, February 1970, pp. 277–278.

KANTNER, JOHN F. and MELVIN ZELNICK, "Contraception and Pregnancy: Experience of Young Unmarried Women in the United States," *Family Planning Perspectives*, Vol. V, No. 1, Winter 1973, pp. 21–35.

———, "Sexual Experience of Young Unmarried Women in the United States," *Perspectives in Family Planning*, Vol. IV, No. 4, 1972, pp. 9–18.

McCANDLESS, BOYD R., *Adolescents: Behavior and Development*, Hinsdale, Ill.: Dryden Press, 1970.

Metropolitan Life Insurance Company, "Patterns of Venereal Disease Morbidity in Recent Years," *Statistical Bulletin*, Vol. 50, April 1969.

———, "Venereal Diseases—Recent Morbidity and Mortality," *Statistical Bulletin*, Vol. 54, November 1973.

MILLER, WARREN B., "Sexuality, Contraception and Pregnancy in a High School Population," *California Medicine*, Vol. CXIX, August 1973, pp. 14–21.

National Center for Health Statistics, "Age at Menarche," *Vital and Health Statistics*, Series 11, No. 133, DHEW Publication No. (HRA) 74–1615, Public Health Service, Washington, D.C., U.S. Government Printing Office, November 1973.

National YWCA Resources Center on Women, *Teen Women Tell About Their Needs*, 600 Lexington Avenue, New York: National Board, YWCA, 1974.

OFFER, DANIEL, "Attitudes Toward Sexuality in a Group of 1500 Middle Class Teen-Agers," *Journal of Youth and Adolescence*, Vol. I, No. 1, March 1972, pp. 81–90.

OSOFSKY, HOWARD J., *The Pregnant Teenager*. Springfield, Ill.: Charles C. Thomas, 1968.

REISS, IRA L., "The Sexual Renaissance: A Summary and Analysis," *Journal of Social Issues*, Vol. XXII, April 1966, pp. 123–137.

———, *The Social Context of Premarital Sexual Permissiveness*. New York: Holt, Rinehart and Winston, 1967.

ROTHCHILD, ELLEN, "Anatomy is Destiny: Psychological Implications of Adolescent Physical Changes in Girls," *Pediatrics*, Vol. XXXIX, April 1967, pp. 532–538.

SCHULTZ, L.G., "The Child Sex Victim—Social, Psychological and Legal Perspectives," *Child Welfare*, Vol. LII, March 1973, pp. 147–157.

SORENSON, ROBERT C., *Adolescent Sexuality in Contemporary America*. New York: World Publishing, 1973.

TORMES, YVONNE, *Child Victims of Incest*. Denver: The American Humane Association, Children's Division, 1968.

VD Statistical Letter, U.S. Department of Health, Education and Welfare, Issue No. 120, August 1974.

YANKELOVICH, DANIEL, "Startling Shifts Found in Youth's Views of Work, Morals," *Chronicle of Higher Education*, May 28, 1974.

YURDIN, M.O., "Recent Trends in Illegitimacy: Implications for Practice," *Child Welfare*, SLIS, No. 7, 1970, pp. 373 375.

ZELNICK, M. and J. KANTNER, "The Resolution of Teenage First Pregnancies," *Family Planning Perspectives*, Vol. VI, No. 2, Spring 1974, pp. 74–80.

THREE

ADULTS

Dear Elders (adults),
I have gone to find peace, love and quiet without hate. You have
not had the time to glance at a single ray of beauty or say a kind
word. Crystal (an imaginary adult) has time for these things.
Please don't cry which would be very hard for you to do anyway. If
you want these things you will find them at the end of the rainbow.
FROM A DIARY (14, *White, small town*)

When adults talk about young people in the 1970s, express their anxiety and often hostility, they make three basic assumptions:

1. There is an unbridgeable generation gap,
2. The family is falling apart and young people especially do not care about being part of the family, and
3. This is a totally permissive country and this permissiveness is the cause of troubles with teenagers.

What did we find?

THE MYTH OF THE GENERATION GAP

Certainly general differences and frictions exist between adults and young people, as they have over the centuries. No generation ever will follow exactly the pattern of the preceding one. Our times do encourage more open communication and self-assertion from anyone who wants to express a sense of outrage and who feels restricted or even subjugated. Young people, therefore, will more openly discuss their differences and stand up for what they consider their rights than at other times in our history. But, very significantly, we found that many of them want to erase the "gap" and one of their loudest cries is for adults to listen and understand. Among adults, too, we frequently find a greater expectation than in older societies to communicate with the young and the same yearning for mutual understanding. Authoritarian societies, like the European and Asian ones from which many Americans came, historically, did not consider communication between the generations important. They simply assumed that the elders would exercise the power and control and the young would submit. "Children should be seen and not heard" was an admonition that included also the adolescent. Apprenticeship in Europe usually meant a kind of slavery in which the young person had to obey his master without question. If the apprentice dared to speak up, physical punishment was considered the appropriate response. The same kind of system applied in fashionable English boarding schools in which "caning" was the accepted mode of discipline. In the past, around 1900 in central Europe, various youth movements fought this system and totally rejected adult society as hypocritical and unjust. The French sociologist, Guerrand, in his book describing the student revolts of the nineteenth century, commented:

> For the educated of this time, the students were first of all enemies. They had absolutely no rights. The only right they had was to be silent, to obey; they must never discuss anything or get together in groups that would even debate some decisions of the authority.[1]

After discussing the student situation, Guerrand went on to quote a ministerial text directed to teachers:

> I want to remind you that it is absolutely forbidden that these forms of organizations elect a president, have an office, carry any kind of sign or that they think they can establish any kind of rules. In our public schools there is only one authority and that is the personnel that is in the administration of education and supervision. Students of any age must only communicate with their teacher on an individual level. If one allows some kind of group association, that would be only under very exceptional circumstances and only for very definite reasons such as a school assignment.[2]

This highly authoritarian directive is dated October 20, 1928. Guerrand reminds us that it was not changed until August 1945.

In the "good old days," therefore, the generation gap was probably far wider than it is today, but there was very little *expectation* that it would be narrowed. Today, communication is sought, though frequently not achieved. Attitudes expressed by girls toward adults—adults in the family as well as others—fall into about three categories:

1. I am close to adults. I can talk to adults about personal problems, and I feel I can confide in them;
2. We get along all right but not when it comes to personal things; I can talk to adults about general things;
3. I am not close to adults; there is no adult I can turn to; I cannot talk to adults at all.

Our data show that most girls feel close to adults. An impressive 75 percent of the girls who talked about this attitude fell into this category. Many

[1] R.H. Guerrand, *Lycéens Révoltes Étudiants Révolutionnaires au 19e Siècle* (Paris, Les Edition du Temps, 1969), p. 36. Translated from the French by the author.

[2] Ibid.

girls were very realistic about what to expect of adults and did not think that they had to be perfect.

> I have people that I look up to quite a bit, but I don't think they're perfect because everyone has his faults. My brother-in-law is somebody I can go to talk to and tell my problems to; he's really understanding.   (16, *White, urban*)

And they do feel that they are equal human beings.

> Cause everybody has got a child in them and an adult in them and so adults can be children and some children can be adults. I don't see why you should be treated differently.   (16, *White, small town*)

A few girls said that they got along all right with adults, but more on a tenuous level. They felt that they must be careful not to cross the adults.

> I get along pretty well with adults. But I don't talk a lot. That's one thing that I have going for me when I get with adults. I just like to sit and listen to everybody gossip. I just indulge myself in gossip and just sit there and listen. And they say, "Oh, she's a nice girl, she doesn't talk, she doesn't do anything."   (14, *White, suburban*)

> I get along with adults. But I can't really talk to adults, you know. Like as far as them being my friends, you know; I think of adults as adults, somebody you watch out for, not to push the wrong button and everything. They scream at you when they get mad at you sometimes, then they just get all upset with you. They don't want to talk to you, or they push you to one side or something like that.   (15, *Black, urban*)

> I like most of them. Most of them are pretty friendly. I get along with them, but I've never been close to one particular adult.   (18, *White, urban*)

The smallest number, only 7 percent of those who talked about adults in general, were totally and completely alienated from them:

> I just don't think very much about adults. I don't think adults understand teenagers very well, and they don't try to understand them. I just think that . . . well, I will be happy when I am free and do not have anybody around telling me what to do all of the time.   (16, *White, small town*)

> I hate a lot of adults, and maybe some adults are neat. But I've grown up hating adults, and it's real hard to kick the habit.   (14, *White, urban*)

Among the alienated ones were mostly girls who had been adjudicated delinquent and had gone through very damaging life experiences. Some of these girls yearned for their lives as children, the period in which adults were more giving and protective of them and when they themselves followed adults unquestioningly:

> *I wish I was a little girl*
> *Pretty as could be.*
> *My hair just one long curl*
> *That's what I want to be.*

I remember when I was little
My life so fun—
And me so brittle
Just living in the sun.
What mistake did I make
Growing up so fast?

ANONYMOUS (17, *White, rural*)

Yet a number of the younger girls could not communicate with adults under any circumstances. When we enter the arena of deprived and assaulted girls, the picture of "golden childhood" changes into a horror scene.

Girls were outspoken in regard to qualities they disliked and admired in adults. Significantly, these qualities fit in with the value system of our general society, regardless of age. Here are the qualities we found that girls disliked in adults (the first four were mentioned most frequently):

They don't respect us; they don't listen or try to understand us; they think they are too good for us and they are always right.

They push their ideas and expectations on us and force us to do things; they are demanding.

They are too strict; they don't trust us to do anything.

They are old-fashioned; they want us to do things the way they used to do them when they were kids.

They cuss and yell at us all the time; they are hard to get along with and they are hard to please.

They are generally unfriendly.

They don't act maturely like an adult should.

They stereotype kids; they judge people on the outside.

They are phony; they are always lying to us, saying one thing and doing the other.

They are grouchy; they nag us all the time.

They don't care about us; they don't have the time for us; they are seldom home.

They cannot be trusted, they tell on us.

They are nosy; they butt into other people's business.

They laugh at us and the things we do.

They do not like us kids.

They are greedy, selfish, and self-centered.

They are often jealous of other people.

They despise us, look on us like dirt and trash.

The grievances of all groups who feel powerless and frustrated are here again—not respected, not listened to, not understood, regarded as inferior and treated as incapable of thought and action. This is the way the young women put it:

They don't understand the maturity we attain by the time we get to be sixteen or seventeen . . . they kind of still look upon us as a child and they treat you in that respect; when actually by the time you're that old, you're almost old enough to vote and get married and things like that. And you should be mature to accept more responsibility than they're willing to give you.   (17, *Black, urban*)

When they try to treat you like you're a little kid, like you're so much below them, that bothers me a lot. But there's just been a couple of people that have treated me like that, that I can think of.   (17, *American Indian, urban*)

Adults who won't listen to you no matter what you have to say, and they're always right because they're an adult.   (16, *American Indian, urban*)

They disliked being stereotyped.

Cause some adults . . . think minors are all alike. They are somebody with long hair or somebody that would look like a hippie, and they think that they don't probably have anything to say, or know anything. I guess I admire adults that wouldn't judge a person by the way they look. I guess I admire adults that give a person, you know, a fair chance at anything they want to do instead of just saying, "Well, he can't do this, he can't do that."   (18, *Black, urban*)

They hated phoniness, adults saying one thing and doing another.

I hate for someone to tell me not to do something and turn around and do the same thing. I don't mind if they tell me not to do it, so long as they aren't doing it either. I just don't like to be told not to do something with no reason.   (16, *American Indian, small town*)

They hated to be belittled.

I don't talk to my counselor. When I talk to him, he always has something to do and he don't listen to me and you can't understand him.   (16, *Black, urban*)

Parents. They make me feel so little, so small, like dirt. I don't think they ever told me that they loved me or anything like that, out loud.
(16, *White, rural*)

I don't like an adult who's always telling a teenager this, "You don't know what you want," always tells me to shut up. Things like that. And the type of adult that always says things haven't changed, like my father, he's the type. You could tell him its raining, but no . . . and it could be pouring down rain, but if he says "It's not raining," it's not raining.   (16, *Black, urban*)

It hurt them to feel they were not trusted.

The kind that don't trust you at all, don't let you do anything. They don't let you out at night, 'cause they are afraid you will get kidnapped, and that's all.   (14, *White, suburban*)

My father drives us kids crazy. He won't let us out of the house past dark.
(15, *White, small town*)

But they also did not trust adults, and they gave their reasons.

I don't know why. I just don't feel that I can go out and tell adults my problems because a lot of them have big mouths, like the women who go out and gossip and tell everything that kids tell them and everything. So I really feel . . . not too safe telling adults my problems. (14, *White, suburban*)

You can't talk to social workers or some people like that, they go back and they tell people about your problems, your parents and things like that. And that's mostly why I don't talk to 'em about it. 'Cause I don't want 'em to go back and tell. So I just keep it to myself. (15, *Black, urban*)

And they certainly resented being yelled at, being beaten, being nagged.

I would get caught all the time when I ran away. They would call me names and they'd say "You were out in the streets and selling yourself," and stuff like that. And how would they know? Some of them don't understand you. (14, *White, small town*)

People who nag, try to tell you what to do, and tell you what's right and what's wrong. We know what's right and what's wrong, but they keep on telling us and telling us. Those people I don't like. (16, *Chicana, urban*)

The ones I really dislike are the ones that's always nagging you. Like if you're doing something very special that you like to do, well, then they'll tell you to get up and do something like clean the living room or put the dishes away. (14, *Black, urban*)

Yet the majority of the girls liked adults.

The following is a list of qualities the girls most admired in adults. The first three were the most frequently mentioned:

They are generally friendly; they are fun to be with.

They are understanding; they respect us; they listen and care about us; they are helpful to us.

They are older, more experienced and knowledgeable; they tell us things, the rights and the wrongs.

They are easy to get along with.

They are good people; they help those who are in need.

They trust us.

They respect us for what we are.

They are patient with us.

They are fair and just.

They are independent; they speak their own minds.

Here are some of the girls' comments on such qualities:

I admire an adult . . . who doesn't dedicate herself to her own self but to give some to others; an adult who sits to talk to an adolescent or with a child, understanding him and not trying to inculcate him with a lot of adult ideas, but understanding his innocence . . . that he has not gone through a lot of experiences. (18, *Inuit, urban*)

For me, most of the adults I know are understanding. They are not necessarily young, but they are young at heart. They think they should make it a better place for the youth. They've been through a lot of what we are going through. I like most of them that I know. I don't think they hate kids. (16, *White, suburban*)

[An admired woman]: She's intelligent. She's determined to do what she wants to do, even though her husband objects to it. And she's got a lot of insight. She's very satisfied.   (16, *Inuit, small town*)

[On a YWCA leader]: She's just herself, she don't pretend to be nobody else.
                                                                    (14, *Black, urban*)

Although a large number of girls said that they felt close to some adults, one cannot draw the conclusion that they actually felt close to the total adult generation. It is striking that the vast majority of adults who ranked highest in their list as people who understand them were *family members.*

Next to family members came older friends.

Adults outside the family were mentioned comparatively rarely. Since schools play a very important part in the life of adolescent girls, teachers occasionally become important.

Adults in youth organizations were mentioned by only seven girls in the total population as someone most important to them.

One gains the impression that adults as an intimate, helpful source of communication outside the family are not especially significant to the girls—certainly always with exceptions. But adults for this generation at least seem not to be any more the "faceless" stereotyped kind of paper dolls that the delinquent girls talked about in my study approximately ten years ago.[3] They are real people, disliked and feared at times, yes; but they are people. Girls do relate and want to relate to them. This relationship was frequently purely emotional, but the girls we interviewed also discussed issues with adults, even if they did not always agree with them. The girls repeated often that times were changing and that some adults did not seem to understand that. They were not resentful of an adult who did not understand this change, but they did object to adults who thought that their way was the only right one. One of the girls said:

There aren't many adults I feel free to talk to. But I wish there were. It's just kind of nice to have another adult besides your parents that you can just go to and discuss things with.   (14, *White, urban*)

There is a generation difference, there are even generation conflicts, but there is not a gap in the sense that it cannot be bridged.

The second assumption concerns the family.

THE MYTH OF THE FALLING APART FAMILY

Loneliness is missin' your family, it is not knowing what to say.

[3] Gisela Konopka, *The Adolescent Girl in Conflict*, Englewood Cliffs, N.J.: Prentice-Hall, 1966.

Loneliness is walking in the park all alone,
crying and sobbing because no one is there.
It is hurt and sorrow, long pain.
Loneliness is emptiness having no rain.
It is falling, falling deep, very deep.
Loneliness is a heart that's broken
hanging on a string.
Loneliness is not being loved or loving.
Loneliness is not reaching out or getting
help. It is having a problem and being
depressed.
Loneliness is darkness in the night.
Never ever seeing the light.
Loneliness is when stars don't come out
or even shine. It is not believing in
God or having one or even a heaven or anything.
Loneliness is being alone. It is the painfullest
of all sorrows.

TERRI WALD (17, *White, urban*)

The family—their own family—was a source of joy, contentment, stimulation, pride, hope—it was also confinement, torture, humiliation, fear, the source of hate and shame. It is the most powerful influence on a girl's life. Surely this is the time of life and stage of development when all young people move closer to their own generation, when friends (who earlier were already an influence) become more and more the "significant others." But the people at home—especially the parents—still spell the difference between a life of strength and hope or a withering period of hate and despair.

This does not mean that parents are responsible for everything their children do. The terrible confusion between "influence"—a close relationship—and "cause and effect"—everything a parent does is emulated by the daughter or son—has overwhelmed some parents with guilt and has distorted juvenile justice. Judges have rebuked and punished parents for the deeds of their children.

Every human being carries his or her own uniqueness, different from every other one, this X factor that we cannot explain either by heredity or environment. Two persons (young and old), who may take from the same environment different nourishment, act differently. Environment, especially the human one, is *most* important but it does not completely *determine* everything. And environment is complex—it includes family, neighborhood, adults, peers, teachers, newspapers, television, the mood of a country and the world. A girl's *behavior, attitudes,* even *feelings* are influenced by all this as well as by the physical environment: the barrio, the crowded slum in a huge city, the ugly cells of a detention home, the warm beauty of a family dwelling or the open spaces of farmland. Environment, inner forces—they are complex factors. I would like to carve this into our minds, so that we understand the vast significance of physical and human environment, but stop blaming one aspect of it—especially the family, the parents—for all the damage done.

Having said all this, I return to the significant discovery that parents are not only important to adolescent girls, but that the girls we interviewed listed them highest in their regard for adults. Yet, as in every other subject the girls discussed, we discovered a broad spectrum of feelings ranging from wanting to be exactly like parents:

> I guess if I could grow up and have the attitudes like my parents, I would be happy. They teach me everything I know. I guess it is the way they brought me up, that I believe everything that they believe in as far as how to do things, how to get along, and that sort of thing. I think if I could be half of what my mother and father are, I'd be happy.   (15, *White, urban*)

or to total rejection of parents:

> I hurt a lot, I would cry a lot and dad would say "Crying isn't going to help," so I put my feelings inside of me. I shed no tears around him, and there was no communication at all.   (15, *White, urban*)

There were all shades between these two attitudes. This is what we heard:

1. The large majority of girls named *mothers* as the person they felt closest to among all adults. And even those who felt alienated from them or from the total world of adults yearned for a mother. The gifted Pearl Nestor wrote thus about her runaway experience:

> *The first night was cold—*
> *   damn cold.*
> *And walking around the avenues,*
> *   we would mock the whores.*
> *The big man and his badge would*
> *   give us a cold eye.*
> *And without hesitation, we*
> *   would flip him a bird.*
> *I wished for my mother,*
> *   and I wished for sympathy—*
> *For a warm bed, and not the cold*
> *   shipyard or the park swings.*
> *I feel really old for 15,*
> *   there just isn't any place to go.*
> *Mama, I miss you—*
> *   and I just spent my last dollar for cigarettes.*
>   PEARL NESTOR (16, *Inuit, urban*)

The mother they yearned for does exist, as described by one of the girls:

She takes a lot of time for her kids and she listens to what you have to say and she's understanding. Some marriages have divorce problems or something, but our parents got along good for 20 years. She seems to always understand. Like, before payday comes, you don't always have that much money, and so you kind of have to skimp on the food, but she makes something. My brother has swimming lessons and hockey. She takes him over there and back and that type of thing. (14, *White, urban*)

In my earlier study on delinquent adolescent girls I had seen many girls in great conflict and in competition with their mothers. At the time, I thought that this was a universal phenomenon. I have to contradict myself today because our data clearly indicate that this is not so. This new relationship may have to do with a change in women's position in our society. The emphasis is far less on "pleasing the male." Thus mother and daughter meet as persons and not as competitors.

The girls described their relationships to their mothers in various ways. Over half of those who talked about parents stressed their closeness with them, sometimes an inexplicable, inarticulate closeness, a deep under-standing and a sense of friendship on a mature level.

She's helped me with all my problems and she's talked with me about things. She tries her best to make it better for us because she said she didn't have it so good way back then. She says she understands all my feelings and she wishes that I could talk to her more about them.
(14, *American Indian, small town*)

We talk woman to woman, it's not mother to daughter. I mean, that's the way I feel it should be since I'm supposed to be so mature and everything.
(16, *Black, urban*)

She's given me confidence in myself and sometimes she tries to make me understand her point of view, then when she says something and it's right even though it hurts me, I kind of listen to her even though I pretend I'm not listening, I turn my face, and she makes me believe in myself, even when I'm down. (18, *Chicana, urban*)

Others stressed their view of mother as a positive model, as someone they deeply admired and respected. Sometimes they saw mother as an important career-oriented woman, sometimes as an enjoyable homemaker, as supportive, and sometimes as a person who could make do with so little to support her family.

She's just fantastic, especially with the kids. She can yell at us but we really respect her. And she's always there to help; she understands. She works and she knows who she is. (15, *White, small town*)

I like talking to my mother cause I learn a lot of things from her. She's a very intelligent person. I respect her as a person, not really as my mother. If there's any questions or what, I have to ask her, I just go to her and I ask her. If it's anything to do with taxes or sex or money or anything she just gives me advice as best she can. (14, *Black, urban*)

It seems to me like she can take a lot, because she's gone through so much: the divorce and four kids, and, like my dad, he never used to stay home . . . yet she took us camping a couple of times every summer, and stuff like that. And I've always thought she did a good job.   (13, *White, urban*)

Girls appreciated *doing* things with their mothers. Many of the activities they described centered around the home, where they could talk. Mothers were those who—if parents did it at all—provided sex information and who were contacted first if the girl was in trouble. But the favorite kind of things that girls described doing with their mothers were the everyday activities like shopping—buying things, looking at things. They also talked about going camping, going to movies, going on other short trips. They described how activities such as housekeeping or working in the garden or cooking the meals were combined with casual talk on personal problems. Talk about public affairs or political concerns was mentioned mostly by girls whose mothers worked professionally.

Our picture of feelings toward mothers will be misleading, though, if we stay exclusively with the positive ones. About a quarter of the girls who talked about their mothers stated that they either felt not very close to them or actually disliked them. This always was said with regret, sadness, pain. A working mother's absence was sometimes regretted, but it was understood, and the regret was leavened by warmth.

I like to dream that we were a few thousand dollars richer a year and that my mother was home and able to take on more responsibility in the home, and she would be able to help so much in things I'm doing in school and with parties and stuff.   (14, *White, urban*)

They did resent—as in all adults—arbitrary authority. They resented not being accepted as an equal, and they especially resented constant distrust toward them based on their mothers' fear of possible pregnancy. Here are some examples of what the girls said:

My mother and I are in complete conflict because she tries to baby me because I am her only child. And I want to get away; I can't stand being imprisoned. And when she found out that I was planning on moving out in a year or two, she started crying and I just can't hack that. I'm trying to grow up and she's not letting me.   (17, *White, urban*)

Me and my mother have never, never sat down and talked like mother and daughter, you know. I don't know what's wrong. I've tried but you can't.
          (17, *Black, urban*)

Well, like this thing about getting pregnant, "Now that's just going to get you in trouble." If you think of anything that is just not perfect, she's going to say, "Now, I don't like that idea at all." You can't sit down and say anything. She always tells me, and I just say "yes" to her, you know, and not really mean it. But what can I say? If I say "no" or what I think, then she just blows up. So, I just don't even say anything.   (17, *Black, suburban*)

It was not the strictness that most girls resented but being "put down," being treated like little children. Strictness in itself, if combined with respect, was appreciated.

> My mother is strict on me. She knows things; she's really looking out for me; she really cares. It bothers me that she tells me I can't do something, or come into the house at a certain time. But deep down inside, she really cares.
> Like a lot of my friends' mothers, they just roam the streets, do what they want and their mothers don't really care. But my mother . . . she looks out for me.
>   (16, *Black, urban*)

The girls were bitter about mothers who had become negative models for them, women they did not want to emulate. Frequently, this attitude was related to their fear of becoming like their mothers.

> She says, "I just don't want to hear anymore; go back to your room." And I think, as a human being, she shouldn't be able to say that to me without getting my response back; I just don't feel that's right. And I'm, I'm going to be sure to give my kids that right.   (14, *White, urban*)
> My mother is the type of person where she works and goes home. That's all she does. And like, that's what she wants me to do. I can't do that, cause I like to have my friends and I like to go out and have a good time and everything. I don't know, she doesn't understand it.   (16, *Oriental, urban*)

Alcohol was often the source of conflict. Yet it is impressive to hear girls trying to understand, wishing they could change their mothers. Whether they were in an institution or in their own home, the cry was "If I could only help her to change!"

2. In the girls' minds the relationship to the *father* appeared different from that with the mother. About one quarter of those who talked about parents said they were close to their fathers, but these were mostly girls who related positively to both parents. Often fathers seemed almost invisible. Some were actually absent or not at home much. Others just seemed remote. Fathers were frequently the authoritarian parent and the one with whom the girl was in conflict on social issues. Fathers seemed to be less communicative, or they "yelled." Repeatedly, girls said that their fathers did not want them to grow up, wanted to keep them "their little girl."

When girls were close to their fathers they saw them often as a counselor, as somebody they could look to for decisions, or he was the protector. In general—again with exceptions—one got the impression of a much more formal relationship than with mother.

Let us hear, first, some of the positive comments.

> My dad's pretty special. Cause, I don't know, there's not many fathers like him. I mean, I don't really mind not seeing him that much . . . but you know, he's always there. If ever I have a problem I can call him at the office.
>   (14, *White, suburban*)

He's an all right guy . . . he'll sit down and have long talks with me about trouble at school, you know . . . he wants to know like just what we'll be doing, what's going on, where we'll be going. He worries about us.   (16, *White, urban*)

I always look up to him if I have any problems or anything . . . he always knows the right answer to everything.   (15, *Black, urban*)

Me and my dad just like to go out, just go out and go camping, and everything else. We're like . . . I'm his little boy.   (13, *White, rural*)

Father served also as a positive model. Not that the girl wanted to become a man, but she appreciated qualities in him that she wished for herself.

Like my dad, when he wants to learn about something, he'll stick with it; he won't just try it out. And he's a little discouraged, but he'll stick with it.
(17, *White, urban*)

I admire him for being so smart and strong, and able to withstand problems.
(17, *Chicana, urban*)

I'd like to be able to work as hard as he does. He really tries, shows me a lot of ways like, when I totally disagree with him, he has taught me how to argue out the responses and kind of debate things.   (16, *White, urban*)

He knows a lot of things. He knows how to build things. He can help me with problems and he knows how to survive.   (15, *Black, urban*)

It was usually working ability, stamina, and as one of the girls said, "the quality of survival," that girls admired in their fathers.

Activities with fathers were somewhat different from those described with mothers. These were mostly recreational activities, sports, camping, hiking, outdoor activities.

Girls talked about discussing issues with their fathers. They often disagreed, especially about sex attitudes and race relations. When he became very authoritarian, the girl no longer talked about that particular issue because of fear.

I'm really scared, I'm afraid of what he's going to say. I've done it a couple of times, not very many times, but I just can't go up and say "Hi, let's talk." Because when I say that, I'm so afraid of what he will say.

Well, when I do it, he will say, "Well, look, I don't want to talk to you," or "There's no way we can get along; you mess up too much; you don't understand the rules around here," and stuff like that. Or sometimes he will say, "Well, what do you have to say?" And that's when I get scared and I will just say, "Well, let's kind of reason," or I will just say, "I'm sorry," just to get him to start going along. And then he will say, "Okay, I'll forgive you, but you know I'm right" or "Next time you will know better," and it's just a short conversation.   (15, *Chicana, urban*)

The authoritarian father was deeply resented. Often a girl would say after some angry outburst that she "still loved" her father, a sign of guilt, confusion, and yearning.

It's a feeling of not really hate, but close to it. My dad was one of telling, "Do this, do that." And that's where my hang-up is. I can accept things when people ask me, but it's a lot harder when people tell me.   (15, *White, urban*)

Daddy isn't much of a talker; he's more using his hands, his fist, that is his way of saying "no," he doesn't like it. (16, *White, rural*)

We speak to each other, but we don't have too many things we do. My father mainly tells me to stay in a young lady's place. "And if you do that, you can avoid a lot of things that aren't necessary," he says. (17, *Black, small town*)

I can't talk to him. He's just too set in his ways. He is right, you're wrong. "You don't have a problem, it's all in your head." (17, *White, rural*)

Often the girls saw their fathers only as someone who was merely around, but better avoided.

I'm not that close to him. I just know him as the father and that's it. (16, *Chicana, urban*)

I get along but, I mean, we're really not that close. Like he's got his business and I've got my school work. He just doesn't seem interested in what I do. (17, *American Indian, small town*)

It don't seem like, he really don't understand, about my feelings. So I hardly talk to him. (15, *White, small town*)

The major conflict involved fathers' suspicious protectiveness in relation to the girls' sex drives. This attitude has been resented by girls for years, but today when girls establish real friendships with boys, which do not always involve sexual relations, this protectiveness becomes especially insulting.

My father is way too over-protective. He gets upset if I'm five minutes late from the store; he goes into a rage. If he were less protective, that would be really neat. (16, *White, suburban*)

My daddy's the type that, since I'm the baby girl . . . he's not the type to just let you go anywhere without knowing where you're going or how you're getting back. (15, *Black, urban*)

He expects me to be his "little girl" all my life and I think he is just not realizing that he can't have that; and that, I think, is what he expected out of me for a long time; he just wanted me not to do anything. (16, *White, rural*)

If the protectiveness indicates true concern, not based on suspicion, the girls actually appreciated that and accepted limitations.

My father always checks on us at night. He checks our lessons and what we have been doing in the day and where we have been and so forth. But I do not mind this because he is interested in us. (15, *Chicana, urban*)

He never does try to tell us what to do but if he thinks it's gonna be wrong and hurt us, he tries to talk us out of it. And he usually wins . . . because I agree with my father mostly. (17, *White, rural*)

Girls want relationships with their fathers and regret their absence. But their absence is frequently accepted with cool resignation, indicating a cultural attitude that fathers are still not yet expected to be close to their growing-up female children.

He's gone an awful lot, and really, I haven't ever really known him that good. I mean, I know him, but just to be around him and when he's around lots of people and everything. I'm not really that well acquainted . . . it's just me and my mom there.   (17, *White, small town*)

We haven't really done anything together, I guess in a long time, because he works. When he doesn't work he is tired.   (17, *White, urban*)

I don't want my kids to be without a father. Because I had to be that way, and it was very hard. There's a lot of times I was so hungry I'd cry, because I was so hungry and . . . he has never cared whether I was alive or dead. He never sent us money or nothing and I just couldn't see my kids going through life like that.   (17, *American Indian, small town*)

Girls talked about their disappointment with fathers who neglected them just as they did about their mothers. Most frequently, alcohol was the cause.

My dad has given me the idea not to be like him. . . . He drinks quite a bit and has been in a car wreck and my mom has worked all her life to keep him in alcohol. . . .   (16, *White, rural*)

My father hurts me sometimes when he gets drunk which I don't like. I don't like to see anybody, especially somebody who has a brain as good as he does, pickle it, just completely waste it, and become something worse than childish. I'm hurt when I see somebody change themselves into somebody that's worse than they are.   (17, *White, urban*)

Alcohol has wrecked my dad's life up. I think I've only seen him sober once and he's been drunk the rest of the time I've ever known him. And it messes him up, it messes the family up, it's just no good at all.   (16, *White, small town*)

But nevertheless, many adolescent girls tried to understand the problems of their elders. One girl, for instance, talked about her father who had abandoned the family.

When he was my age he used to get into trouble . . . he doesn't have anybody that really cares about him, so he doesn't care what happens.
                                                      (17, *White, urban*)

3. The ideal to practically all the girls we interviewed was *loving parents* who understand their children and were their friends, but also protectors. They longed for harmony in the family. Conflicts between parents were difficult for them to accept. I talked earlier about their great fear of divorce when they had lived through it. They talked about the quarrels of their parents and how these disturbed them.

I don't like for my mom and dad to argue and when they argue they get loud and everything and it kind of affects me because I just like for it to be a lot of peace around the house. I just sit and wonder what they would do. I guess I think they wouldn't be sitting here fussing if I wasn't here or something like that. Some of the times it's about me, the argument is about me . . . they try to control it but sometimes it just can't be helped, I guess.   (14, *Black, urban*)

The fighting made them feel desperate and unwanted. A 17-year-old wrote in her diary:

> Last night my sister and I talked about Mom and Dad, for about two hours. I don't like Dad much, but something inside me is telling me if they do separate or divorce, I'll miss him. I call him a bastard and everything else because of what has gone on. He deserves it. But inside real deep, I just can't understand. I try so hard but I can't.
>
> Mom says she doesn't love him and that's the truth. But I try to talk to her about her shitty marriage and she just tries to tune everything out. She says she doesn't want to give in and let him out so easy, but meanwhile she's miserable. She's so cold and bitter against him. So why doesn't she ask for a divorce? I have no idea. It gets to be infuriating.
>
> I don't really want summer vacation to come. It's so boring! Unless I could get a job somewhere. Mom and Dad are getting worse. They've been fighting about his job. Everybody's getting raises and promotions except him.
>
> Tonight Dad came home for dinner and all day had been having a beer or two with the guys.
>
> I feel awful. I have a cold and I might be getting that shitty flu. Mom and Dad have been talking about divorce. Yesterday morning every time I'd walk into the living room they would stop talking. So that night at dinner, I asked what they were talking about and she said, "financial stuff" and then in a real low voice she said "about our marriage."
>
> I want to take off from home. Just for a week or two. If I had somewhere to go I'd leave right now. I'd like to have a place where I could go to school here but not live at home. But for only a couple of weeks.   (17, *White, urban*)

The girls who enjoyed their families talked about their parents without sentimentality but with a calm assurance.

> I guess really they're the most important. Because they're always there and I can always go to them and they always say something that will make me feel better. And they support me in my activities and I don't know. They're just good all around.   (17, *White, urban*)
>
> They have given me life, which is the first thing, they have given me a home, a good education, I can't complain because they have been very good. Sometimes they reprimand me, but I know that it is for my own benefit . . . they are everything for me.   (16, *Puerto Rican, suburban*)
>
> They're always there when I need them; they're always giving me what I need, always helping me out with problems, whatever.   (17, *Chicana, urban*)
>
> I'm very, very close with my mother and my father. We talk about everything. There's nothing that I wouldn't tell them.   (16, *White, urban*)
>
> I love them. I don't want nothing to happen to them because if it wouldn't be for them, I don't know where I'd be.   (15, *Black, urban*)

In general, the girls did not expect their parents to be "ideal." Several of them said "there exist no ideal parents." Their standards were reasonable and not hard to meet. They did not expect parents to be perfect. One of the more outspoken girls probably summarized this attitude best:

I suppose that an ideal parent is not of such a different species. I'd consider an ideal person someone who could accept other people without first tacking on things like, "Oh, that person's younger than I am," or, "that person's older than I am," or "they grew up in a different part of town," and would start by looking at people as potential friends and seeing them in that way, more optimistically, perhaps, than thinking, "I won't get along with them."

And I suppose, try to understand—that your children aren't just old individuals for you to mold, to turn out exactly like you, that they are people, and they want to do things, to see what life is like, and that they have the right to explore as much as you do, within certain confines—you don't want to let them kill themselves just to see what it is like.

But I think that acceptance of other people, and other ideas, and an openness to them—although that doesn't necessarily mean compromising your own ideals—are really important things for a person to have. And I suppose not being hung up about different roles or games that people have to play—not just masculine/feminine sorts of roles, but roles about parents and children, and people having to have power over each other. You know, it doesn't have to be that way, and I think it is really important for it not to be and for people to understand that.   (15, *White, urban*)

4. Next to parents, the family members who are often seen as the most beloved, and in whom one can confide, are *grandparents*, especially the grandmother. A 15-year-old talks about her grandmother:

At first, when I was little, I used to live with her a lot . . . she told me a lot that happened to her and everything. She doesn't put me down and everything because of the things I've done, cause she says that other kids have done them . . . you know, I'm not the only person in the world that's done something wrong and that . . . she just understands my problems.   (16, *White, rural*)

Another:

Well, I like my grandfather, he's close to 95 years old and I can sit down with him anytime and talk and play with him, and laugh with him, you know.
(18, *Black, urban*)

Grandparents do not have the same responsibilities for raising children that parents have and therefore can enjoy them more and be less hard on them. It is most helpful to a girl to have a way out when the relationship with parents becomes too tense.

Several girls mentioned that they did like older people because they seemed to be more experienced and shared with them these experiences. Perhaps people beyond the parent age are also not quite so self-protective and are more willing to admit their mistakes to adolescents. It may also be that in relation to older people, girls feel more a sense of interdependence instead of being forced into either a dependent or totally independent role. They feel they can be helpful to older people while at the same time the older ones are helpful to them. And finally, older people frequently have more time and are willing to listen. This is the essence of what the girls need.

These ideal older people do not always have to be their blood relatives. To the adolescent girl they are admired because they have a long life behind them and have "achieved."

> I see Katherine Hepburn as kind of an ideal. I have a tutor . . . I think she's about 65 who's good friends with Katherine Hepburn and the two of them probably represent the biggest heroes of my life. One has made it in the world . . . where she's very famous and she lives her own life; she's her own woman. And the other is just a really nice human being. There are some people who are really true human beings. And I feel she is, she's just a really beautiful person.
>
> (16, *White, urban*)

Home, the family, especially the parents, are so important that the girl who is denied them cries out as much as the girl who loses a beloved boyfriend. The wish for a close family life is strong, but not for one that represents an authoritarian power structure. One flees it when one feels constantly censored. The terror of silent and spiteful treatment by the family is a terrible burden to bear.

> My parents don't pay any attention to me. . . . I felt kind of left out. . . . I'm pregnant and they didn't like that, and they didn't like him being Black. My sister was pregnant before and she had the baby and gave it up for adoption. . . . Now I feel like they have hurt me more than I could ever hurt them the way they treat me. I don't think they ever want to see me again; that's the way they make me feel. I'm living at home and I'm very uncomfortable. I feel like I'm just totally left out, like I really feel they don't want me there.
>
> Like they say that "We figure as long as we get you through school and feed you, that's all we got to do." My parents would talk to my sister who had been in trouble but not to me because my fiance is Black. My parents told me that they had made two mistakes in raising us kids . . . they didn't tell us how to hate or how to be prejudiced. You know, I couldn't quite understand that!
>
> (17, *White, small town*)

And another girl cried out:

> *"Dear ma, may I come home?*
> *I'm so sick and tired of being alone*
> *I've been sitting here day after day*
> *the pusher keeps coming anyway*
> *the reason I left is cuz the stuff had me down*
> *I was high I needed to make a touchdown*
> *so, may I come home?*
>
> ROSSLYN RIGGINS (15, *Black, suburban*)

In addition to the myths about the "unbridgeable gap" and the "falling-apart" family, adults speak of a too "permissive" society.

THE MYTH OF PERMISSIVENESS

Permissiveness, in the sense of *laissez faire,* is frequently presented as the hallmark of relationships between the adult and the young in the United States. It is condemned in thundering sermons all over the country and it is the stereotyped picture created abroad of the typical American family. The picture painted is that children can do what they want to do; adults let them run wild. The result of this supposed permissiveness is anarchy, rebellion, and rising delinquency.

Any careful investigation into American institutions, such as schools, the correctional system, and the family, for example, proves that this assumption is overexaggerated. The findings from our study, which relate to family relationships, and especially the relationship between parents and young girls, belie the myth.

In our study, we examined the relationship between parents and children through the words of the girls. It is their perceptions that we describe here, but it seems to us that our conclusions are accurate. We found an unusual amount of very close and very positive relationships between parents and children, where there was genuine cooperation among family members and where girls were treated as persons, with respect. Obviously, it is this kind of family that allows girls to develop their own personalities, and that includes the acceptance of reasonable limitations. In such families, girls take on responsibilities and show an appreciation of other family members, young and old, and accept their own capacities or shortcomings. Here are some examples of such family relationships.

> In our family we go from nineteen to three years of age. It's a pretty big span. It's neat too, because we . . . the older of us have gotten the benefits of it. It's almost like having our own kids because we babysit for 'em and mother 'em, when Mom and Dad go out and things. And they have the benefit of . . . they'll have older brothers and sisters to go to if there are ever any problems and they don't want to go to Mom and Dad. Although I don't really see that, because we're really close to our parents. (15, *White, urban*)

Obviously there are demands made on these adolescents, but they see a purpose in what is asked of them and they respond to it.

> I respect my father a lot, though the way it is now, a lot of times he doesn't get home until it is late. I never see him very much, but I want him to think highly of me. It upsets me when he gets mad.
> My mother teaches pre-school and I'm very close to her. I feel like I can share things that happen in school with her and tell her the good things and the bad things that have happened to me. . . . If I come home and say I want to go to a party Friday night, she'll want to know where it is. When I tell her, she'll usually let me go if I think it's right.

> My parents usually . . . they'll let me do just about what I want, but they don't let me make always my own choices, like about what time I want to be in. We have to compromise. (15, *White, urban*)

Here again is a calm, but not over-permissive, relationship.

Totally different is the family situation that is based on parental authoritarianism. It is the totally nonpermissive, strict authoritarian family that breeds frustration, distrust, anger, rebellion, and violence between parents and children. Treatment of children ranges in such families from constant nagging to extreme violence and brutality. These are the families that produce delinquency. Though we did not make a special study of delinquency, we found that twice as many delinquent as nondelinquent girls recounted violent treatment at the hands of families. Those same girls then spoke about their own violent gang fights, their own extreme outbursts, or their complete sense of defeat. I would like to burn into the reader's mind the incredible and terrifying experiences under which some of the girls live or have lived. At this time in our history, we are very concerned about and have become more aware of the "battered child," but mostly in terms of the very young child. Without looking for it, we found the "battered adolescent." The girls talked about beatings, rapes, adult molestation, and about resulting suicide attempts, flights, and a general sense of their being "all bad." I will let the girls themselves talk, starting with the "milder" forms of attack they suffered, to the utmost abusing invasion of their bodies and souls.

> My mother makes me mad. I just sit there and get all puffy and I'll start humming to myself like I'm not listening to her just to make her mad. I can't stand to hear her fuss. . . . She'll grab me and I'll stay home and I'll find something else to do. . . . I'm afraid to talk to my father. (17, *White, small town*)

Another one:

> My father was always too strict. Since I was thirteen he never let me out of his sight. I think he did a lot of bad things when he was a youngster and he remembers and now he is afraid. He also wants that we are always his little girls. (15, *White, urban*)

The next one was a girl who constantly ran away.

> I am running mostly from my father because he's very dominant, very hostile and things like that. And the other times, I might have a boyfriend that he disapproved of or I shouldn't see, so I ran to see him. (15, *Black, urban*)

A girl of about the same age, from a professional background, described her life in a restrictive punitive atmosphere:

> I felt hurt when my mother said that I could never possibly love someone, and that me and my boyfriend were just a Romeo and Juliet, and that I wasn't capable of loving someone, and that my boyfriend couldn't possibly love me. And I felt very hurt when I ran away from boarding school and came home and

my mother told me to go back, that she wouldn't have me, and she called the boarding school and told them where I was at. And when they . . . and when *I* wouldn't go back with them, she called my father up and told him to come and take me. I felt very bad when I got kicked out, no, I didn't get *kicked* out of the house, she just said that she couldn't possibly live with me and "You are going away to boarding school whether you like it or not, so you better pick one out now." So I just picked one out that was closest to my boyfriend's boarding school, and I was always in trouble for never being on campus. . . .

I've never had a weapon used on me, except my mother has chased me around the house with a bottle in her hand.   (15, *White, urban*)

This same girl also resented her mother's hypocrisy, as, for example, her objections to the girl's use of drugs although she herself kept a fresh lid of marijuana in her room. They fought about it.

Yes, I used a knife, but the only thing I have stabbed was a door. Like, when my mother had that lid, I held a kitchen knife in one hand and the lid in the other hand, but it was small. . . . I held the knife in one hand and the lid in the other and said "This goes nowhere until the police come." So to show how "violent" I am; my mother grabbed the lid from my hand and ran to the bathroom and flushed it down the toilet. And here I am with the knife in my hand, only saying, "God damn it." I don't have the guts to stab anyone, I would have to be super, super mad.

Another described a suffocating restrictiveness.

My mom wouldn't really let me join any clubs. I always wanted to join the track team at school. She never would let me. . . . My mom, she's really weird. She wouldn't let me go to basketball games and she wouldn't let me go to school dances or . . . she wouldn't let me do about anything except go to church. Cause she's . . . my mom's really religious. She wouldn't let me wear pants. I would always have to wear real long dresses and stuff. So I ran away.

(14, *White, urban*)

But the actual "battering" of the young person is far more serious. It does not present a pretty picture. It is a mistake to think that physical abuse occurs only in low-income families. There were some violent beatings reported by girls from middle- and upper-income homes. It is likewise a mistake to think that child beating is *exclusively* an urban phenomenon, although more than half of the girls who talked about such violence came from the cities. Nor is parental violence predominantly confined to minority groups; approximately half of the girls who talked about violence were white. The other half consisted of girls from a variety of minority backgrounds: Black, American Indian, Oriental, Inuit and Chicana. They expressed their horror of a society that either covered up or condoned such behavior. Here are their experiences:

When I do something wrong he beats the shit out of me. If I wouldn't clean the table right, if I did anything wrong, if I talked back especially, or if I start crying or show any feelings, my stepfather would beat me up.

(17, *Oriental, urban*)

There is so much whippings and stuff like that. I wished they would just sit down and talk to us instead of just whip us and drown us. Most of the kids around here are not very close to their parents. You can always hear some kids say, "I can't wait until I am eighteen so that I can get away."

Around our house, my dad makes most of the decisions and Mom is afraid too. She's afraid he'll get mad. She always said "Wait and ask your daddy" but you know she has just as much authority.   (16, *White, rural*)

The girl in this family expressed—probably without consciously realizing it—how much of what she lived through was related to the traditional position of women. Even her mother was totally subjugated. The fathers probably thought that they were doing the right thing in terms of their own upbringing.

Other girls were abused because of their fathers' or mothers' own despair and twisted feelings.

I got beatings as long as I can remember, for different things, for stupid things. When I was twelve I wanted to go trick or treating and she beat me over the head with a broomstick. "You aren't going anywhere." She wouldn't let me go nowhere. She beat me with braided ropes, extension cords, yardstick, boards, whatever she could find when she was mad.

I was always at school, she made sure of that. She would always drive me to school.

And my dad, he always made my brothers walk across hot stoves and everything. But me, I was his pride and joy. He showed me off to all his lady friends and everything. That's what my mom told me. She left him . . . so I think she has blamed me for it all along. . . .   (17, *White, urban*)

My mother is the biggest disappointment of my whole life, cause I went out and I thought she had straightened up and I was going to see a new mother, she was going to straighten up, she'd be acting better. She was worse. She'd get drunk, she'd just sling me like a piece of spaghetti, you know, she'd make me wear long sleeved blouses, not to show the marks, but you know, I just look back on it sometimes and laugh at it. I've heard of mothers being brutal and things like that, but I didn't think my mother would be like that.   (16, *Black, urban*)

This particular girl made every effort to try to understand her mother. She said at one point:

I don't hate her, I feel sorry for her, cause my father used to tell me, she always wanted a child but she was still a child herself when she had me. She still wasn't finished running around with her friends and everything—so I feel sorry for her.

This girl did not become delinquent and perhaps one of the reasons is that she could live a part of her life with a grandmother who really took care of her.

Other examples of brutality:

I took some pills when I was in seventh grade, or eighth grade, I took some pills and tried to kill myself. . . . I just got sick and then I ran, and when they found out they called my parents, and then I felt that my parents wouldn't take me back. . . . I took sleeping pills because I just felt awful because of the way I did my parents and the way they treated me.

They beat me. That's mainly why I've been doing these things, because it hurts me real bad inside. And it hurts right now. I have bruises and scars all over. They hit me with a butcher knife. I was frying potatoes and I burned them and my mom grabbed the knife and she cut me. I've got a lot of bruises, and strap marks.   (17, *White, urban*)

My mom was always beating me up and everything . . . so they put me in the Hall for my own protection on a dependency charge . . . but afterward I kept getting busted and busted and busted. If that first time wouldn't have happened I never would because I didn't know what Juvenile Hall was . . . until then. . . . Every time after they picked me up they put me back home and my mother just egged on things and beat me so that I'd leave again or run, or something.   (17, *White, urban*)

My step-dad raped me, when I was five . . . he messed me up really bad over it. Like he came home late, loaded one night, drunk, and he was going to teach me the facts of life . . . and I didn't really understand what was going on. He told me that if I ever told my mom that he was going to kill me over it, so I never told my mom until I was twelve . . . and that was the only time . . . until later on when he tried it with my younger sister, the sister next to me who's fifteen. I told my mom then and I didn't care what he said or I didn't care what he did to me. My mom left him and we moved off and I haven't seen him since then.   (17, *White, urban*)

What became of this particular girl? We listen to her continued story.

I used them [drugs] only because I'd had a bad marriage and I got beat up a lot by my ex-husband and I lost my son from that. I think that's one of the main reasons I ran to drugs . . . was because I thought I could get away from it all. I just thought it was a bad dream and drugs would help me to get away from it. . . . I beat up a guy one time. He pulled a knife on me and I didn't like it and it made me really mad . . . so I beat him up . . . in the street. I did, boy! I just tore him up. It was funny because he pulled a knife on me and he was going to stab me because somebody said that I had done something and I didn't do it and I didn't like it and he was going to kill me for it. So when he pulled that knife I kicked him and he fell, and I jumped on top of him and I picked up his head, like you know, and banged his head on the cement. . . . I busted his skull. I messed him up really bad. I really didn't mean to do it, but I guess you do weird things when you get mad.

Another one told us:

I skipped out of school two days and my dad found out and he just gave it to me with his belt. I had bruises all over my hands and all over my legs. And my mother couldn't do anything about it and she was upset with me at the time, so that Friday I ran away and hitchhiked.   (15, *Chicana, urban*)

The tragedy is that the girls often received the same kind of brutal treatment in those institutions that were supposed to "treat" or protect them. This girl was placed in a delinquency institution.

If you did something wrong, you couldn't even go up and tell anybody, to tell them what was the matter. . . . When he asked me if I was ready to go back to class, I turned around and told him what I thought of him, and he just took off his belt and just laid it on me—this man up there. So I just left, I said "forget it" and I just ran away.

(15, *Chicana, urban*)

My brothers, sisters and cousins and me went to the park and drank some wine and I got drunk. When I went home to mama, she said "You drunk, ain't you?" and I said "Yeah." So she started hollering and carrying on like that. I said "Well, they paid me $35 to do it." They didn't, you know. I didn't know why I said that, but I said it. And so she got mad and she said "You get out of my house. You going to juvenile center." So the police came over and so they talked it over with mama and me, you know. "No, we don't want to take her down there like this." So the policeman said "Well, if that was my daughter, I would beat her with a police belt." So he said "Here, here's a police belt" and he gave it to my daddy. And he beat me, you know, I was laughing while I was getting a whipping, you know. I didn't even feel it. And so everybody said that I was down on the floor laughing, talking, about like I got seizures, you know—and he was beating me. So then later on he got through with me and sent me upstairs to go to bed. So I went upstairs and I started vomiting and stuff like that.

(16, *Black, urban*)

Who could live normally through such terror? How often must they suppress their anguish because of fear.

My stepfather was also my teacher. And I hate him, I just absolutely hate him. This is . . . I'm glad this is confidential . . . he used to beat me up all the time and stuff, and I don't like him at all. He makes me crazy, he drives me crazy. I just hate him . . . my stepdad told me if I told anybody that he beat me up that he'd kill me. That's what he said. And so, you know. . . . Finally I have a chance to tell *somebody.*

(13, *White, urban*)

I dislike my father, he drives us kids crazy. He'll get mad and start hittin'. He hits hard. One time he hit my sister and put a big wart right across her face. . . . I think if a girl needs help with her parents they should have someone like counselors or something that can come to your house and talk to you both at the same time. The way it is now, if you go up to the police station for help and talk to the cops, the cops are always for the parents, they're never for the kids.

(15, *White, small town*)

The girls reacted in many different ways. Some became as violent as their parents. An 18-year-old from a very affluent family talked about constantly being adjudicated for assault and battery.

When I am angry I get really mad and I start fighting with people. . . . When I've gotten angry I've beat up people for it. I was so used to beating up people. I used to ride in tough gangs like the Hells Angels, I used to go around knocking people over the head with bike chains and stuff you know. It was just like something I wanted to do. . . . But my hands are my only weapons. I get into fist fights. . . . I don't believe in fighting if you have to use a switchblade or a gun or anything else. At least if you have to fight, fight with your hands. . . . I did see people being killed. I saw one girl killed by this one girl I knew very well. She took a knife and stabbed her thirteen times. But I couldn't have the guts to stab anybody. . . . I don't really enjoy fighting. I wish I hadn't learned how to fight. . . .   (18, *White, urban*)

This same girl talked about her fights with her mother.

My mother chased me around the house with a metal pole that holds two glass doors . . . it was not hard metal, it was aluminum . . . she pulled it off the door when she got mad at me, so I got one off the other door and it was just, like . . . I just dropped it and I just hit her with my fist and she just charged on me. . . . Later, my foster mother was loaded. She was stoned, and she started beating me up, and I had to protect myself, so I fought back. She looked worse than I did because I really got it back hard on her. That was it. She thought it was her fault for what happened and she didn't charge me with it.

She was one of the girls who returned violence with violence. Most of them ran, ran away.

My mom, see, she has hit me with sticks and my dad has thrown me across the room, hit me with his fists and everything else. . . . I took it for five years. I don't blame them for doing it because I deserved every bit of it. They don't do it all the time, but when they get mad, they do. And when they did it, I knew I deserved it. So I never did fight back. Then one day I got tired of it and I just said "Forget it. I'm not going back there. I'm not going back to a place where people hit me to death."   (16, *White, urban*)

When the girls ran away, they were usually adjudged delinquent and they began to feel like this girl. They were bad! They were incredibly confused—about themselves, about their parents, about the world around them. Continue listening to this same girl and feel her despair and confusion.

I was just charged with being ungovernable and I was only running away for about fifteen minutes before the cops picked me up. I ran because I didn't think they cared about me. The night before, my mom told me that they never liked me. She says, "Go live with your friend." And then she goes, "I don't give a damn about you. Just get the hell out of here. I never want to see your face in this house again." Then my dad took me over to my girlfriend's house, and from there my girlfriend and me went to school. And I go, "I can yell at my dad if I feel like it." And we started fighting, and we started hitting each other, and I blacked out and I didn't know what I was doing but when I woke up, my dad was hitting me, hitting my arm, hitting my head, jerking me and everything else, trying to get me off of my mom because I was choking her. I blacked out 'cause I didn't know what I was doing. But after I came to, I just let go of my mom. And Mom had her hands around my neck and she was trying to choke me. But I never held that grudge against her, but she held that grudge against me. And she started hitting me with sticks ever since then.

In spite of this treatment, she still said in another part of the interview that her mom and dad were the people she cared most about. She herself felt worthless. We saw this same sense of worthlessness and hopelessness in many of the girls. One of them said sadly:

I ran away from home because I'm no good. If I were good, why would my parents beat me all the time? (15, *White, urban*)

Because, if I go home I feel that I will mess up. I don't like my mom drinking and beating the hell out of my sister. My mother hurt me way too much and I am sick of it. . . . (17, *White, small town*)

Another expressed her total sense of abandonment.

I can't pick out a future. . . . I ran away because our step-dad beat us all the time. . . . I can't see any adult I dream to be like. . . . I never seen a good life . . . I am lonely all the time. (14, *White, adjudicated*)

One can only be surprised that the delinquency in girls has not become far more violent than it is and so many survive such assaults against body and soul and still retain some belief in themselves and other people. What helps them, we do not always know. There is a basic human resiliency. Perhaps, in the lives of some of these girls, there may have been a few other positive experiences that at least allowed them to be resigned about their parents' behavior and to have a slight sense of confidence in themselves or others. A 15-year-old expressed this kind of feeling.

My dad raped me when I was fourteen. The charges I pressed against him were for attempted rape, because my brother and sister were little and I couldn't see them being put into a home, like I was being put in and I hated to hurt my parents more than they had to be hurt. I was really hurt too, 'cause I was close to my dad and it kind of tore me up. But like I kept thinking, "Well, you can do without your mom and dad." Because I had friends to support me and help me get through what I was going through, and that's all I really needed. It's like, if my parents were going to do that to me, I was going to have to do without them. (15, *White, urban*)

It must be stated earnestly and with emphasis that there is no proof that permissiveness is a cause of delinquency since according to our data, hardly any permissiveness existed. We can say with absolute confidence that the brutal invasion of a human being's self-respect does produce angry, violent, and desperate reactions that may lead to delinquent acts.

It can also be stated with confidence that too many of our so-called correctional institutions simply intensify feelings of worthlessness and frustration. I personally know of a number of delinquency institutions that increase the girls' sense of failure and distrust of themselves and others by their harsh, insensitive, and depersonalized treatment. It is not the place here to go into an intensive discussion of what can be done about this situation. But from everything we heard during our interviews, we know that there is in these girls a yearning for a sense of integrity regarding their bodies, their minds, and emotions combined with a desperate wish for self-esteem. One girl in an institution told an interviewer of winning a speech contest sponsored by one of the local community civic clubs. It was the first time in her life that she had ever succeeded in anything. She said: "I never thought I was worth anything." It showed how important it was for her to succeed in something that enabled her to express herself as a person.

In my office stands a beautiful sculpture of a striding figure, arms swinging freely. This sculpture was done by a 13-year-old girl in a delinquency institution and had been entered in a contest sponsored by the Junior League, which gave it to me. This particular girl had never before worked in art and had never experienced a sense of accomplishment. When I met her and told her how exciting I found her work and how much meaning it conveyed to me, she almost broke into tears. I still, after some years, feel her arms around me and her choked, "Maybe I can be somebody!"

SUMMARY

1. From our interviews we are convinced that there are differences between young people and adults but not a generation "gap" that is unbridgeable.

2. Young people yearn for relationships with older people.

3. Their ideal adult is one who can listen and understand.

4. Adults to whom they feel closest, or to whom the majority of girls feel closest, are parents, especially the mother.

5. Other adults who are important to the girls are, at times, grandparents, teachers, and for the adjudicated girls, social service personnel.

6. There is a yearning for a warm accepting family life based on mutual respect.

7. There is no evidence of permissiveness in families. There is evidence of democratic as well as very authoritarian families.

8. There is an evident correlation between brutal and authoritarian upbringing and various forms of delinquency.

9. We found in the girls a surprising emotional resiliency against violence.

10. We found evidence of adolescent girls being "battered" in their homes and in institutions that exist to serve them.

BIBLIOGRAPHY

BERDIE, RALPH F., DOROTHY R. LOEFFLER, and JOHN D. ROTH, "Intergeneration Communication", *Journal of College Student Personnel*, Vol. XI, No. 5, September 1970, pp. 348–354.

Center for Youth Development and Research, *Youth Encounters a Changing World*, Seminar Series No. 3, University of Minnesota, Minneapolis, Center for Youth Development and Research, 1972.

DAHLEM, N.W., "Young Americans Reported Conceptions of Their Parents," *Journal of Psychology*, Vol. LXXIV, 1970, pp. 187–194.

GUERRAND, R.H., *Lycéens Révoltes Étudiants Révolutionnaires au 19ᵉ Siècle.* Paris: Les Édition du Temps, 1969, p. 36. Translated from the French by the author.

HERZOG, E., C. SUDIA, B. ROSENGARD, and J. HARWOOD, "Teenagers Discuss the Generation Gap," *Youth Reports No. 1*, U.S. Department of Health, Education and Welfare, Children's Bureau, 1970.

KONOPKA, GISELA, "Barriers Between Generations—The Issue in Perspective," in *The Function of Rebellion. Is Youth Creating New Family Values?*, pp. 1–14.

LITTLEFIELD, ROBERT P., "Self-Disclosure Among Some Negro, White and Mexican American Adolescents," *Journal of Counseling Psychology*, Vol. XXI, No. 2, 1974, pp. 133–136.

MEAD, MARGARET, *Culture and Commitment.* Garden City, N.Y.: Natural History Press/Doubleday, 1970.

SCHAB, F., "Adolescent Attitudes About Parental Controls," *Journal of Home Economics*, Vol. LXII, 1970, pp. 54–56.

SIMMONS, LUIZ R., "The Real Generation Gap," in David Gottlieb, ed., *Youth and Contemporary Society*, Beverly Hills: Sage Publications, July 1970, pp. 219–224.

FOUR

FRIENDS-LONELINESS

Hand in hand, we scan the park.
Hand in hand we smell the flowers.
Hand in hand we smile together.
Hand in hand we sing a love song.
Hand in hand we are free together.
Hand in hand we love each other.
Hand in hand we will remember each other.
> DAWN COMEAUX (14, *White, small town*)

There is one generalization one can make about adolescence. It is the age when one greatly needs one's contemporaries; when one must interact closely with them to try out one's capacity to think, feel, and make decisions; the time when one becomes truly part of one's *own generation.* We did not have to do a survey to reconfirm this. Friends are the life-blood of adolescence, trusted adults as well as peers, as we saw in the preceding chapter.

> If I were in any trouble, I think I would go to my friends first and see what they would think. I don't know if I would go to my mom and dad first.
> (12, *White, urban*)

> The only thing I ever wanted to do, was to be able to do it with my friends and have a good time. I have never wanted any money, just being with my friends makes me happy and that's all I want. (15, *American Indian, small town*)

Nearly all girls in every age group distinguished rather clearly between "friends" and "very close friends". They frequently spoke about huge circles of friends, at times forty or fifty. But they also talked about only one or two very close friends, both boys and girls.

Most girls talked about having friends of the same ages that they were. Only a few had younger friends. And very few talked about older friends. It may be significant, though, that adjudicated girls frequently had more older friends than did the non-adjudicated ones. I think it indicates their desperate need for protection and possibly earlier physical maturation. We also found among them more frequently the very lonely girl who needed a person to provide the support that they did not get at home or in school or at work or who may have been sometimes exploited by friends.

We learned a great deal about the girls' needs and hopes from the pictures they presented of desirable qualities they searched for in friends. Two themes stood out clearly.

1. A friend is someone you can *trust*, who does not speak ill of you behind your back, who can keep secrets, and who is available when you need him or her.
2. Friends must be able to listen, to understand on a feeling level.

I think [a friend is] somebody that is loyal. Somebody that would stay on your side no matter what anybody—well, if somebody started a rumor and everyone believed it, somebody that wouldn't believe it. Or somebody that, if they knew you did it, they wouldn't say "Aw, you did it" just to be like everybody else.   (14, *White, rural*)

[A friend is] someone who . . . when you really need them, they will come. Someone who sticks close and is truthful and, y'know, I won't really have to worry about them goin' out and tellin' your business or somethin' like that.
                                                    (15, *Black, urban*)

A friend don't talk behind your back. If they are a true friend they help you get out of trouble and they will always be right behind you and they help you through stuff. And they never snitch on you. That's what a friend is.
                                                    (14, *Black, urban*)

Often the girls expressed a deep fear of being "cheated," which related to a general mood of distrust and yet an enormous wish for honest human relations.

I don't have any close friends because I don't trust anybody . . . well I trust them but not all the way.   (13, *Black, urban*)

But there were friends who made it possible to live through a period full of doubts and pains.

My best friend I love very, very dearly. She has gotten me through a lot of hassles and problems that I could never talk about with my mother.
                                                    (16, *White, urban*)

A friend is someone who I can talk to, a girl who'll understand, and don't turn you down and say they don't want to listen and they don't want to hear what you're having to say.   (12, *White, rural*)

I like people that are willing to listen. . . . My friend and I, we talk to each other about our problems and we help each other . . . with our ideals and things.   (17, *White, rural*)

These qualities parallelled the ones they looked for in adults. The constellation of values was very consistent: People should be trustworthy, honest, understanding. It is surely not a "new" constellation. The only sign of "changing times" was the fact that these young women expected an *open* expression of those qualities. Communication was expected to be very outgoing—verbal.

Some girls were aware of the fact that listening and understanding were not the same. They searched for closeness, which would come partially from similar interests and sometimes from background.

All of my friends are a lot like me. You know, none of them are carbon copies, but enough like me so that they can understand me and I can understand them. I think understanding is really important to a relationship because if you don't have it, then you spend too much time explaining things and you never get around to really helping each other or being more personal and deep. They have a lot of the same attitudes that I do, so that really affects your actions. So, I don't ever have to worry about them doing something I'm not going to do or me doing something that they would disapprove of. So when you go out you know that you're not going to be embarrassed by them, or vice versa. We would enjoy the same types of things.   (17, *White, suburban*)

Others consciously wanted to get along with girls who had had different experiences. They learned that it takes an effort to understand one another.

I have a lot of girlfriends, but most of my close girlfriends are Mexican. I get along with them really good and I feel that I can tell them about anything. They feel the same way towards me but they talk about white people and against white people. But then they say, "but not you." It makes me a little mad. But what can I say when white people have done things to them all their life.   (16, *White, urban*)

A few girls were searching for genuine friendship and intimacy.

It's important to have more than one friend, because you can't expect one person to fulfill all the needs that you have. So I have different friends who fulfill different needs. I'm sure I fill the same sort of spot in their lives.
(15, *White, urban*)

Well, I only have about three tight friends, because I don't trust that many people with my feelings . . . the rest of them (friends) I consider acquaintances.
(15, *Black, suburban*)

Most of the girls had met their friends in school. Very few girls who talked about friendships said that they had made friends in church groups or organizations or teen centers. Even fewer said that they had made friends with other young people from their neighborhoods.

The only girls who talked with strong emotion about their belonging to highly organized groups were the very few who belonged to gangs. Among the 920 girls we interviewed, we found only a few urban girls, exclusively in California, who belonged to such gangs. They had actively participated in gang fights, were not merely auxiliary to boy gangs as girls had been in the 1940s. Yet they basically feared and disliked the violence.

We had two different gangs of girls and we fought with knives and whatsoever. I have scars and things. I've got a scar down my back, my hands and legs . . . we fight with a gang because we don't get along. They are in different territories than we are and they start spreading rumors to other people and when it gets down to us they say, "Well, this gang wants to fight with you." And at this one time we got mad, we just had to fight, and the cops busted everyone.

I don't like gang fights. You see a lot of blood and it's really not worth it. It scares me. Some of the guys will be shooting guns and all this and no telling who's going to get hit. It's not just the girls, when we fight we fight all of us, the girls and the guys. . . . It is really scary, once you are in a gang and you get to fighting. I have seen some friends die. Sometimes it makes me think, "Should I leave the gang?" because next time it may be me. But if you leave your gang, it's like betraying them. But I am worried that I might die too.

(14, *Chicana, urban*)

I was a War Representative. You go, like, we have informers and, like, they come tell us whether or not there is going to be a fight. The War Representative from my section goes to meet the other War Representative through a neutral gang. Like if the X and Y gang are going to fight, we'd go into Z territory to meet. And we'd have protection from the Z's and so would the X's. And the girls will usually set it up, because usually the fight would be over some girl going with some other gang. And me and the girl would talk, and if we didn't work out an agreement, we would fight. . . .

I saw one of my friends get shot and stabbed. It was just bad. No policeman came. . . . The only time police had come is when it's out loud, when we do things out loud and there is too many witnesses. I've seen a lot of girls get stabbed, a lot of girls get shot—dead. Policeman's not around. They don't even care, they don't care . . . they are scared, they are scared to get involved, because too many teenagers have guns, too many, and too many knives. . . .

I have been shot at and I have shot at somebody, but I didn't hit them, didn't miss them by much, but it didn't hit them. As far as stabbing, yes. Even when I was little I used to play with knives. Blood doesn't bother me. But when I got older, girls would have run over me if I didn't fight back, so that was one reason that kept them from me. Cuz you know, when I had gang fights, I would just slash up girls a lot, so I really didn't have no problems. A lot of girls left me alone. . . . (16, *Oriental, urban*)

We heard also of individual violence besides the gang fights.

Everyone stays out of my way when they know I'm mad. This girl—I got in a fight with her. . . . I gave her a big black eye. I remember it was swollen shut.

(14, *White, urban*)

I got in a fight with this one girl, the first fight I ever got in. She had braces on her front teeth and I knocked her front teeth out. (16, *American Indian, urban*)

Frustration and anger fed the physical violence. These girls moved in an environment that hardly would have allowed them to survive if they could not defend themselves. The tragedy is that it was again they who were penalized. So-called rehabilitation—usually by institutionalization—focuses exclusively on the girl instead of the total life situation that provokes such actions.

Girls told us what they did—and liked to do—when they were with friends, or what they enjoyed doing when they were with friends. More than half the girls responded to that question and by far the most frequent theme that emerged was that they liked to "go out" with their friends. By this they meant riding around; walking in parks; window shopping; attending movies, dances, concerts; and physical activity. It tells us how strongly the need for adventure and novelty is in girls, as it is in all adolescents.

> Sometimes I sit around in their [girlfriends'] houses when they can't go out. That drives me crazy . . . 'cause I like to go, go, go. And when I stay at somebody's house, like when it's a bunch of us girls sitting around, I get bored and leave. I don't like to be around the house.   (17, *White, urban*)

And another:

> I like being outdoors a lot. I hate being inside and it really bugs me. Like in the summertime, I like to go swimming and water skiing and camping and I like just walking around—just stroll around the lake and say, "Hello world, I'm here." And in the wintertime . . . I love to throw snowballs and roll around with people in the snow. . . .   (15, *White, urban*)

The next most frequent response to what girls did with their girlfriends was that they *talked* with them.

> Well, if we're together alone, then sometimes we get into really deep conversations about other people, but usually about ourselves, our surroundings, our families and stuff.   (16, *White, urban*)
>
> The best things [friends and I do] is we talk to each other about our problems and we help each other.   (17, *White, rural*)

Only about 10 percent of the girls who discussed activities talked about activities at home. Among such activities were watching television, listening to music, playing cards or games, and doing some cooking and baking. Only thirty-nine of the girls mentioned illegal activities as their *major* pursuit with other girls. They told about drinking, taking drugs, or breaking windows. This small number is not necessarily the whole picture. It only tells us that either such activities were not significant to the girl or she did not value them. The girls did not fear retaliation in these interviews, but some of them may have been embarrassed to discuss illegal activities. A number did talk about delinquent activities as part of the things they did while doing other things.

> We like to go to the movies and we like to go downtown . . . windowshop . . . buy a lot of stuff. Like to listen to records. Sometimes we'll sniff paint or something like that . . . or I'll show them the stories I wrote . . . that's about it.   (14, *Chicana, urban*)

All of these activities really do not add up to a picture of a "new generation." They point toward an enormous need for adventure, for an outlet for energy. This thirst for adventure has always been strong among the young. But girls today know more about the wider world through television and movies and they have whetted this appetite. Girls also now expect to have the same opportunities and freedom as boys.

The majority of young women had both female and male friends. It is important to realize that the word "boyfriend" no more means a coy sex-oriented relationship. Boys are regarded as *friends,* as *people.* Girls often talked about the same activities with boyfriends as with girlfriends and in a very relaxed manner. Sex may have been or may not have been part of the relationship, but it was not the exclusive goal.

> We usually go to a show or go out and get drunk. But my boyfriend, he likes to go bowling. He doesn't like to drink and stuff because he figures you can have a friend without drinking . . . make your own fun, like going to shows and stuff. (15, *White, small town*)

> I like to have sex with my boyfriend; I like to go to parties with my boyfriend. I like to go cruising, I like to be seen on the drag, and I like, if we are on a road and there is no cops around, we race the nearest people who are willing to race. (17, *White, urban*)

The most highly valued quality in boyfriends, as in girlfriends, was that he be loyal, understanding, considerate. He should be somebody one could talk to and who could feel with them, one who was close.

> *Come, walk with me as twilight fails and crimson*
> *   splashes in the sky*
> *In shadowed pathways, you and I.*
> *Come, walk and dream, and, high upon some windblown cliff,*
> *   which overlooks the sea,*
> *Come, watch with me*
> *The restless waves that spill upon the sand.*
> *Come closer, love, come, walk with me.*
>
>   ANONYMOUS (16, *Chicana, urban*)

She was described as inarticulate by the interviewer. And yet, her poetry is beautifully eloquent.

> I always dreamt of somebody that understands, or he tries to understand, you know. He's not the type that will come and beat you up in front of everybody either. What he has to say to you is between you and him, not nobody else. And that's the same way between me and him. What I have to say is between me and him. (16, *Black, urban*)

> Looks don't really matter. He should be considerate of me. And he should like to go places with me and he wouldn't like, say, two-time me. . . . (16, *White, urban*)

> He wouldn't be tall, dark and handsome. I think I take somebody who would like to have fun, like to go hiking, who would just understand a lot. I'd like to travel with him across the United States, around the world. I've always wanted to do that but not by myself. (17, *White, urban*)

The adjudicated and distressed girl especially looks for this quality of gentle understanding and describes it intensely. Since she rarely has an adult to confide in, the young man becomes her major support. Several girls interviewed stressed the fact that they and their male friends had helped each other to move out of difficult life situations and felt better for it.

He is really nice and he has really settled me down a lot. Before I would go out with a different guy every night and it got so people would talk. . . . He has really straightened *me* out. I haven't gotten into hardly any trouble since we started going together. It helps because at least you know somebody cares about you. It was like nobody cared and you could do whatever you wanted.

(16, *White, rural*)

This is about the first year that I have had medium self-confidence in myself. I'm just starting to get it. I always feel inferior. The main quality I like most in him is that he is full of self-confidence. If he makes up his mind to do something, he's going to do it. He made up his mind to go to college and to make good grades.   (17, *White, small town*)

Most of the time when I am down, he is usually right beside me, you know, helping get me back up and everything. Most of the time he is right there. He tries to get me back up in spirit and everything.   (17, *White, small town*)

Still, certain physical characteristics frequently were termed desirable. Traditionally, some girls wanted a boyfriend who was taller than they were and who was handsome.

He would be nice. . . . Neat, comb his hair and . . . you know, he should care for himself. . . .   (15, *Black, urban*)

He'd be tall; he would be handsome; I guess he'd be a wrestler because I know this one that's a wrestler and I like him in a special way.

(14, *White, rural*)

He'd be tall, handsome; I'd like him to have dark hair with dark skin like me and, um, I don't know, he'd have blue eyes. . . . (17, *White, small town*)

Emphasis on physical appearance was often followed by a "but" that stressed other qualities.

He'd be very masculine built. He would be taller than I. I would like him to be six feet, four inches, something like that and handsome . . . but handsome to me in a variety of things, you know; I like him to be intelligent and I would like him to know how to please me and just know how to cope with life.

(17, *Black, urban*)

Older girls looked for interests they might have in common with boys. They talked about moral values and a certain sense of responsibility.

I have more close male friends than I do female. I always seem to find fault with girls. She's too flighty or something like that, so I don't associate as much with girls as much as I do guys. It depends upon the person. If I can find something in common I can become friends. If I can't find something in common, I'll dig until I do. If I have absolutely nothing in common with them, there's not much I can do because I have nothing I can relate to them. To get to know them better. I'm not the type of person to go out and learn something just so I can become friends with the person.   (17, *White, urban*)

We found depth and a great yearning for love in these young girls, as we have always found in adolescents. There was gentleness and a wish for lasting and mutual relationships. Increasingly they wanted these relationships to be equal. They resented boys who regarded them only as sex objects. They wanted to be respected.

> He wouldn't just use me, he'd respect me.
>
> He wouldn't play around.
>
> He would protect me from people that might be a threat to me.
>
> He wouldn't run out on me if something happened.

Some wanted a traditional relationship.

> He would be possessive.
>
> He wouldn't go with other girls; he'd just want to stay with me, wanting to love me.

Others took a less traditional view.

> Well, if I was to go with somebody else, he'd say, "That's all right." Being tied down to one person, you know, that's foolish. . . .   (14, *White, rural*)
>
> He wouldn't have to be faithful and loyal—I wouldn't expect that of him. Just have respect for me. Everybody wants respect.   (18, *White, urban*)

Their range of lifestyles was evident, but their underlying motivation was the same—the wish to be respected as *people*.

> I think he's got to be really nice, he's got to understand me, that's one thing; and I sometimes think the biggest problem is, sometimes guys think they can just use a girl and that's not right.   (17, *White, rural*)
>
> One that isn't thinking about sex all the time. One that isn't too forward or too pushy. One who respects you and just wants to go out and have a good time, I mean go to a show or something. Well, one who expresses his feelings but isn't too overbearing; who lets you have your feelings too, just kind of half and half.   (15, *White, small town*)

The girl who has little support at home or in regular friendships, at school or in the community—unlike her counterpart of ten years ago—does not so much idealize the boy whom she loves, but rather is more realistic about him. What she expresses is simply a desperate fear of losing him and therefore her willingness to do almost anything for him. One such girl, when asked what she considered the ideal boyfriend, said spontaneously, "One that never would leave me!" Even very sophisticated sounding girls betrayed the same terrible fear of abandonment.

> I like older guys because they're more experienced and they understand more about life, and they've got more dope, because they've got more money,

and they've got cars. I wouldn't hang around little kids, you know, your own age. All you can do is walk to a movie with them and they have to be in at a certain time.

I think girls get to do a lot more stuff than guys do. Most girls say that guys get to do more stuff than girls do. It is really not true. Girls develop faster than boys, and that gives girls the advantage. Cause then older guys go after them, you know. They say, "Look at that little sexy thing," and you don't tell them how old you really are; you say "16." You just lie through your teeth. I know, I do that a lot. That's one thing girls are good at. I'm a great liar. Boys can't lie as good as girls. . . .

There's one thing I can't stand; it's when people leave, when people leave me. My friend is leaving from here and I am just going crazy. She's my very best friend. I can tell her anything. There is no one else in the group that I can just pour my heart out, like to her.   (14, *White, suburban*)

And the desperate pain when being actually abandoned:

> *A girl freezes in a telephone booth.*
> *In her draughty overcoat she hides*
> *A face all smeared*
> *In tears and lipstick.*
>
> *She breathes on her thin palms,*
> *her fingers are icicles.*
> *She wears earrings.*
>
> *She'll have to walk home alone, alone,*
> *Along the ice-bound street.*
>
> *First ice, the very first time,*
> *The first ice of telephone phrases.*
> *Frozen tears glisten on her cheeks,*
> *The first ice of human hurt.*
>
>   ANONYMOUS

Much has been written about the loneliness of the aged. There comes a time in life when close friends die, when children leave the home, when self-confidence cannot any longer be built on a job, when physical capacities sometimes diminish. The bite of loneliness and fear can be harsh in late adulthood.

Yet, it was the young Anne Frank who wrote, "Youth is lonelier than old age".[1] Maybe it is not lonelier but—as so many other experiences at that age—it is new and one has not experienced a certain strength that comes from having overcome it. One of the girls said:

> Being alone just scares me. I don't know. Sometimes when I do feel lonely, I don't know how to handle it, because I am definitely not a loner . . . it just scares me.   (17, *White, urban*)

[1] Anne Frank, *The Diary of a Young Girl*, New York: The Modern Library, 1952, p. 278.

If my brother and sister are gone, or if I called someone to do something and I can't get hold of anybody, or if I don't have a book to read, I feel very lonely.

(13, *White, suburban*)

These two girls were not deeply depressed. They had an advantage in having many friends and being active young women. The 13-year-old was involved in skiing, tennis, and swimming, and the 17-year-old was a member of a youth organization. Both had opportunities to talk and associate with others, to discover that others shared their anxieties and loneliness. Others were not so fortunate. Though none of the girls we talked to said that she had no friends, several had no close ones and suffered for it. They often considered themselves somehow guilty for their situation.

I feel lonely when I feel I have been rejected. And I say to myself, "I shouldn't have done this, I shouldn't have done this." There is a conflict between my two selves and I bring myself down. (14, *White, urban*)

Or:

Most of the time when I get sad, it is when I feel no one understands me or I haven't helped somebody. And depressed when I see other friends of mine giving up. . . . Then I get a lonely feeling. Happy is just knowing I did the right thing. (16, *Black, urban*)

I thought about suicide when I feel that my life is not accomplishing anything, and that I'm not really that much a part of anyone.

(16, *White, urban*)

Some found ways of escaping from their depression by becoming philosophical about it.

I want it that way, you know what I mean. You have to be alone. You're alone when you're born and you're alone when you die, no matter how many people are there. You have yourself. If you need something you have to go out and get it. You can't sit back and let people do for you all the time.

(17, *White, suburban*)

Some girls knew about hotlines and used them; others called their friends; some read; watched television; wrote poetry; or sought solace in pets.

I never have been lonely, I always have my pony. (16, *White, rural*)

My cat kind of senses when I am lonely and she comes up and purrs all over me, and I really like her to do that. She is a real good companion.

(14, *White, suburban*)

But the greatest helpers were friends.

After my father raped me, I felt kind of lonely. I felt like the whole world was falling in on me. But my friends kept on telling me, "You know, things are going to get better for you. You are going to make a better life for yourself."

(15, *White, urban*)

Loneliness may drive a girl into delinquency, into drug use and self-destruction. Studies on adolescent suicide attribute the act to "inadequate social life," "broken families," "death of a parent," "loss of boyfriends." [2] Whatever the specific reason, the common denominator is loneliness, no one to turn to. Suicide *wishes* are to be expected in adolescence and are almost universal, according to my own experience. In the 1920s, in Central Europe where I grew up, we considered an adolescent not quite normal who had not occasionally experienced such wishes. "Weltschmerz" (despair about the whole world) was characteristic of young people. I heard of similar death wishes as a normal phenomenon in youth when I visited countries in Asia, in South America, and Asia Minor. Such cultural acceptance of the suicide *wish* makes young people less guilty about having such thoughts. They also do not conceal these thoughts as much as young people do in a culture that considers suicide a crime or an aberration. Most girls we talked to said that they had never considered suicide.

I have a great life.

I'm too chicken to try.

I just know that I never could do that.

It's against my religious principle.

No, I think when a person gets to that point, something is wrong with him, but I have never felt that way. There is no problem that's too heavy, that I have to take my own life or wish I was dead.   (18, *Black, urban*)

It was a strong and proud 18-year-old girl who said this.

Yet there are girls who talked about their suicidal thoughts. They give as reasons conflicts with parents or with friends, either girl or boy, or a general sense of personal unworthiness and lack of meaning in life.

Well, I think almost everybody when they get really depressed or something, they think, "Oh I wish I was dead."

And whenever I used to fight with my mom I used to get to feeling really depressed and I would think, "Oh if I wasn't here, I wouldn't have to go through this." But not seriously, because I am afraid of death.
          (15, *White, urban*)

I thought that if I died that they [the family] might stop arguing and stuff. I don't know.   (14, *Black, small town*)

I can understand the feeling of people wanting to commit suicide; I've thought about it. . . . I can understand that they feel there just is no future. Everything for some reason is impossible. . . .   (16, *White, suburban*)

---

[2] James T. Barter, Dwight O. Swaback, and Dorothy Todd, "Adolescent Suicide Attempts," *Archives of General Psychiatry*, Vol. XIX, November 1968, pp. 523–527; T.L. Dorpat, J.K. Jackson, and H.S. Ripley, "Broken Homes and Attempted and Completed Suicide," *Archives of General Psychiatry*, Vol. XXII, February 1965, pp. 213–216; H. Jacobziner, "Attempted Suicides in Adolescence," *Journal of American Medical Association*, Vol. CXCI, January 4, 1965, pp. 101–105.

Even though the number of girls who reported actually having attempted suicide was small (57 girls), it has to be taken very seriously. In a culture that considers suicide a mental aberration or a crime, 57 out of 940 is a significant number. It is also important to realize that over half of these few girls were adjudicated delinquent. It again indicates how depressed and lonely these girls were. Even if the girl did not actually want to die, her suicide attempts were not "fake." They were a cry for help, for love, and for understanding.

> See, I didn't really want to die. I just wanted to get into the hospital so they would all be worried about me and so that they would go, "Oh my God, they haven't been treating the poor child right, look what we have done."
>
> (17, *White, urban*)
>
> Nobody really understands me. I wonder, "Am I going to kill myself?" I have tried it once.   (16, *White, rural*)
>
> I tried to commit suicide a couple of times but it was just because I figured I was moving away, so why not die before I lose completely.   (14, *White, suburban*)

With a slight sense of humor, she continued:

> Like once I took a whole bunch of Barbs and I was trying to drown myself. But I'm too good a swimmer to do it consciously, great! So, a top swimmer in the club happens to see me "drowning," so he fishes me out and takes me to his house. And I come to on the living room floor, cute! And I'm sitting here; "Why am I still alive?" And he says, "Because, you idiot, you didn't even manage to commit suicide."

And an older girl seriously tried suicide and explained:

> When I am lonely, that's when I want a boyfriend. I'm insecure. I was depressed about a week ago, I felt like quitting school and everything. I was sick of school. I had about three bad days in a row and I was really fed up. But I know if I quit school I will really regret it. But I don't like being depressed or lonely. . . . I think nobody cares for me, nobody loves me. (17, *White, urban*)
>
> I have tried suicide about five different times. I overdosed on sleeping pills one time and I slashed my wrists twice and I was going to jump off a cliff onto some rocks and I got stuck. That's when I first found out I was pregnant with my daughter. . . .
>
> My parents had gone over to a neighbor's house to play cards, and they had been drinking. I was in seventh grade and I was going with this guy who was twenty-two and my parents didn't like him and he was over watching TV. My parents called up every once in awhile to see if anything was going on, cuz my dad knew that I had been having affairs with him and he told my mom about it. I got really upset and I went in the bathroom and I took some of my mom's sleeping pills plus some of my brother's allergy pills, because they made me real sleepy and I just took every single one of them. I told my friend that I was gonna take a bath and I ran the water and stuff. I took a bath and then I remember sitting in the tub and the next thing I knew I was in the hospital, you

know. Here was some nurse looking over me. God, it was weird. I couldn't
believe it. I hurt! It was terrible.   *(16, White, small town)*

This same girl gave us an important insight into the strong longing for
support. She continued:

> While I was in the hospital, some lady—I don't even remember who she
> was—she was in the same room next to me and she was talking to me and I
> really matured with her talking to me. And I realized that I was carrying a
> baby that was part of me. . . . When I left the hospital I really matured.

Someone had broken through her sense of total rejection. Suicide attempts
because of pregnancy have declined appreciably since the time of the
"Scarlet Letter." We found in our population only two who had tried
suicide because of pregnancy. Gabrielson found only 14 out of 105
pregnant girls who had attempted suicide.[3] Problems with parents drove
more girls toward suicide.

> Because my mother had gone into the hospital, well, she had gotten out, she
> went back in, and she has this nervous problem; she says things she really
> doesn't mean. I guess she told me a couple of things that really hurt me, and I
> know she didn't mean them but I still felt them inside.
> At that time my father was drinking too and he wasn't at home, so I just felt
> everybody had left me. I took some pills. I guess, I just felt that way for awhile,
> but I was kind of glad it didn't work. I tried it a time before too. It was a couple
> of years ago, same way.   *(17, Chicana, urban)*
>
> The reason why I did it was because I got really loaded and I had a big fight
> with my parents and then when I went out it seemed that everyone was against
> me. I said "The hell with this," so I just OD'd. I was loaded and then I got into
> a fight and I got really depressed. People I don't know, maybe everyone, was
> just in a bad mood that day or something. It seemed like everybody was against
> me.   *(16, Oriental, urban)*
>
> One day I was about seven or eight and my dad . . . I don't even know how
> to explain it, he just liked to use his belt a lot; that's the only way I can put it.
> And I was playing with these neighbors and my dad didn't like it and he took
> me and he really gave it to me. And his pet, my older sister, just laughed.
> And that's another thing, older brothers and sisters, I just didn't know what
> to do, back then I was so confused. I was just running around in circles and
> back and forth. And, anyway, I was crying so much that I had a headache and
> I went to the cabinet and ate a bunch of aspirins and I told my sister and I said,
> "I hope you are satisfied now." And she didn't tell my dad. She said, "Well I'm
> not going to tell him, because I hope you do die." And my other little sister did
> go and tell him and because I took them, he whipped me again and took me to
> the hospital and then told them it was an accident. I love my daddy and I
> didn't want to say I did it because of him, and I said, "Yes, it was an accident!"
> *(15, Chicana, urban)*

---

[3] I.W. Gabrielson, L.V. Klerman, J.B. Currie, N.C. Tyler, and J.F. Jekel,
"Suicide Attempts in Population Pregnant as Teenagers," *American Journal of Public
Health*, Vol. LX, December 1970, pp. 2289–2301.

Fights with boyfriends drove some girls to attempt suicide. Sometimes it was her way of calling to him—"Look at me!" Often she saw no other way out.

> Yeah, I took, I think, eighteen downers, sleeping pills and then I had been drinking that night really heavy. I was drinking alcohol with the things to set it up real bad and so I was all sleepy. I just wanted to go to sleep. So, when the police told me, "We're going to take you home; just get in the car." So I got in the car and when I woke up I was in the police station. I did it because I had this real big fight with my boyfriend and I didn't talk to him for two whole weeks; then we went to this basketball game and he was there with this other girl. (15, *Chicana, urban*)

> Yes, I did that once with the guy I lived with, the first guy I lived with and had sexual experience with. I didn't like the way things were going, and at home mom gave me everything. I had a nice house and everything. And here I had to start from, you know, fourteen years old, I had to cook. Learn how to cook. Learn how to clean house in this little bachelor apartment; didn't have everything I wanted. I was dissatisfied with my clothes and how I took care of myself alone without my mom helping me.

> My boyfriend, he didn't give me as much attention as I needed, so I cut my wrist and locked the door—so he'd break the door down and catch me right when I'm going to do it. I just wait till he opens the door before starting to do it and then I get all this attention! (17, *Oriental, urban*)

Perhaps the most compelling reason for suicide attempts was a general feeling of helplessness.

> Suicides are in my family, almost all the people I've known. The environment I was in was very, it was a depressing thing, like my mother's an alcoholic, and my aunts and uncles and everybody else, they're all drinking, and they're all so depressed, and their families are breaking up, and they're trying to commit suicide. I even tried to commit suicide myself. Oh, ever since I was little I tried to commit suicide all the time because I was very unhappy. And I just felt that life was, really wasn't worth living. . . .

> And I didn't like myself; I didn't like the life I was living, and I didn't like the world around me. And ever since I was little, my mom kept saying, "I wish I was dead; I wish I was dead. Life isn't worth living. It's nothing but pain and misery." And she says, "When you get married, you'll see; you'll be sorry and you'll wish you was dead." And I used to always wish I was dead because I was always in a depressed mood; I'd never know what love was. And even now I don't know what love is.

> I'm still trying to sort out the reasons why I'm very depressed. What is really being happy? I just found out being happy is being content with yourself and with the people in your surroundings. And that's very hard to do because the surroundings sometimes aren't very good. And people are always having things worrying 'em, and people are always griping—they wish they weren't alive, and they wouldn't have to accept the responsibilities and stuff.

> Main problem is when you have a boyfriend and you break up. . . . There was some times that I was going to get married, and I loved him very much and

things didn't turn out and it really hurt me really bad. And I didn't want to live then; I felt that it was worthless. I'm just empty feeling. It was like life had no meaning for me.   (17, *American Indian, small town*)

As in many other instances, the societal institutions that were supposed to help, frequently added to the despair.

I am being pushed around from institution to foster home. . . . What have you got to live for? No place to go; no place to stay where you're at; nothing to, nothing to want to get up in the morning for. I always feel lonely. I've got my friends, you know, but something's missing. . . .

I figure, well, there's no place for me to live. They don't want me here, and I don't want to go there. So I figure, why should I live, you know? What is there in life? I cannot see—as hard and clearly as I'm trying to look—I can't see one thing to live for.   (14, *White, urban*)

And a girl in a delinquency institution:

It is sad, a person being stripped down—what they, what they've built up for themselves and what they are. One day someone comes along and just does that and starts tearing them apart. And that really gets me 'cause that person had to work a long way to get where they were. And the other person didn't have to, so they really had no right to do what they did. They just come up and say, "Well, you're fired," or something. "I got here the easy way, 'cause I'm cool."

I get hurt by things that people do—seeing my best friend do some of the things she does, for instance, seeing those kids in here and what they come in for. They all have no right being here; they should be home with their parents, instead of running around. When I see something get killed, like an animal by a car—that hurts.

I am depressed a lot of times. Lately I've been waking up pretty depressed. I get really rowdy when I'm depressed. . . . I can't really talk to my own age because they—nothing ever gets across.

After I tried to commit suicide, I was cooped up in the hospital; that was bad. I OD'd on tranquilizers on my mom's, a whole bottle. Reasons? My mom, home, school, job and my boyfriend—and me. I just found myself getting farther down each day and not going anywhere. I was just in one place, and I was going back and not going forward.   (17, *Black, urban*)

We saw a combination of personal problems, a sense of hopelessness in trying to cope with life, a despair at ever seeing a meaning in life, an abandonment by others, and—as a new factor—a depression induced by barbiturates and alcohol. To the girls we interviewed it looked as if there was no one, but no one, who really cared. From several states these words spilled out to us:

> *Loneliness is a silent jail*
> *Without cellmates, parole, or bail.*
> ANONYMOUS

SUMMARY

Our findings showed that:

1. Peers were as important to these adolescent girls as they always had been.
2. Both boys and girls were viewed by most girls as *persons* and not as totally different species.
3. The quality most important in friends, regardless of sex, was trustworthiness.
4. Also highly valued as friends were persons with whom one could talk, in whom one could confide, who could listen—the same qualities that were admired in adults.
5. For girls who had had many problems in their lives, boyfriends represented the givers of warmth and emotional satisfaction, which they craved.
6. Most girls did not want to be looked upon purely as a sex object by boys, though they would have sex relations if they felt close to a boy.
7. A number of girls, especially in the inner city, gave way to violence, individually or as part of a gang, but disliked violence.
8. Suicidal tendencies were rather frequent. Actual suicide attempts were not so frequent but were significant in number and implication. They stemmed from a sense of utter loneliness and worthlessness. Alcohol and drugs added to their depression.
9. Societal institutions, established to help girls, frequently added to their depression by offering no basic security and by separating them from their friends.

BIBLIOGRAPHY

BARTER, JAMES T., DWIGHT O. SWABACK, and DOROTHY TODD, "Adolescent Suicide Attempts," *Archives of General Psychiatry*, Vol. XIX, November 1968, pp. 523–527.

DORPAT, T.L., J.K. JACKSON, and H.S. RIPLEY, "Broken Homes and Attempted and Completed Suicide," *Archives of General Psychiatry*, Vol. XXII, February 1965, pp. 213–216.

FRANK, ANNE, *The Diary of a Young Girl.* New York: The Modern Library, 1952, p. 278.

GABRIELSON, I.W., L.V. KLERMAN, J.B. CURRIE, N.C. TYLER, and J.F. JEKEL, "Suicide Attempts in Population Pregnant as Teenagers," *American Journal of Public Health*, Vol. LX, December 1970, pp. 2289–2301.

HANSON, KITTY, *Rebels in the Streets*, Englewood Cliffs, N.J.: Prentice-Hall, 1964.

KONOPKA, GISELA, "Adolescent Delinquent Girls," *Children*, Vol. XI, No. 1, January 1964, pp. 21–26.

MILLER, WALTER B., "The Molls," *Society*, Vol. XI, No. 1, November–December 1973, pp. 32–35.

ROBLY, AMES, RICHARD ROSENWALD, JOHN E. SNELL, and RITA LEE, "The Runaway Girl: A Reaction to Family Stress," *American Journal of Orthopsychiatry*, Vol. XXXIV, No. 4, July 1964, pp. 762–767.

ROTHMAN, ESTHER P., *The Angel Inside Went Sour*. New York: David McKay, May 1971.

SEIDEN, R., "Suicide Among Youth— A Review of the Literature, 1900–1967," *Bulletin of Suicidology*, supplement, December 1969.

FIVE

DRUGS AND ALCOHOL

Sometimes
When you get up high
you can see
people walking
talking
smoking
laughing
crying
moping
happy

Sometimes
When you get up high
you can see
people running
walking
riding

Sometimes
When you get up high

you can see
people fighting
cussing
punching

Sometimes
When you get up high
you can see
all walks of life
poor
rich
in between

You can see through them
sometimes
by the expression on
their faces

It's an experience

ANGEL CRAIG (16, *White, urban*)

The use of drugs or alcohol is, as the girl says in her poem, a very personal and important "experience." Practically all girls, an actual count of 92 percent of all the young women we interviewed, expressed opinions about drugs, often spontaneously. From a comparatively very early age, at least from about the onset of puberty and at times even earlier, the girls were aware of drugs, had opinions about the use of drugs, know a great deal about the various kinds of drugs and alcohol, and know where they were available. We found no girl who had her first encounter with drugs later than at the age of 17. We encountered 8- and 11-year-old girls who had tried drugs. Almost all girls had tried alcohol at one point or another, but did not consider it worthwhile to comment on it, except incidentally. Unless it becomes addictive, adults rarely regard alcohol as a serious problem. In spite of its seriously damaging effects, just like any other drug, it has been accepted for a long time. The general attitude is that alcohol is benign and not really so dangerous as drugs. As one girl expressed it:

> I'll say about it [alcohol]: In some ways it's better than drugs because everybody says that with pot, you are going to go on to some harder stuff.
>
> (17, *White, urban*)

Other studies have shown recently that alcohol is increasingly popular among both sexes.[1]

From our interviews with them, we gained four major insights about drug use among girls.

1. A little over half of the girls who talked about drugs said that they had never used any drug, excluding alcohol.

2. About a quarter of the girls who reported personal experiences with drugs said that they had experimented only once or twice. Others talked about infrequent use or only on social occasions. They used mostly marijuana and alcohol.

3. The smallest percentage of girls said that they used hard drugs and felt they were addicted. These girls used a great variety of drugs, including alcohol.

4. Almost unanimously the girls disapproved of *hard* drugs, even if they themselves had used or were using them.

In general, more urban than rural girls were users of drugs, but the rural girls were by no means ignorant of drugs and their influence.

But let us hear from the girls themselves, and first from the majority of them who were against drugs and had never used them. It is significant that they were consciously rejecting drug usage themselves but that in general they showed an informed tolerance toward others who used drugs.

As far as that goes, I'm pretty straight. I don't use anything, probably because I have a really strict attitude about my own body. I want to be really healthy when I'm old. I want to be able to get out and hike and dance and sail and do everything I do now. And I just don't want to do anything to my body that would make it less efficient.

And most of my friends feel the same way, either for that reason or just because of the fact that the things are illegal or for moral or religious reasons. And since all my close friends are against drugs now, I don't hear a whole lot about it. I hear fringes of things, and I've run with different groups at different times that do the things, and I've been exposed to it, so I don't think my decisions against it are based on ignorance or on closemindedness.

I think that pot ought to be legalized because of the legal hassle that people go through, and the potentially good people who get thrown in jail and ruin their lives because they don't happen to feel that pot should be illegal. I think

[1] See Janis Rosenberg, Stanislav Kasl, and Rosalie Berberian, "Sex Differences in Adolescent Drug Use: Recent Trends," *Addictive Diseases: An International Journal*, Vol. 1, No. 10, 1974, pp. 73–96.

The News (Mexico City, December 1974, p. 6, Column 4) reports on a drinking study of 2,000 high school students from 25 areas across the United States conducted by Grey Advertising of New York. The findings were that half of the nation's high school students drink alcohol at least once a month, drink mostly away from home, and again half of those admit they get drunk at least once a month. That means that the percentage of high school drinkers is about the same as the percentage of adults who drink. This study applies to both boys and girls.

that it should probably be placed on the same basis as alcohol. Because I think it's a burden on society the way it's set up right now.   (17, *White, suburban*)
   Drugs? It's bad. I can't see myself taking anything like this. All the people I have seen die and mess themselves up. I have never experimented with drugs. I don't know about other kids; I know some of them are walking around, smoking weed, grass. I've seen some of them pushing . . . my sister found a needle . . . and alcohol, I don't like the smell of it. Parents don't want their child taking nothing like that because I know they want their child to grow up and be somebody.   (14, *Black, urban*)
   I don't see any sense in them. I think people who take drugs have got emotional problems so deep that they can't cope with them and they're trying to find an escape.   (16, *White, small town*)
   I get mad sometimes when I see someone on the road and they'll be drinking and I don't like people to drink, you know, especially on the side of the road. It's all right if they're at home. But, I'm always afraid someone is going to get into a wreck and get hurt or something like that when they're drunk.
        (16, *American Indian, rural*)

Girls who had only experimented with drugs usually explained why they stopped taking them. Those who took them intermittently explain why and when they took them. Let us hear from them.

   People, they get a nice high, you know, and that's how I feel, I mean I really despise a person when they just abuse their body by sticking needles in their arms, and dropping all different kinds of pills and all that. But, like myself, every now and then I may smoke a joint or something, and sit back and relax. But like I smoke a joint, I know I'll be at home somewhere; I don't be driving or anything like that. But I really feel sorry for somebody that really just misuse their body by shooting up and taking all that different mess.   (18, *Black, urban*)
   I've taken speed, but I don't like it. Like, all my friends, they can't believe you know, that I don't take acid and stuff. I've never taken acid but I've taken a drug called Qualudes a couple of times. They're not good for you, so I don't take those anymore. They just screw you up. So I don't want anything that'll screw me up, you know. I've taken maybe two hits of speed, you know; I don't like it, so I don't take it. Besides that, I have not taken anything.
        (16, *White, urban*)
   I've tried acid. I've tried mescaline. I've tried cocaine and downers and reds. I've probably tried just about everything but heroin. I've eaten psylocibin mushrooms. I've taken peyote buttons. But I'll never eat any of 'em again. Because, for one, I tried most of those drugs just because I wanted to find out what they were like. I was really curious about 'em.
   And the drug that I tried was acid. And if I wouldn't have freaked out as bad as I did, I probably would be into drugs. But I freaked out really bad, was almost taken to the hospital, and it's just . . . to me, they're just not anything I want to fuck around with.   (16, *White, rural*)

There were girls who used drugs more frequently, but several reported that they have stopped or that they were not too happy with them. They also explained why drugs or alcohol were necessary to them.

I take drugs a lot you know. I think it's okay but I wouldn't want my kids to, cause I know how much it messed me up. (15, *White, rural*)

About once a month or something. I don't take it (marijuana) unless my friends, you know, really offer it to me, because I really don't want to feel left out of anything. So that's the reason why I take it.

And it makes me feel good and happy when I'm down. And that's the only reason. (13, *White, urban*)

Well, when I was taking them, I thought it was pretty neat. You have beautiful, some beautiful trips, but then others aren't too beautiful. And when you come down you don't want to go back again. But you may have a really good trip and when you come down you want to go back up and have the same trip but you may not have it; you may have a bad one.

(15, *American Indian, urban*)

To let out my energies. I think when I smoke, it makes me what I am, because when you smoke you don't care what other people think. I like to drink because it makes me happy and I'm more open. Usually I'm pretty quiet and I keep things to myself. And when I drink, I can talk and have fun and laugh. (17, *White, rural*)

I smoke marijuana every once in a while, and I don't like to get drunk. I just like to sip and taste. Um, I'll go into a bar, or my neighbors'll bring over a bottle of wine and I'll just sip. I never get drunk. I don't like the feeling.

(18, *White, small town*)

Some girls brought up some serious delinquent behavior related to drugs, such as stealing and dealing in drugs.

I was addicted to reds when I was thirteen. I was taking a lot of reds and I still do now. I often wonder if that's going to mess me up, doing what I want to do maybe ten years from now.

I sniffed paint, glue, mainly paint. When I got busted, I went to a psychiatrist and he said if I didn't stop sniffing paint, I would ruin myself and all this. It seemed like I stopped for awhile but then I went right back to it.

I figure a lot of that happened when I was fighting with my parents. They were arguing a lot of the time and I thought it was because of me.

I had to buy reds but when I'm not buying them—like I have a friend who is a dealer who gives them to me and my girlfriend. Or—we'd steal things and we stole money. . . . I don't like doing it; I stopped drinking; it got me sick because I was mixing up all this stuff together. (14, *Chicana, urban*)

One girl who was selling drugs talked feelingly about how her own family as well as others regarded her as inferior. She described how she came to live with her grandmother, one of the few people she loved and respected, and how she stopped pimping and selling dope because, "I was showing respect for her so I just had to sell legitimate ware to get my money. I didn't want to beg it from her." She made much less money legitimately than when she was "pushing."

It was a lot of money during just one day. . . . I had a lot of young ladies doing it, and they'd bring in $500, $300, and I never got under $100. . . . I had a few people that was dealing for me. I had this housewife I'd go to all the time; people would be waiting there for me to come so they could buy the dope . . . and so I would bag it up and I made $700 in just about two hours . . . because there was a lot of kids and different people there.   (15, *Black, urban*)

As a dealer she was "big" and "loved." Yet, for the one person, the grandmother, whom she respected and who trusted her, she gave it all up. Now she wonders what her future opportunities are.

The very few girls who continued to take drugs and felt that they could not stop, expressed the following sentiments:

Well, I have smoked marijuana, taken "whites," "reds," "yellows," "acid," "rainbows," "keminal," "mescaline," "speed," "cocaine"—that's about it. I was nine and a half when I smoked marijuana. All of my friends were getting high. I had older friends so I decided to get high with them.

(16, *American Indian, urban*)

I'm a speed freak and I still am. But I don't like to be down, and . . . and I can't get high without it.

I don't see why they should have a drug law so hard because no matter what it says, it's a person's own decision and you have to make it yourself. To put 'em in prison for ten years, and they'll come out and if they want to, they'll just do it again.   (17, *White, urban*)

We also asked the young women whether they thought boys and girls took drugs for the same reasons. In the past, published findings on alcohol and drugs made very little distinction between men and women, not only in the use of drugs but also in their reasons for taking drugs; the largest population studied was adult males. In recent years there has been increased interest in the female population. The research shows an increase in drug use in white adult women, mostly related to depression, confusion about their own position in society and, at times, what is called the 'empty-nest" syndrome, after children grow up and leave home. Rosenberg and his associates[2] in their review of recent research findings, pointed out that there also has been an increase in the use of drugs by adolescent girls. More adolescent females than males prefer barbiturates, tranquilizers, and amphetamines. The authors of these studies speculate that this preference, especially the use of amphetamines, may relate to specific needs of girls. Many girls want to look slim and attractive and these drugs depress appetite and induce a certain sense of euphoria. On the other hand, young women, more than young men, seem to admit to and talk about their emotional problems, and seek relief from tension and depression through the use of barbiturates. Since we based our understanding on informal interviews, not questionnaires, we have the advantage of having girls give their reasons. We did not need to guess about motives. In listening to the girls, it became clear that to them the major

[2] Janis Rösenberg, Stanislav Kasl, and Rosalie Berberian, "Sex Differences in Adolescent Drug Use: Recent Trends," *Addictive Diseases: An International Journal*, Vol. 2, No. 10, 1974, pp. 73–96.

reason for taking drugs was to get away from problems, mostly related to relationships with parents.

> Girls are doing it for a specific reason, maybe they need attention from their parents. (15, *Black, urban*)

> I take drugs when I get depressed or when I get upset or when I feel I can't handle a problem or when I've really got a bad problem on my mind. I take drugs to forget about it at the time. (15, *Black, urban*)

> Because the pressures they are put under . . . you have to have a way to escape, you have to have a way to relax, you've got to get away from having to learn so much so fast and having to grow up so fast. (17, *White, suburban*)

> Probably mostly they take it because they have problems at home . . . they just don't have anyone to talk to. (13, *White, suburban*)

The problem is dealing with one's feelings. Some take drugs because they feel very rebellious.

> I got involved because I was trying to rebel against my father because he never let me do anything that I wanted. You know I couldn't talk to boys until this year. It was really upsetting, and I just turned to drugs for an escape. (17, *White, urban*)

Others were forced to hide their feelings.

> Girls are a little more emotional. Boys take it just to get loaded, the kicks, the feeling. Girls take it to hide their feelings and not face them. So therefore we use them more. (16, *Oriental, urban*)

But there were other reasons too. Peer pressure was strong, as was a wish for status, for being "grown up."

> I think we are trying to prove something and we don't know what we are trying to prove. Maybe we are trying to prove we are growing up. (17, *White, rural*)

> I'm not really sure why girls take drugs, but a lot of times they do it just to be neat and their friends do it and they want to be just like their friends. They think they will be cool and they will like them. . . . (13, *White, urban*)

> Some girls they use it for escaping problems; but some girls, like if they are gay or something, they want to get sent to an institution where they'll be with all girls, you know. They do that stuff to get up here [detention home]. (16, *White, small town*)

Less frequently mentioned, but important to the individual girls, were:
1. The wish to be popular with boys.

> Probably we feel inadequate . . . because men these days can make you feel inadequate if you let them. Uh, we feel inadequate. We feel rejected, maybe, we feel like that makes us popular with the boys when it really doesn't. (15, *White, rural*)

2. Curiosity, sometimes aroused by drug education.

> Oh, it could be because their friends use them, or this class that I was taking this year, in Home Economics, said that it stimulated you; it gave you a sex drive or something like that. That's what they experienced and that's what they liked. (18, *Chicana, urban*)

3. Pleasure, it made them feel good.

> I don't know too many kids that shoot dope or anything like that, but I know a lot of grass smokers but I don't really consider that a drug. . . . I think they smoke grass to have a good time. They really have a good time if they are in with people that smoke grass. People who are alone are probably the type that sit around and say, "What am I supposed to do with myself tonight?" Well, I always feel pretty good when I smoke grass, so I guess I'll smoke grass.
>
> (17, *White, urban*)

This particular girl was very active in youth organizations and felt that her occasional use of grass made her more efficient. Others expressed similar thoughts.

> It's kind of a nice high; it's the best way I can explain it. They want the pleasure now, not later. When they want it, they get it and that's the way they want it. (15, *White, urban*)

Many girls said that girls used drugs and alcohol for the same reason that boys did, but about an equal number assumed some difference. The only significant difference, at least the way it was perceived by the girls, was that boys took drugs to prove their masculinity. One would have to talk to the boys themselves to see whether the girls' perception was right.

> Yeah, and I know lots of boys that do it only because somebody calls them a chicken . . . if somebody calls them a chicken, that's it; they have to prove that they can do that or die. (17, *White, rural*)
>
> Oh, I think it's just a natural instinct for dudes to drink. (16, *Black, urban*)
>
> I feel most boys do it because they want to go have some fun.
>
> (16, *Black, urban*)
>
> I think boys use them more than the girls 'cause boys sometimes do things like that to show off, you know, who can drink the most, who can, you know, do this the most, like that. (16, *Black, urban*)
>
> I think they just want to act cool and tough, but I don't think it does anything, really. (14, *Chicana, urban*)

The girls saw themselves as more burdened, with more problems than boys.

> The boys they take it for enjoyment and everything else, and to me a girl takes it because most of the girls that I know that have problems get it off their mind, so they do it. (18, *Inuit, rural*)
>
> The boys just get high every day and act crazy. And like the girls . . . something might happen between her and her boyfriend, and they want to go out and get loaded. They'll be having problems with their mother, real sensitive about it . . . the boys, cuz that's what they like to do. (15, *Black, urban*)

It is quite evident from all our interviews that drug education may prevent girls from taking hard drugs—it does give them information on the subject. Yet if the information is not accompanied by some change in a dissatisfying life situation, it does not help basically. The girls themselves have to decide to abandon drugs. This motivation comes either because they feel more satisfied with their lives or they do not want to risk the effects of drugs for a specific reason.

> I just don't want to do it anymore. If you take speed, the baby will be retarded . . . that really scares me because I don't know what I will do with a retarded baby. Really, I blame it on myself if I did that. I'd say, "Well it's because I took acid" and that scares me because I love kids and I want one. My mom had one on Sunday, the other Sunday, two weeks ago. And I got to hold it and everything, and it made me want one more than I did.
>
> (17, *White, small town*)

> It's not a problem to me, but everybody else considers it as a problem, because it's against the law. I know it's dangerous to my health. It could kill me, give me brain damage. But at the time when you be doing it, you don't be worried about whether it's against the law or it can give you brain damage and stuff like that.
>
> (17, *Black, urban*)

> I mean, the person that brought up the drugs, I don't know why, it's just ruining the whole world! Just ruining the young, the young kids.
>
> (14, *Chicana, urban*)

Only 4 percent of all the girls gave a positive response to the effects of drugs, whereas 89 percent described negative effects. (It is important though to remember that the negative response was mostly related to hard drugs. Marijuana and hash were very frequently considered harmless. Most believed that they should be legalized.) Perhaps one girl's own description of her "trips" speaks loudest.

> *I swallowed it.*
> *I didn't hear anybody.*
> *There were all noises,*
> *different noises.*
> *I never heard them before.*
> *I was scared.*
> *They looked like blobs of air.*
> *Different loudnesses—it was bugging me. What could I do?*
> *What happened? Where am I? Everything's white with flowers.*
> *Am I. . . .*
> *Cliffs, mountains, the echoes tore at my ears. All over I*
> *heard their cries. Running like an animal I was frightened,*
> *scared. Like I was being hunted—hunted, trapped—*
> *trapped like an animal chased, I heard their cry, their*
> *howl. My head, oh my head. Then behind me, there they were.*
> *I was caught, trapped by my deadliest enemy—MAN!*
> *Animals! Animals!*
> *Coming! Coming!*
> *After! After!*
> *Me! Me! Me!*
> *Help! Help! Help!*

Die! Die! Die!
Help! Help! Help!
Dead! Dead! Dead!

ANONYMOUS

I'm on an acid trip. I'm the only person. I'm falling—not falling, but drifting. I hear the birds talking to me. They are angry so they try to kill me. . . . I wake up. Outside the wind is blowing but the birds are singing. They are happy so I sing with them.

It's very dark. It's spooky. Terrible noises, strange things. I am on a planet by myself. I'm walking, walking, walking—gone.

I am on acid, by the river. I am drowning and now dead and birds are flying above my body.

I'm out of the world and everything and nobody can reach me. I'm trippin out—I'm dying—I'm a spirit—I'm alone—I'm dead!

Who are you? What do you want? Tell me, please tell me. What do you want? Back, go back! What have I done? Go away—leave me alone. Back, I say, back! Ahhhhhhhhhhhh!   CATHY MATHISON (12, *White, urban*)

Marijuana, grass, barbiturates, dope
now there is no longer hope.
Funkies dying in the street,
not knowing drugs can't be beat.
Red ones, blue ones, heroin,
I often wonder if drug's a sin.
Uppers, downers, L.S.D.,
Acid, reefer, none for me.
Red devils, black beauties, yellow jackets
Some take an overdose if they can't hack it.
Is there really need of crucifixion?
Most is done by drug addiction.
Pushers, pushing every day
Drug addicts can't get away.
Shooters, shooting all the time
Believing they'll have a happy mind
Some sniff cocaine, some sniff glue,
watch out, little brothers, and big brothers too,
don't let the habit get to you!
I hope the kids of the drug generation know it's true
the modern crucifixion all is new.

ROSSLYN RIGGINS (15, *Black, suburban*)

And she sounded a deep cry for help.

Hello God are you there?
Well, listen to me God, please, listen
Oh God, Oh God
Please, please don't let me die!

I don't want to die, I want to live!
I want to live!
Why? You ask me why,
Well, why should I die?
What have I ever done,
Except want a little fun.
What did I ever do,
Except sniff a little glue!
And you ask me why?
Well, why not
because I want to live!

ROSSLYN RIGGINS (15, *Black, suburban*)

Parents were often pictured as totally unaware of their daughters' taking drugs. The girls sometimes mentioned that "they figure what they don't know won't hurt them." In relation to both alcohol and drugs, but especially to drugs, the importance of the peer was overwhelming. They were the ones who urged the girls to experiment with drugs, but they were also the only ones who seemed to be able to support the girl who wanted to give up drugs or avoid taking them altogether.

SUMMARY

1. The girls knew about drugs, were well-informed about them from a very early age, frequently at grade school age.
2. When girls take drugs they may start very early, often around 12 or 13 years, but also earlier. No girls reported starting later than age 17.
3. About half the girls reported never having used drugs and never wanting to use drugs, but most of them were tolerant of others who used them.
4. The largest number of girls who admitted having taken drugs either had experimented only a few times or used what they consider harmless drugs (marijuana and alcohol) only occasionally. Very few girls considered themselves addictive and continuous users of hard drugs.
5. The overwhelming majority of girls who had taken drugs considered their effects negative. But this attitude applied predominantly to hard drugs.
6. Their major reasons for taking drugs were:
   a. to escape from problems,
   b. peer pressure.
7. Drug education alone seems to have had little effect in preventing a girl from taking drugs or ceasing to take drugs.
8. The reasons for either not taking drugs or ceasing to take drugs were:
   a. strong motivation in regard to other life goals, such as wanting to have healthy children, wanting to have a healthy body, or

b. pleasing another person (boyfriend or girlfriend).

9. Drugs, including alcohol, have a strong personal meaning to the girls whether they take them or not, as evidenced from the fact that the majority of girls addressed themselves to this question.

BIBLIOGRAPHY

FORT, JOEL, "Youth and the Drug Crisis," in David Gottlieb, ed., *Youth and Contemporary Society*. Beverly Hills: Sage Publications, 1971, pp. 191–210.

Minneapolis Star, January 23, 1975, Section C, p. 1.

Minneapolis Tribune, February 6, 1972, Section B, p. 15 (Gallup Poll—"51% of College Students Admit They Tried Marijuana").

TEC, NECHAMA, "Some Aspects of High School Status and Differential Involvement with Marijuana: A Study of Suburban Teenagers," *Adolescence*, Vol. VII, No. 25, Spring 1972, pp. 1–28.

The News (Mexico City), December 1974, p. 6, Col. 4.

TRAUTMAN, EDGAR C., "Drug Abuse and Suicide Attempt of an Adolescent Girl—A Social and Psychiatric Evaluation," *Adolescence*, Vol. I, No. 4, 1966, pp. 381–392.

WIDSETH, JANE C. and JOSEPH MAYER, "Drinking Behavior and Attitudes Toward Alcohol in Delinquent Girls," *International Journal of the Addictions*, Vol. VI, No. 3, September 1971, pp. 453–461.

SIX

SCHOOL

Here I go for another boring day. I hate most teachers. . . .
The day is so long. Well at least it's Friday. No more teachers for
the weekend. But still, more painful adults.
Every day, first I go to school and listen to Mrs. A. try to quiet
the class, maybe give out a few detentions. Then to Mr. B's class to
hear him talk for 49 minutes. Then wonderful ten minute break
and a few cigarettes. Ph.Ed. with Mr. C. and basketball. Science
with Mr. D's stuffy room. Then lunch with leftovers. Then math
with Mr. E. I could and never will be able to do math. Spanish with
Mr. F. I can't do Spanish either. Finally speech. Quite a
boring class. Poor Mr. F. can never get the class's attention. Then
home on the bouncy bus. Throw my books and coat on the bed.
Then to take my frustrations out on the poor piano. That is a very
boring day in my opinion.
(FROM A DIARY OF A 14-YEAR-OLD, *White, urban*)

It is not unusual for girls to describe their educational experiences, as was done in this diary. But during our interviews we heard also very many positive comments. Whatever the comments were, school was most important to the young women.

I want to remind the reader that our findings are not based on questionnaires with preformulated questions and opinions, but that we purposely used open-ended interviews to find out which kinds of subjects were most significant to adolescent young women. We saw that their searching into themselves, their own family life, especially the relationship with their parents, and their friends were of primary concern to them. School matched these other interests in intensity. Because it represented a very large part of the young women's lives, it had significant intellectual and emotional meaning.

Schools certainly have been most important to young people for centuries. Their content and purpose have changed over time. Schooling originally was restricted to the upper classes, predominantly to males in the Middle Ages, and retained its privileged character until quite recently. It became a tool, not only to prepare the young to "make a living" but also to instill in them virtues considered important at a given time.

Obedience was probably the major virtue inculcated through schools throughout Europe and Asia for many centuries. Teachers, too, were expected to be obedient in reflecting and accepting the manners and morals of their particular cultures. They were to impose strict discipline on their pupils and teach them only what was prescribed by the school curriculum.

It is probably not accidental that most teachers in the agrarian New World were women. They were supposed to be submissive by nature and therefore receptive to the obedience/discipline criterion. In the college preparatory schools, most teachers were men; these schools catered primarily to boys.

After World War I a new wind blew into the European and U.S.A. educational systems. Some class distinctions were erased. The North American school system especially moved toward a more nearly equal education for all. True, inequalities continued between urban and rural schools and schools for the white majority and minorities. Still, compared with European schools, the American school system was far in advance of its European counterpart in terms of compulsory basic education, a comparatively warm and informal relationship between teachers and children, and a certain encouragement of creativity and of teaching based on the understanding that learning is more than a purely cognitive process.

The advent of Sputnik reawakened in the United States the odd inferiority complex that Americans often have in relation to Europeans. Suddenly they felt compelled to imitate the kind of system that placed heavy emphasis on purely intellectual pursuits, directed predominantly toward technical competence, which left no room for and placed no value on other activities. Students were increasingly forced into a competitive mold. I remember in pre-Sputnik times a principal of German schools visiting this country and exclaiming admiringly, "Oh, in this country young people really *like* school!" In the post-Sputnik period emphasis on teacher-student relationships was diminished and the main criterion of a good school was often based on the amount of technical knowledge pumped into the heads of students. Elitism, intellectual conceit and dogmatic belief in test scores robbed schools of much of their human quality.

The 1960s saw a welcome reaction. A most interesting development was the establishment of various alternative schools, not based on race, sex, class, or intellectual distinction, but simply on various forms of approaches to young people with active consideration of their variety of interests.

This period of transition, with its variety of educational philosophies and innovations, was clearly mirrored in what we heard from the young women in our study. Perhaps what was most surprising was that many girls had a very positive attitude toward school. Almost three-fourths of the girls who expressed an opinion about school in general were positive about it. Only a minority, about 20 percent, were strongly negative. It was not that they seemed incapable of doing acceptable school work. We can only again speculate about the reasons. They were often girls who were alienated from both adults and other young people, who came from backgrounds in which education was not much supported, and who received very little support and satisfaction from the school itself.

The most significant positive aspect of school was that it was a place to *meet and be with friends*. Schools seem to underrate this part of their function. They often consider it only a by-product. But this function is the most significant one to the young people themselves and has a deep impact on their whole attitude toward people and learning.

> Yeh, the main thing I like about it is going and whooping around with my friends. I get good grades and I study hard but the main thing that really makes me get up in the morning and want to shoot out there is that I know my friends are there. The fun part is social, and the learning part is a must.
>
> (16, *White, suburban*)

> Well, I like school because you get an opportunity to meet other teenagers of your age and make new friends.   (15, *Black, urban*)

> Well, I think school is really fun because you learn a lot and I'm with my friends all the time. And you get opinions from them, and the teacher really helps us a lot. I like it and I like to go to school. And when it comes to the end of the week I wish it was Monday again.   (13, *White, urban*)

The social aspect becomes especially important in a society that is still racist. When girls talked about problems in social relations in school, they often mentioned racial problems.

> Our school is 85 percent White and 15 percent Black. If you are walking down the hall and the football players are all White, and they tell you to move. . . . I have gotten into a lot of fights because of that. . . . I got into fights when kids tell me I am nothing. I don't really pay attention to that, but when they come up to you and start teasing you about your color. . . . I am proud of what color I am and not what they want me to be. And I don't think I should be any other color. And nobody wants anybody to talk badly about their parents and that's when they really get me mad.   (13, *Black, urban*)

> My friends at school are a lot different from my friends outside of school. My friends at school are obviously mostly white. They don't fit into the same category that my friends outside of school do because after school I don't usually see most of these people because, for one, I'm on the other side of town. . . . Well, see, most of the people that I go to school with live in "suburbia," you know. It makes it kind of difficult to get back and forth. And really, I don't have that much desire to be with that many people outside of school. We're not interested in the same things. Usually they're more interested in going to the Country Club. And obviously, since I can't get into it, I have no affinity for them.

> I doubt that it occurs to them that the Country Club won't post swim meets because they won't have Blacks swimming in their pool. Also, we were talking about the senior prom, and they wanted to have it at the Country Club. My mother said if they had it there I couldn't go because they discriminate. So we

brought this up . . . the Black people in the class. But their parents weren't as anti- as my mother. We suggested the Athletic Club. And they didn't seem to think, since it affected so few members of the class, that it was that important to consider. So I'm sure it really doesn't bother them unless they are really a friend, and then they would speak up and say something about it. I have some friends that did, but still it wasn't the majority and they said, "Oh, your mother doesn't really mean it." But she does.

Some of the people in school are ignorant. Like some girls would ask me why I wouldn't vote for George Wallace. That's kind of an obvious answer.

And then there are some people that know since it's not affecting them they take the attitude of, "Why worry about it, it's not my problem and I'm not going to make it my problem." It's this way everywhere. If it's not affecting you then don't worry about it. Everybody is afraid to put themselves out on a limb to help somebody else because if they really cared they would say, "We'll make it somewhere, so that everybody can go regardless of race, creed or color." But as long as they are having their good time and having their prom with their right kind of ritzy friends, and their long rich dresses, then it's all right with them. I guess in a way this is not really callousness, it's just apathy or something.

They may have a lot of money, but culturally they're quite ignorant. Like they thought that everybody that lived below X street had food stamps. I don't even know what food stamps look like. Granted, my parents aren't rich, and my mother works, but still, I can afford to eat three meals a day and have heat in my house and stuff like that. Culturally they're deprived cause when they graduate they're going to a private white college, and they're just building a wall between themselves and the rest of the world that they're never going to get out of. And they're just going to grow up to be like their parents, trapped in their little worlds of glitter and ritzy parties and stuff like that. And they're never going to realize what the world is really like and it's going to be too bad. They're going to bring their children up to be the same way. And the world isn't ever going to change at that rate, if they just keep on with their little circles.   (17, *Black, urban*)

The plight of the girl who belonged to a minority was very critical even if the social differences were not so apparent. At a time of life when social interaction is most significant, it is difficult to find oneself considered "special," "different," and therefore having to struggle so hard to find friends. One of the girls described this feeling very sensitively.

It's a private school. Well, academically it's all right. But socially it kind of lacks . . . as far as I'm concerned . . . there are fourteen Black people there, and 500 or so White people. After four years, that tends to kind of put you out in the cold. . . . No, I don't think I have an identity problem. But it doesn't help any to make you feel accepted because you have to fight harder to have friends outside and inside school in order to get along.   (17, *Black, urban*)

There were problems between two of the minority groups.

Sometimes those colored people, when you do something wrong, they'll get kind of mad and start cussing at you or something but if you ignore them they'll go away. I guess that's all.   (14, *American Indian, small town*)

The race relation picture was far better when the varied populations were of approximately equal size and there was a conscious effort on the part of school administrators and teachers to include social life as a significant part of their educational program.

I think this new school has really helped me out a lot because here is more of the real world, because you have the racial differences, you have religion differences . . . like last night there were a bunch of all different kids . . . it has helped me in really relating to people. Education is where you end up memorizing and everything else, but myself, what I think is important right now is to get to understand people and to get to understand myself. Because if you get out of the world of school, and you don't know yourself, that can be a very bad thing.   (16, *White, urban*)

Well, what I mostly liked about high school was meeting people. That's the only thing I really liked about going to school everyday and being able to communicate with different people, you know, different races and getting to know people. I really didn't dislike anything about school. (18, *Black, urban*)

But certainly there were also young people who themselves were strongly prejudiced and had difficulties moving in with a different group.

Well, I don't like the school I'm in now because it's . . . it's integrated and, you know, that's really cool if it would just work, but it doesn't. We've got fights in our school all the time between White and Black and girls and boys and stuff and always kicking and pushing around the hallways and. . . .

These schools, public schools are really behind the other ones. I mean here you hardly ever get through a whole book. And you just go in there and you just mess around. The teachers, you know, they can't do very much with you. I think it's because like at the beginning of the year, they said, well, the kids are just getting started to school so we'll give 'em a break and be kind of easy on them. 'Cause, you know, there's a lot of tenseness and stuff because the whole school is mixed Black and White, and the principal is a Black woman and most of the staff is Black, and there's a bunch of White kids that are real prejudiced and don't want to be around Blacks, and it's the other way, too.

(13, *White, suburban*)

Racial problems are intensified by the way adults relate to racial or ethnic groups. The girls were very sensitive about this. A 15-year-old tall and attractive Black young woman spoke very calmly, but one could feel her suppressed anger.

The teachers are sort of scared of Blacks here. I'm not the kind of person that shows how much I hate them. I just sit back and do mostly what I'm supposed to do. But teachers are still scared. If I ask a question, some of the teachers just ignore me. And I sit back and I watch this and I feel it.

(15, *Black, urban*)

The young girls from minority backgrounds were basically often gentle and thoughtful, but because of their color they were looked upon as fierce and frightening. And they resented it if teachers did not consider them capable of thinking and reasoning.

> She's always saying we're not good enough, and she's always saying stuff, jumpin' on to us, comparing us with the sophomores, saying that they're better than we are. She's prejudiced against us, because she's a different nationality than we are, and she's used to different things, and we're not, and she wants us to be like she wants us to, and we can't change. And she thinks we should. I don't think that she should change, but I think she should get used to us, like we've had to get used to her.
>
> And she just tries to push us too hard. She says we never do anything right. And that isn't encouraging us a bit. (17, *American Indian, small town*)

> They didn't want to take up no time with you, you know, and so I . . . that's what really made me mad and. . . . Because I figure if they wasn't trying, I'd just cut. And then I just started fighting in school and fighting the teachers and everything. Getting suspended. I just gave up. (16, *Black, small town*)

> It's all right, being one of the only eight Blacks, but some kids, they are bigots and they just give you a hard time. Like in my sociology class they say things like, "They don't know any better," pertaining to Black students. Or, "They'll never make it in this school," and things like that. (17, *Black, suburban*)

> If a white kid did something, they got away with it. If a black kid did something it was suspension, expulsion, probation, or just plain ole kick you out of school. (15, *Black, urban*)

> They always put Indians down and that's not fair. When they put Indians down, that's when I don't like them. (16, *American Indian, urban*)

Some young white girls still accepted the myth of Black inferiority as fact and talked like their bigoted elders.

> No, I don't like school. I just don't like the way they run the school. Just the Blacks have, you know, got into fights and everything. . . . So far, integration is okay, but we're getting a little ugh . . . well Blacks are just . . . are getting fed up with all of us. I don't really pay much attention to them but—some of them are nice. Integration has affected my education because the teachers are giving us easier stuff. Because, you know, Blacks can't learn as much I guess. . . .
> (13, *White, urban*)

The teacher's attitudes had a strong effect.

> I don't like teachers because they are prejudiced against Blacks. . . . Like they think Blacks are dumb and don't know nothing. Like they put us in slow groups and stuff like that. (15, *Black, urban*)

> School doesn't help Black-White relations because the teachers allow kids to call you trash or nigger-lover or honky-lover. (14, *White, urban*)

> In grade school I was pretty smart. When I got to high school—I had always been brought up people to people. When I got to high school it made a difference between Black and White. I got suspended about three times for fighting because people would say something about it. . . .

> Some of the kids we get along like sisters and brothers but there's always one that comes along and makes it different because you're Black. Or some Blacks come along and make it different because you're White. . . . (16, *Black, rural*)
>
> I feel that Black teachers are discriminating against students of their own race.   (17, *Black, urban*)

One girl described the condescending attitude of the teacher in a boarding school for American Indians.

> We had a teacher that liked Monopoly. We were supposed to be studying and she got us to play Monopoly, even during school hours. But if we didn't get our homework done we'd have to stay after school. (15, *American Indian, rural*)

Prejudice and discrimination were also strongly felt by Spanish-speaking girls, especially if their English was not perfect.

> It was not so hard for me because I already knew how to speak English. But for people who do not speak English well, it is very hard. . . . I am making good grades and I hope to be able to finish high school. (15, *Chicana, urban*)

Spanish-speaking children were treated like little animals to be "trained."

> When I was in school I had to go to the bathroom, you know, once in a while, because I can't hold it too much. And the teacher only lets us go two times a day. That's all, we can't go no more. Every day, if we go three times a day, we have to stay after.   (12, *Chicana, urban*)

And racial problems arose partially out of the very different experiences and life goals of the girls. We found that young Black women often were highly motivated to learn and criticized the negative attitudes of some White middle-class girls toward school. Here is an example, related by a 17-year-old Black girl who went to a 95 percent White school.

> Seems like the White kids are kinda . . . hippy freaks. They are really something else. I mean, like just recently, you go in the bathroom and they put cigarette butts in the toilet, you know, and stuff like that. They write all over the walls and stuff, where before it wasn't like that. It was clean and everything. It's getting trashy around here.

Social relations were important to the girls. Racism was a major barrier to their really enjoying one another.

Many adults who think that the young do not want to learn may be surprised at what they usually consider major goals of school. Learning, working at intellectual tasks, and preparing for the future were mentioned very frequently by the girls we interviewed. Most of them mentioned preparation for the future as a school function and considered this positive. Through schooling they hoped to "be educated and productive" and to learn "what's going on in the world today."

> My favorite is humanities which is one of the hardest classes I've had, just because it makes me think and want to work. I also like newspaper because its a

fun class and you are kind of on your own and can develop whatever you want, your own ideas. I'm not very smart when it comes to math, but I keep taking it because I know I should learn. And I take French. . . . I really want to learn; I know it is one of my needs because there is so much to learn. (18, *White, urban*)

I really like school because when I am here I get involved in student government activities and I get deeply involved in my work and I like to learn things. I really don't come to school just to be here, I really love to learn and every day I find out more and more good things that I never did before.

(17, *Black, urban*)

See, my step-mom, she used to pressure me a lot to always do my work and stuff and that used to make me mad, so I wouldn't do it. Until this year she told me, "Well, just do the best you can" and I got to thinking, "Well what do I want to be when I get older? Do I want to be an old maid?" you know. So I started working. I've been coming home with A's and B's; I made the Honor Roll this time. And my mom was just thrilled to death, cause last year I got F's and D's. And so I don't know—just because she wasn't pressuring me I decided to do something. (16, *White, urban*)

I just like to go to school a lot. I just like to go to school because, you see, I want to learn and I like the idea of changing classes, you know, and having different teachers, not just one teacher for all day. (17, *Chicana, urban*)

I've got a values class and you learn about your values and there's a lot of things in there that have brought me to realize what my values are and I kind of think it has been good for me and that's why I like it. (18, *White, suburban*)

The most favorite subject area seemed to be English, followed by mathematics, physical education, and art, including creative writing. There seemed to be an almost even distribution among those four preferred subjects, between the academic and the more artistic ones. Girls wanted an education to "get ready for the world, and know about things one needs to know," and also "to get an education so you can get hired for jobs." The latter purpose was stronger among the girls who had experienced hardships at home. A 13-year-old girl from a family that had known unemployment said that education for a job would be useful to her.

I like some of it; I like the parts, you know where it gets me ready for a career. I want to get an education because nowadays, you know, you have to get an education but some kids, they don't want to get an education and they don't care what happens. (13, *American Indian, urban*)

Another one from a low-income background expressed the same attitude.

Yeah, I think so; school helps. I want to do a lot of secretary work and then I'd like to be involved with doctors a lot. I want to help a lot of people.

(14, *Chicana, urban*)

Her contemporary, whose father was a rural laborer, agreed.

Purpose of school is to try to teach us things, and to try to get an education where we'll get a better job from. (14, *White, rural*)

And one 13-year-old said simply:

> I want to be a highly educated person.
>
> (13, *American Indian-Inuit-Russian, rural*)

The creative arts give outlet for joy and sadness, for feeling. But to many, and especially the adjudicated girls, school was not giving them what they wanted.

> I don't really see any purpose in going for all those years and taking the same thing over and over and over again. Even with a high school diploma, you can't get no better job. There's nothing else to do, so I go to school here. The main thing I look forward to in school is getting out at the end of the day. That is my purpose in going.   (17, *Black, urban*)

And the same frustration is expressed by another one.

> Right now, the only thing that really ever gets me really, really down is going to school. But sometimes I enjoy it. Like today I ran down the hall—it was really pretty weird. A friend of mine, she was standing at one end of the hall, I was at the other end. And she was down there, so I just started screaming. I was going, "Ahhhhh"; I was screaming my head off, running down the hall, and everybody was just looking at me. But, you know, it felt good after I did it, you know, because I hate it, 'cause I usually just walk down the halls, you know, just go from one class to another class, never even talk to anybody. 'Cause it's . . . school just bugs me.   (16, *White, suburban*)

In schools in which girls could choose subjects, in which there was a very positive relationship with teachers, there were no such expressions of boredom.

> Well, let's see, about school—I really like it. I enjoy it. I know that I'm learning something. I find it enjoyable. It gives me a chance to take whatever courses I want to take, and the school I go to is pretty liberal—I take what I want, and that's the most important thing.   (16, *Oriental, urban*)

> I feel free at school for one thing. The classes I have, a lot of them are discussion classes and I feel that I can say what I want. And if other people disagree or don't like it, I can say, "That's too bad."   (16, *White, urban*)

Such expressions do not mean that girls in such schools wanted complete freedom. Many of the girls talked about discipline and talked positively about it. They did not want a harsh and demeaning discipline, but over and over they mentioned that they wanted teachers who could keep order in the classroom. To them a part of discipline meant a fair teacher and one who could keep young people interested in a subject.

A girl who went to one of the alternate schools expressed those thoughts.

> I like about school the informality, I guess. You call the teachers by their first names and all that. I have been used to that 'cause I've been going to schools like that since the sixth grade. The reason why I like this school is because of the people, including teachers. . . .

But she didn't like one of the teachers because she . . .

Doesn't control her classes at all. She knows it but she can't control the kids. Otherwise she would be a really good teacher. Well, the kids gotta respect the teacher. I suppose you got to like them first if you're gonna respect them. You can't respect somebody without liking them. You have got to remember that they know more than you do. They are just trying to teach you.

(14, *White, suburban*)

Some girls wanted more rules.

Well the school I am going to right now I don't see sense in it. It does not have strict enough rules. They are so interested about communication they don't want to be harsh on you because they know how you all feel right now. So they are giving us easy, everything is easy. They are going to the extreme they are trying to please you so much. . . . (18, *Chicana, urban*)

Some girls, only a very few, favored very strict discipline.

I think they [the kids] need more discipline. If they want to take dope and all that, skip classes, kick 'em out of school. They don't really care about it then. If they're going to smoke in the restrooms instead of going to class, there isn't any use for teachers to give out grades to 'em. (16, *White, urban*)

It is significant that this suggestion came from an adjudicated girl who probably had to fight very hard within herself to overcome some of the tendencies she wanted punished so harshly.

In discussions about discipline, racism again crept in, with both White and Black young people feeling discriminated against.

Teachers, you know, paddle people and give hours . . . and they are afraid of niggers. You know, colored people. And you know, if a colored person is after somebody, the teachers won't do nothing to the colored people but they will to the White. (15, *White, small town*)

She favors the Black kids. Like she's real hard on the White kids and if the Black kids are noisy or cutting up in class, it's okay with her. But if a White kid says something or does something out of order, she gets up a case about it.

(18, *White, urban*)

I dislike school 'cause of the teachers there; they are too strict and prejudiced. Like they get after the Black kids and don't do it to the White kids. And the colored teachers are like that, too. (15, *Black, urban*)

As might be expected, reactions to teachers were very strong, since they really were "the school." Obviously, there are very beloved teachers, there are very much hated teachers—as there have always been. The teacher was the *person* who made the difference between learning eagerly or hating it.

Teachers are the most important thing. Whenever you sign up for a class . . . I think the person teaching the class is really what you sign up for. Some classes which I have, which are very difficult for me, aren't near as difficult as I thought they would be, because the person teaching can really communicate with the kids. Whereas some courses which should be snap courses, so to speak, have become really problems because there is such a barrier between the student and teacher. (17, *White, rural*)

The girls wanted their teachers to be human beings; they wanted them to be able to relate to and respect students; they wanted them to be understanding and warm and—interestingly enough—to have a sense of humor. They expected them to be competent, to know their material, to help them learn. They also wanted them to keep control and discipline in class without becoming harshly authoritarian and unpleasant. It was a very reasonable choice of qualities consonant with a basically human atmosphere. The girls did not reject the significance of the teacher as an adult who should know more than they did, but they did not want them to be conceited or patronizing.

> If you get a teacher that is really hung down, just straight from the book, nothing deviates from the straight pattern, you fall asleep. . . . But a teacher does make a difference if they really get with it. . . . A teacher has got to have a sense of humor or they just won't survive. Kids are really liberal and if a teacher is really strict, the kids will probably boycott him.

> They have to know what they are talking about. Most teachers will say, "Well, I've got a master's in this and a master's in that," but they have to know what they are talking about and they've got to know today's generation.
>
> (17, *White, urban*)

Here are some comments from girls who had good rapport with their teachers and could explain why.

> Well, I like school and I like my teachers, and we get along. I like to help around the office and I help my teachers and all. I like going to school, and my favorite subject is math. It's a challenging subject.   (14, *Black, urban*)

> You feel respected. An answer may not be correct, but if you can back it up, you don't have to agree with them. They listen and they take the time to build a relationship between the student and the individual teacher. I'm as much a friend of my teachers as I am a student.   (15, *White, suburban*)

> Well, he's young and he laughs and he smiles and he's easy to get along with and he remembers how it feels to be a kid, and he can understand many of our feelings about school, and about teachers and about writing papers. He's easy to talk to.   (16, *White, urban*)

> When a teacher sort of devotes himself to the students, you know, and tries to do everything to help you understand what he is trying to explain to you. Thats what I like best about a teacher who tries to do—some teachers, they just say and explain it once and if you don't understand it, that's just your tough luck, and I have had several teachers like that.   (15, *American Indian, small town*)

> They were a lot of fun to be with, they make you laugh and talk about things that you like to talk about. They were old, older people.   (18, *Inuit, rural*)

In the context of this girl's culture, the word "old" had a positive quality. Clearly the ideal teacher was an older, respected, and respectful friend, but also someone who could teach.

> Ability to understand kids, to get along with kids, and the ability to teach them so they enjoy learning and they are getting something out of them.
>
> (17, *White, urban*)

Someone that can make the students understand; they don't have such a high vocabulary that you don't know what they are saying. One that will help you at your rate and not go too fast.   (17, *White, rural*)

The girls also wanted individual attention.

I could take all my problems to her and when I needed help with something, school or something I'd just call and she was at home, she'd stay after school with me, she took me home; she took me different places. I just got so used to her.   (16, *Black, urban*)

Yes, I like the teachers. It's not a teacher/student basis; it can be friend to friend. I get along with all the teachers. I'm on the tennis team and a lot of times on Saturdays my teachers and I go play tennis. I like to associate with a person more mature than I am so I can learn.   (17, *Black, urban*)

They aren't afraid to show that they are people. They're very sympathetic to the needs and to the tastes and to the different ways of thinking that different students have. I guess basically that's it, just a tolerance for people who have other ideas.   (17, *White, urban*)

They wanted to be exposed to good teachers.

They make it so you enjoy your classes. Like once in awhile they crack jokes. And they make the subject interesting, like they won't make you work, work, work all the time. They'll talk and sometimes the kids in our class will really get into conversation about the subject and it gets really good and they just know how to communicate; they just know what to do; it's really fun. I like the teachers.   (15, *White, rural*)

The way they teach. Like some teachers they just tell you, they just tell you, "Do that!" and they don't explain to you and you know, some teachers they act it out to show you to make you understand it.   (14, *Chicana, urban*)

She shouldn't be too hard on you but she shouldn't be too easy either. She shouldn't let the kids run over her and yet she still shouldn't be too strict. Most of the time the strict teachers are the ones that most the people like the best after they grow up.   (13, *Black, urban*)

Treating you human. A lot of teachers treat you like a student and you aren't human.   (13, *White, suburban*)

There was also sharp criticism of teachers who did not come up to these standards and who made life miserable for the girls, did not respect them, or did not know how to make a subject interesting. It is not always the dull girl who dislikes school. It is often a very intelligent and spirited girl who cannot take constant regimentation.

I dislike the regimentation of school; I dislike the feeling of inferiority I get in school; I don't like the feeling that the teachers are always an authority. I don't like being dictated to and are punished if you don't do this or that.
                                                            (17, *White, urban*)

. . . I didn't have no interest in school because nobody showed no interest in me.   (16, *Oriental, urban*)

Well, a teacher, it probably sounds strange for a student to be saying this, a student doesn't like a teacher to be out of the room so much; but I have a teacher that he'll give you—"Here, read this chapter and do this work"—and then he goes out and talks to other teachers. He doesn't stay in the classroom to explain the chapter to you or anything, and he just doesn't spend very much time with us.   (13, *White, small town*)

Obviously, many girls did not want to just sit and do nothing. They recognized condescension when it was disguised as laissez faire.

Well, it's kind of hard to talk to them when they just let you do anything you want. Like they really don't care. They don't care as long as you are in school.   (16, *Inuit, rural*)

Or when it was hidden by fancy language.

Some teachers, they just say and explain it once and if you don't understand it, that's just your tough luck; and I have had several teachers like that.   (15, *American Indian, small town*)

Sometimes, I don't understand what they are saying. The teachers, they talk but when you go up to the desk and ask what they mean, they don't say nothing. They just say, "Go on and do it!" They don't explain. They just say, "Go back to your desk and do it."   (14, *Chicana, urban*)

The girls genuinely wanted teachers who made learning possible.

I'd change school so that I'd get enough teachers that would be strict enough for enough students to get a good education, and not let the students run over the teachers.   (16, *Black, urban*)

And my dislikes are: some of the teachers don't give you attention or try and help you. They expect you to more or less know, and they don't want to take individual time.   (17, *Chicana, urban*)

Some of the teachers they don't help you and stuff. Like, my English, I cannot get up in front of the class and talk. I asked my teacher if I could do anything, and she just laughed it off.   (15, *White, small town*)

For the adjudicated girl, school was—and is—mostly a place where she met constant defeat, had to struggle with subjects she did not understand, subjects that were not explained to her, and that therefore bored her. School seems to have no place for her. This is expressed even in the absurd handling of young people who are absent from school without excuse. They often are excluded from school for a considerable period of time. Their response is a very simple one, "I don't like school!"

A recent report published by the Children's Defense Fund stated that the nation's public schools have systematically excluded more than 2 million children. The report cited hundreds of examples of children being pushed out of school, mainly because they were "different."

We found that if a child is not white, or is white and is not middle class, does not speak English, is poor, needs special help with seeing, hearing, walking, reading, learning, adjusting, growing up, is pregnant or married at age fifteen, is not smart enough, or is too smart, then in many places school officials decide that school is not the place for that child.[1]

The people in school who are supposed to help with curriculum and individual problems are the school counselors and school social workers. We heard very little about school social workers, probably because they do not exist in many school systems. School counselors do exist. About half of the girls who talked about schools mentioned school counselors, but not spontaneously. They responded only to questions asked by the interviewers. Girls regarded school counselors mainly as people who should arrange class schedules or enforce school regulations. Very few young women talked about counselors as job or career advisers. Only twenty-six girls mentioned this function at all, and fourteen of those indicated that counselors were not helpful in that respect. More than half the girls said that they had either no contacts or very unfavorable contacts with school counselors. Their point of view was expressed something like this:

They don't act like they want to help.

They don't understand your point of view.

They never really have time to talk with you.

You only go to them when you are in trouble for breaking some regulation.

They don't listen to you; they just tell you what to do.

Their only job is changing classes, you have to have their permission.

They won't respect confidentiality.

They ought to help you with real problems, not just bureaucratic matters.

Other unfavorable comments were:

I think counselors are terrible. You go in there and start to explain your problem and they give you something else, you know, some kind of answer that doesn't even apply, or "We'll work on it." I have had three different counselors during my four years of high school. Most of them, I don't know, it didn't seem like they really cared.   (18, *White, urban*)

I usually don't get along with them because they are super establishment. They don't try to listen to kids most of them, and if you find one that does, that is good. They don't listen, maybe they are too busy; I don't know what it is, but they don't have enough time to listen to anyone's problems.

(16, *White, suburban*)

School counselors ain't no help at all to me. I mean, they sit there and they tell you what classes that you should take. But when it comes down to real problems, things that they should really be counseling you on, they don't seem to understand. Like when you say you're having problems between you and your teacher, you and the teacher don't get along, "Well, I'm sorry we can't help you there; you just have to go in there and take care of it yourself."

(17, *Black, urban*)

[1] New York Times Service, Washington, D.C., quoted in *Minneapolis Tribune*, December 22, 1974.

Some girls' impressions were favorable.

> You talk to them about your grades, your classes. If there is any problem in your schedule, or just problems that you're having in school. If you want to talk to them they'll be glad to help. They are always glad to help you.
>
> (16, *Black, urban*)
>
> They are very good. I was an aide for a counselor last year and they help a lot of people. If you don't feel like you're learning in your classes because you are failing it, they'll try to talk to you and find out why you're failing. And if they feel like you have a good reason why you're failing it—like your parents or just not up to that level of work—they'll try to get you out.   (17, *White, urban*)

It is tragic that a service which was introduced into the schools to give young people access to immediate help seems to be quite ineffective. This lack of assistance may not always be the fault of the individual counselor, but results from the position they seem to hold in many schools. They are not considered very important. A girl who appreciated her counselors said:

> Well I never went to any because I never really had any problems. But I would feel comfortable in going. Not too many people go to him. . . . Kids wonder what is the need for him because they go to the teachers with problems.
>
> (12, *White, suburban*)

If this were true, counselors would not be necessary. Yet our survey clearly indicated the great need for individual and small-group help for girls for whom school had become a nuisance, burden, or even nightmare. School social workers and counselors who can work sensitively with girls, teachers, and parents are essential.

A general observation about schools must be underlined. In the comments of the girls, two "styles"—both legitimate in my opinion—appeared as desirable:

1. The orderly "old time" school with set curriculum, and
2. The open school that stresses student choice and involvement.

But both styles demand teachers who respect their students.

Although school is the major work that an adolescent faces, it still has very little relationship to their other work experiences either in the home or on the job. Practically none of the girls we talked to were expected to contribute essentially to the financial needs of their families. This situation, which applied across geographic, economic, and racial strata, is different from societies of poverty where very young children are expected to contribute to the family income. Most girls in our study had to take care only of their own specific needs, such as lunch money or money to take small trips or buy clothes. Their work experiences were definitely related to those needs and not to any stimulation for some future career. In rank order their work experiences were:

Babysitting
Waitressing/counter service
Reception/secretarial work
Saleswork/cashier
Helping with club activities
Volunteer/work in hospitals/clinics/with children and aged
Cleaning help
Factory work
Gardening
Helping parents, odd jobs or work with family business
Picking oranges (in Florida)

Work consisted mostly of routine activities and allowed them little opportunity to make decisions. Many girls accepted it because it was a way of bringing in some money. We can say that we heard some very responsible attitudes expressed toward work. Girls who were babysitting commented on the need to be on time and to be concerned about the children. They actually wanted to work and they would have liked to learn something while working, but that was not always possible.

I'm working on a part time job and I'm working at night. Well, I work right after school, maybe 4:30 to 9:30 but I get very little hours now because it's going so slow right now. I don't especially like the job. I'm not working enough to benefit from it really. I work maybe twice a week and I want to learn more than I am learning. You can't learn enough working two days a week. We have new registers and I don't know them that well yet. . . .   (17, *Black, urban*)

I worked at a dry cleaning place. I took in the clothes and gave out the clothes. I hated it because it was kind of a rotten dry cleaner and there wasn't too much business and I sat around most of the time and I thought it was a waste of time.   (16, *White, rural*)

I'm sort of a receptionist at the place where my dad works. . . . I don't really like what I do; I would rather be outside working. I have to stay in and answer the phone and I don't like that.   (18, *American Indian, small town*)

They did not discuss their work experiences very frequently. They had too little meaning for them.

SUMMARY

1. Most of the girls liked school, but most adjudicated girls did not.
2. Positive aspects of school were:
   a. opportunity for social contact
   b. opportunity to learn
   c. contact with understanding adults

3. Negative school aspects were:
   a. poor opportunities for social contact
   b. racism and other forms of discrimination
   c. not enough choices of subjects
   d. non-caring, disciplinarian, or racist teachers
   e. little help from school counselors
4. A variety of school styles is required to fulfill the different needs of many very different students.
5. Most girls worked outside of school to earn money, but the work they performed was not regarded as preparation for a career.

BIBLIOGRAPHY

BUXTON, CLAUDE E., *Adolescents in School.* Forge Village, Mass.: The Murray Printing Co., 1973.

JACOBS, RUTH HARRIET, "School Identity and Success: Adolescents in Gloom," *Youth and Society*, Vol. IV, No. 3, March 1973, pp. 275–290.

McCANDLESS, BOYD R., *Adolescents: Behavior and Development.* Hinsdale, Ill.: Dryden Press, 1970.

New York Times Service, Washington, D.C. Quoted in *Minneapolis Tribune*, December 22, 1974.

SEVEN

YOUTH ORGANIZATIONS

On midsummer's eve the moon was high in the sky.
We danced all night in the moon's smiling, gleaming face
We ran about the park with youngness and freedom
We sang songs of old and new.
We played on midsummer's eve as though it were never to leave us.
The morning soon followed, so we left.
But we will be back on midsummers'.

DAWN COMEAUX (14, *White, small town*)

Youth-serving organizations usually lose many members when girls become adolescents. These organizations constantly question why this should be so. These organizations were started because there was a growing recognition of the value of voluntary associations in fulfilling the needs of the young.

We all know that adolescents, whether boys or girls, must have the opportunity to test themselves, to experiment, to get to know the world in a new way. They learn by experiencing, by daring, by adventure. We also know that adolescence is an age of beginning commitment to other people and causes, today probably more so than ever before. There is an urgent sense of selfhood, the need to make one's own decisions. And finally, we know that it is an age in which one tries to find oneself, partially by searching within oneself, partially by being with others of one's own age, and partially by confiding in trusted adults. Most youth-serving agencies are aware of these adolescent needs, but do they really offer the opportunities that young people must have to satisfy their needs? How did the girls whom we interviewed perceive such organizations?

Our research design stipulated that one-third of our population be girls who then were involved in youth organizations. We found in addition a large number who previously had been affiliated with some major youth-serving organization and also with school or church groups. Only a minority of girls had never belonged to any organization. Yet it was significant to learn that 83 percent of the girls who had once belonged to an organization were no longer affiliated at the time we talked with them. They had withdrawn from them earlier than we had expected, most of them at ages 12 and 13, during the critical period of early adolescence.

To understand better this phenomenon, we asked the girls why they had originally joined an organization. The reasons given were:

The program and activities
Pressures by parents to join
Wanting to find friends or friends suggesting that they come to meetings
Personal convictions in terms of the importance of the organization

As might be expected, the most frequently mentioned reason for joining was the interest in program and activities. This interest was frequently also the reason why girls continued in the organizations. Many girls gave no reasons and simply discussed their belonging or not belonging. Only some of the older girls we interviewed explained that they stayed with an organization out of a strong ethical conviction to serve.

Those who answered in terms of programs and activities enjoyed especially those that offered adventure, "going places," "meeting people" and also expressed pleasure with individual accomplishments. They talked about awards or a sense of satisfaction at having achieved something.

Here are some examples of very positive experiences that kept them in organizations.

I am vice-president of personnel of a company in Junior Achievement. That's an interesting job because we're supposed to call the people and see if they're coming and if they're not coming, are they going to drop out. You know, talk to 'em and find out exactly what was wrong; and we try to give suggestions on how to improve the company and things like this.   (15, *Oriental, urban*)

I love to help people. And that's the way it is in Campfire. You go different places and help each other.   (14, *Black, urban*)

I am happy I've been in Campfire Girls because I have a lot of friends that I wouldn't have otherwise, if I wasn't. We really enjoy the meetings and stuff. Last night we had a potluck supper and played charades all night. And we really enjoyed it. It really gets kids together and things like that. Every so often we do stuff with a Boy Scout troop, other Campfire Girls.

Campfire Girls our age are supposed to be working on patches and stuff like that but most of us are not doing this. I think we use the group just to get together, and stuff like that, rather than working on the program.

I think it's really great that kids get to do stuff and even though their family doesn't. Like a lot of kids get to go camping out into the wilderness. A lot of kids wouldn't have been able to go camping if it wasn't for some form of organization.   (14, *White, suburban*)

I really like 4-H and I think that has opened me up so much. I have won trips to the state fair, to the market show, and when you go there you meet so many kids, and I think that's really great. You can't help but make friends. I have a lot of fun there.

I have taken a lot of projects like clothing, foods, home improvements and I've been taking livestock like sheep and beef. That can really get you involved, working with animals. It gets you involved with other kids, too. Right now I am president of the club and I think I am getting to realize my responsibility.
(17, *White, rural*)

Yeah, I thought it was fun. Cause we could do anything we wanted to, like dive, I loved to dive, and swim.   (14, *White, suburban*)

We have projects where you individually achieve, you set your own goals, there are trips as a result of these projects, there are heartbreaks. Most important is that you are out of the little community that you are always brought up in. There are so many kids; that's what is wrong with them; they are always in this one environment. They have to have a change and 4-H provides this through trips. You get trips to Washington, New Orleans, Kansas City; you meet people all over the United States. If you are like me, you might not ever win one of the trips but you still have the opportunity.

(17, *White, rural*)

What were the reasons for leaving youth organizations? The one reason repeated over and over again was that the program was boring. "They do childish, babyish, silly little things." Or, "they just had meetings." The comments were numerous.

All you did was sit around and listen to the leader talk, did projects that didn't interest you. (13, *Black, urban*)

I was in that organization until about the 5th grade and then I got kind of bored because it was the same old thing. We sat down and made scrapbooks for people in nursing homes and things like that. (17, *White, urban*)

We didn't do nothing, just went to meetings and ate our snack and made something or studied the rules. (15, *White, urban*)

It got boring; they really didn't teach us anything. They gave us little angels for Christmas trees. We didn't go on trips or nothing. (16, *White, urban*)

I think it would have been fun to belong. I like the outdoors, camping out and stuff, but they never did anything. (17, *White, urban*)

Another major reason for withdrawing was bad experience with the leader. Girls complained about leaders being not understanding, and especially being too domineering.

The leader thought up the projects and the girls didn't get a chance to see if they wanted to do them or not. And I didn't care for the leader because she was always calling your ma and asking if you could do such and such and if you couldn't do it she would kind of get mad at your mother and then take it out on me. (13, *Black, urban*)

I wish we could have had leaders that understand you more because they were just as bad as a lot of people. They didn't really care. (14, *White, urban*)

This same girl entered another program, a neighborhood involvement program, and was very enthusiastic about it.

I don't think I will ever want to leave this group. We talk about our home life, our friends, and last week we really opened up one girl that had been constantly cutting herself down. We made her open up and told her that she was a great person and we were all really happy after that. Everybody was almost crying and everything. I just love it; it made me face up to things with my problems at home and try to help them.

Or again about the leader:

For one thing, the leader was very snotty like, real bossy. (15, *White, urban*)

I dropped out because there weren't any good leaders. I just didn't enjoy it; we just go to meetings and sit there and they yell at us for a while . . . then we leave. (17, *White, small town*)

Some girls disliked it especially that their mothers were leaders and that meetings were just the same as being at home.

There was also a feeling that clubs were often much too large and that they could not get any attention either from the adult or the other girls.

The lowest amount of girls at one time I seen was 22 and I don't think they can give each girl that much attention if they have that many.

(12, *White, suburban*)

When we asked them what would make a good leader, the qualities they mentioned were pretty much the same as for good parents or good teachers. The one most often mentioned was someone who listened, understood, and really cared for them; someone who did not demand respect simply because she or he was a leader but earned respect because he or she really knew how to help them and the program. They stressed that they did not want to have too strict, authoritarian leaders. Decades ago, those in the forefront of youth work—Grace Coyle,[1] Gertrude Wilson,[2] and Harleigh Trecker[3]—rejected the term "leader" because of its authoritarian connotation and called them "group workers." [4] An additional quality girls expected of youth workers was an ability to organize, someone who could get things done, and help them to carry out plans.

Age of the "leader" did not seem to make much difference. Some wanted younger ones because they would better understand them—they hoped. Others wanted older ones for the same reasons. They wanted someone who let them make their own decisions but helped them with them. They wanted calm and patient group workers. It was interesting that many wanted to have as a group worker someone who could appreciate the different needs and capabilities of individuals and could offer individual help.

Very few felt able to go to the staff of youth organizations to which they belonged and talk about personal problems. Even when organizations included counseling or told them "Come to us anytime you have a

---

[1] Grace Longwell Coyle, *Group Work With American Youth: A Guide to the Practice of Leadership*. New York: Harper, 1948.

[2] Gertrude Wilson and Gladys Ryland, *Social Group Work Practice: The Creative Use of the Social Process*, Boston: Houghton Mifflin, 1949.

[3] Harleigh Trecker, *Social Group Work: Principles and Practices*, New York: The Woman's Press, 1948.

[4] Gisela Konopka, *Social Group Work: A Helping Process*, 2nd edition. Englewood Cliffs, N.J.: Prentice-Hall, 1972.

personal problem or are in trouble or need help" very few girls felt that they could respond to that. Not a single girl who did not belong to an organization, considered going to a youth worker for help. In fact, many girls mentioned that youth workers could not be trusted because they violated confidentiality. In general, the girls thought that these organizations existed for *good* girls with no problems and that they would not accept any other kinds of girls. Therefore, if even the "good girl" had problems, she would not go to the youth leaders with them.

> I was getting into a lot of trouble at that time and those kids were pretty straight. I couldn't get along with the kids because they hadn't been through a lot of things that I had been through. . . . I didn't believe a lot in what they were doing and they were pushing me too much into many things that I just didn't believe in. And I was still getting into a lot of trouble and they were telling me to give up all my old friends, just forget them.
>
> (16, *American Indian, urban*)

Some girls described themselves as tomboys and therefore unable to fit into those organizations where:

> They are all goody goodies and they never do anything wrong and they do their homework. (15, *Black, suburban*)

The girl who said this was trying to destroy this stereotype because she enjoyed the activities of the organizations she belonged to. But she struggled with this image.

Some girls were almost apologetic about belonging to a youth organization.

> Well, I feel kind of embarrassed because people say "Oh you are in the Scouts, how stupid, ish." Sometimes I like the organization but whatever people say about it sometimes influences me and sometimes I intend to quit. A few of my friends are in it but when they ask you about it in school, you get all embarrassed. (14, *White, suburban*)

And even harsher words:

> I kinda have a dislike for what I call a "goody-two shoes" and that's who I consider being in these organizations. I picture all goody-goods in these organizations. Like Girl Scouts, and the Y and stuff. I was a member of the Y for awhile, and that was a "trip." But we weren't like the way you see them on TV, all sitting around the campfire and stuff, racial integration on Nabisco Cookie level, you know. When we were in the Y, we were really abusing it, 'cause one of the counselors was my girlfriend's fiance and we would go up to the mountains and get loaded on a camping trip, and you wouldn't see us on a TV thing.
>
> Otherwise we didn't do or go anywhere. I only remember we made bean pictures with lacquer on it. We had a party once.
>
> I got kicked out for not paying my dues, I couldn't always get a dime, so I just dropped out. (17, *White, urban*)

Lack of money and, occasionally, racial discrimination also were mentioned as reasons for not belonging to an organization. Yet, nationally, some of these organizations—e.g., the YWCA—have been in the forefront of the fight against racial discrimination. The "goody-goody" image surely is often a wrong stereotype, but one gets the impression that even the girls themselves who were positively active in organizations, wanted to be regarded as people who did not associate with girls with serious problems, and especially not with those who get into trouble. They did not see their organizations as a place for such people. They often talked about "they" when they referred to girls who took drugs or got drunk. The "we" were the nice and good and active girls.

We heard about a few other organizations, especially churches, in which girls felt free to discuss their problems. One girl talked about her church group, for instance.

> Its purpose is for people not to be inhibited. We go on field trips and we visited a rape center one time.   (16, *White, suburban*)

Or another one:

> I've just become involved in this and I really like it a lot. It's something that I have been really concerned with because I'm trying to find out how I stand on religion, what I do believe. I go there because it is one outlet I see as a place to question. . . .   (17, *White, urban*)

Usually these church groups were not related to very traditional churches. The girls were quickly sensitive and resentful of any discrepancy they might find between preaching and actions taken.

> I'm Catholic but I don't go to church and I haven't for quite awhile. It started in . . . when my sister was going to get married, and they wouldn't marry her because she was pregnant, and that was the reason he gave. And ever since then I just haven't gone to church.   (18, *White, rural*)

It was quite obvious that many girls sought strong and well-defined ideals, but they were quickly turned off and disappointed when they met with hypocrisy.

When we asked the girls to make suggestions in regard to work with youth organizations, many felt they could not give any. Several expressed a very strong sense of individualism and insisted they could find outlets for their interests by themselves or with close friends and did not seek any organized activities. Those who made suggestions stressed that there should be more exciting activities and especially more opportunities to see other places and people. They realized that the fulfillment of their need for adventure demanded organized support.

Next in number were girls who mentioned opportunities to talk about their problems, and another group wanted to discuss or participate in public events. This desire indicated their strong need to find themselves and at the same time to participate actively in society if given an opportunity. Several spoke of the need for career and job counseling. Others wanted to work with other young people who had problems.

Many—the majority—favored activities involving both boys and girls, although there were some who preferred single-sex organizations. Almost all the girls said that they occasionally liked to get together by themselves, but they did not always want to be separated from boys.

The idea of organized clubs with rules was almost foreign to most of the girls. They preferred an informal atmosphere that allows them to be open with one another and with the staff.

> Everything is too parliamentary procedure. I don't like that. I think if we just had a great big conversation on who is here and not here, and what do you want to do instead of being so formal.   (17, *White, urban*)

> I think I would open up a place just for kids to be there. If they wanted to go and be there, then that's fine. They could come and it wouldn't be a program where you cram things down people's throats or you say this is the way it is. Like I said before, just talk to them.

> And for the staff, I think I would want staff that's been in conditions like institutions or had been through a lot of this stuff, a lot of the drug things, drinking. I know one thing that kids say a lot and I say it myself, it's very hard to relate to people about drugs or about drinking or about things like that to somebody else who has never been into it.   (16, *White, urban*)

Girls mentioned also that they would want a change of image of these organizations. And a considerable number did not consider belonging to a youth organization a viable choice for them.

In summarizing the girls' opinions about youth organizations, we must emphasize that great satisfactions resulted occasionally from participation in them and were expressed with genuine enthusiasm, particularly when the girls saw opportunities for individual growth and for service. Using some words taken directly from expressions by the young women, we can state:

> If affiliation with a youth organization offers active adventures; action-learning; learning to be independent; being productive in meaningful projects; opportunities to be helpful to others; receiving honest and knowledgeable advice and counsel, even if a girl has problems, then affiliation is very satisfying.

> If a program in a youth organization is too childish, too adult-dominated; too conforming to exclusively traditional "girl-roles" and especially if there is no consideration for the various lifestyles in our population, the organization will appeal to only a small number of adolescent girls.

> There was a great yearning in these young women for meaning in life.

Obviously youth organizations, like schools, can appeal to young people if they help them develop and translate their ideals and values into clear action relevant to the lives of these young women.

SUMMARY

1. Girls joined organizations primarily because of their programs and activities.
2. Other reasons for joining were pressure by parents, wanting to find friends, and personal convictions.
3. For some adolescent girls, youth organizations brought the fulfillment of what they have hoped for.
4. Many girls were turned off by youth organizations. The major reasons were that the programs were boring, childish; "leaders" were bossy; there was too little input by the girls themselves.
5. Girls in trouble did not see youth organizations as existing for them.
6. Girls wanted youth workers who were not authoritarian, but rather were creative, attentive, and with whom they could discuss personal problems.
7. Girls wished for co-ed activities, but also wanted to have the opportunity to meet occasionally by themselves.
8. Adventure and the opportunity for active participation were important criteria of a good organization.
9. The girls preferred an informal and individually oriented program.
10. They wanted youth organizations to provide fun and recreation but also to help them with their genuine wish to find meaning in their lives.

BIBLIOGRAPHY

BURK, BARBARA A., M. ZDEP, and H. KUSHNER, "Affiliation Patterns Among American Girls," *Adolescence*, Vol. VIII, No. 32, Winter 1973, pp. 541–546.

COYLE, GRACE LONGWELL, *Group Work with American Youth: A Guide to the Practice of Leadership*, New York: Harper, 1948.

KONOPKA, GISELA, *Social Group Work: A Helping Process* (2nd ed.). Englewood Cliffs, N.J.: Prentice-Hall, 1972.

RYLAND, GLADYS, *Exploring Human Space*. New York: Young Women's Christian Association, National Board, p. 967.

TRECKER, HARLEIGH, *Social Group Work: Principles and Practices*. New York: The Woman's Press, 1948.

WILSON, GERTRUDE and GLADYS RYLAND, *Social Group Work Practice: The Creative Use of the Social Process*, Boston: Houghton Mifflin, 1949.

EIGHT

SOCIAL-POLITICAL CONCERNS

When he left he was alive.
When he went to that cruel war he had one thing in mind.
He was going to do his patriotic chore.
He cares about what happens to this nation.
He was very brave and young.
He wanted freedom more than anyone.
Now his arms and legs are twisted beyond repair.
When he left he was alive! Alive!
When that bomb fell, he was very confused.
He tried to move, but his legs were gnarled.
His fear increased, that bomb fell too hard, and fast.
My dear God, he was alive when he left.
Now he is never ever to be found. He was a good boy,
  a very good boy.
I knew it would happen sometime.
When he left he was alive! Alive! Alive! Alive!

Now he is dead.

DAWN COMEAUX (14, *White, small town*)

Only about 60 percent of all the girls interviewed responded to questions regarding their interest in political affairs. But the number increases if we include social concerns. A 17-year-old expressed this concern with social issues very clearly when asked about her political opinions.

We don't get into that a whole lot. Maybe once in awhile we say something about that; but we aren't serious about that. I guess we just aren't worried about that yet. I suppose maybe by next year when we will vote we will want to understand what they are doing. Right now we just don't talk seriously about it. We talk about *premarital sex* and *abortion* and we've gotten into a few discussions about *religion*. Sometimes we talk about our *teachers*.   (17, *White, rural*)

With my first glance at the interviews, I was struck by an exaggerated individualism and a serious lack of sense of community that they reflected. The girls rarely showed an awareness of belonging to something larger than themselves. Most of those we interviewed not only did not belong to any movements that had deep meaning for them but also did not feel they could participate. Many expressed an extreme sense of powerlessness, saying: "My little vote wouldn't matter anyhow." Or—very frequently— "Politics is boring; politicians are all a bunch of crooked creeps, so there is no point in voting or anything." This sense of powerlessness and disenchantment seemed to be combined with a comparatively low sense of urgency in regard to the preservation of a democratic way of life. It seemed to be taken for granted, not consciously valued.

Having myself lived through the downfall of a promising democracy and having experienced the rise of a disastrous dictatorship, I am deeply conscious of the need in any democracy for well-informed, active citizens concerned with public life. Therefore, for me, the voices of stark disenchantment and the sense of isolated powerlessness stood out and worried me.

> I don't think anybody is interested in voting. I don't know . . . like my vote wouldn't have no effect . . . like if we were voting for President, one vote wouldn't matter; one vote—what's that? It's not that important . . . 'cause they are going to get whoever they want up there anyway.   (17, *White, urban*)

> And that's why all political science and stuff is lying a lot. (16, *Black, urban*)

> We don't really talk about politics that much. We are involved in our little world and don't want to come out.   (18, *White, rural*)

> I wouldn't want to vote; there is nobody there to be voting for. I know a lot of people who could have voted but didn't because it wasn't worth it.
> (17, *Black, urban*)

> I am powerless. I don't have to *feel* powerless. One vote! Even when I can vote, big deal because the ones you can vote for are the rich ones that have all the oil companies . . . the swindlers and whatever. You don't get to vote for honest people so it's no good.   (15, *White, suburban*)

Yet in restudying the material, and listening carefully to what these young women had to say, I realized that I had placed too much emphasis on only one side of the picture. I had not taken into account several factors.

1. We were interviewing at the height of the Watergate discussion, which threw the whole country into a sense of disenchantment with political life.
2. We have to realize that since high school students are concerned with themselves and their own specific tasks in life, they always see social issues in a personal sense.
3. In the total population, even among adults, the majority are not actively involved in politics, and
4. We found actually a high degree of interest in social issues.

We heard from those who were in the middle of the road.

> Concerned about politics? Well, I guess everybody is about the way the economics is going. I don't know, I don't think I could do very much about it, but I do read the papers and I do follow along; but as far as, would I go out and try to be President? I wouldn't.   (18, *American Indian, urban*)

> Last election time was murder for me because I was completely for Nixon and there is this other girl, she's not my best friend, but she's at the same level I am. So we can discuss things rationally but she is completely Democratic. We sit and fight over this stuff, and then Watergate broke out and you feel like

sticking your foot in your mouth . . . it's still disillusioning. You think "Oh gosh, what's happening?" You believed in these people and then all of a sudden, wham, down the drain. But there has always been corruption, and I just say, "Well, the Democrats do it too."   (15, *White, rural*)

And then we heard from those who were actively interested.

I listen to the campaigns because I do care about this world but I am too young to vote. . . . I think to vote intelligently you have to read up on the person, you have to listen to the campaigns, or you should . . . you can't just walk in there and chalk it down.   (17, *American Indian, rural*)

Well for me, it would be very hard not to be concerned with them [politics] because I think they are things which are really important to my future. . . . I think of my responsibilities . . . how in another year I will be able to vote and the decisions I am going to have to make about people.   (17, *White, urban*)

I'm very much interested in political things . . . I'm involved in the Jewish Youth Council . . . the only problem is, in the Jewish community it's . . . it's a very male dominated one. Right now there is only one woman in the Executive position in the United States in the Jewish community. . . . I like to change people's hostility . . . just totally unfounded hostility towards people . . . between the Israelites and the Arabs you know; if you are an Arab you must be bad, you know, and if you are an Israeli you must be bad . . . that's all kind of ridiculous.   (16, *White, small town*)

If you don't like society, you better help it do something. You just can't let it fall to hell. If we would all act and work together, we would be so strong; and like, anymore, the government—it's the government today more than people. The people should count.   (14, *Black, urban*)

Although girls were not frequently involved in political organizations, most of them were aware of political and social issues in the country and the world. The solutions girls suggested were often very idealistic, one may even say simplistic. This evaluation applies especially to the younger girl and is consonant with all findings regarding judgment in the developmental process. Seeing the world with all its complexities comes at a later age. In adolescence idealism is strong.

I'm not really interested in it, but I'd like to know what is going on in the world. I'd like to *change* the *hatred* in the world between countries. So many countries are going to war and everything; supposedly they own this and they own that; but God gave us the world; he didn't give us any specific owners for the world and I just wish that we could really all get together and that countries could lean on one another if they needed something—not be like they are right now.   (15, *Black, urban*)

They feel strongly with the suffering of individual human beings.

I talk about politics, I guess, about as much as anybody, but I don't know anything about it and I'm not really that interested in knowing. My real interest lies with individual people, something which politics ignores.

How could I change things in the world without changing the people? I'm not sure I'd change anything, maybe a few forms of government. I don't think

Totalitarianism is good but even Russia seems to be moving toward Socialism from one end while we're moving towards it from the other. So we're getting closer there.

In some parts of the world I'd change the laws that make it illegal to have a woman go out without a veil over her face and without a male companion. Just unreasonable things like that. But I would change very little, because there's nothing I could change without actually changing the people.

(17, *White, urban*)

The young women were concerned with war and peace, better human relations, and corruption in government because of the Watergate situation. Other concerns, but far less prominent, were:

Poverty (7 percent of those who responded)
Energy crisis (6 percent)
Drugs (5 percent)
Pollution (5 percent)
Crime (3 percent)

Housing, the economy, taxes, and equal opportunities for women were named by less than 1 percent.

The concern with war also involved concern for improved human relations.

I think everybody should be friends and peaceful and not have any problems. . . . I guess when I get the right to vote, I will probably be a lot more involved in it than I am now.   (13, *White, small town*)

I'd vote to stop the wars.   (13, *American Indian, urban*)

I would want to change in the world the lack of brotherhood, and wars, that's about all.   (15, *White, small town*)

I knew this guy and he was out in the war and they shot him. And I just started thinking and wondering, "How come they're fighting against each other? They are just killing each other and it's ridiculous."

(13, *American Indian, urban*)

I think about, you know, where I would like to vote certain issues, like bettering the society, the world in general. I like to have peace.

(17, *White, urban*)

The opposition to racial prejudice was very deep. All girls, from whatever racial or ethnic background, considered prejudice something "bad"—something they wanted to erase. This does not mean that in the course of the interview girls did not express prejudice or fear along racial lines—some did—but it is significant that we found no one who considered it right.

If people would get along, there wouldn't be so much fighting, and if they did, they wouldn't want to anymore. This is what I object to; being prejudiced.

(15, *American Indian, urban*)

I'm not very interested in politics, but the first thing I would change if I could, would be prejudice, and the way people look at people—the way they are, not their skin color. That would be my main task. And then, I think helping out the poor, putting them to work. (16, *White, urban*)

Most white girls showed a constant defensiveness about prejudice saying, "I think I'm not prejudiced, but I don't have any contact with Blacks," or "I'm White; I don't want to hate Blacks." And far more White girls than Black ones said that there was really no difference between the races. The majority of girls, Black, White, or any other racial or ethnic groups, meant by this that people are of equal worth.

For all I know, unless I look in a mirror, I could just as well have black skin and I don't think it makes a difference. I think they are all people.
(15, *White, urban*)

Well, I don't see people as different from the next person. I see them the way they really are inside. That's really where it counts. 'Cause it's not going to get you anywhere if you see 'em on the outside. (14, *Black, urban*)

They're just like us, I mean, there's a Negro woman over where I work. Underneath that black layer, she's the same as we are. And, it's not what's on the outside that counts. . . . (16, *American Indian, rural*)

Ideal boyfriend could be any color or race. That doesn't matter as long as he's nice. (18, *Chicana, urban*)

I haven't found anybody that is actually different than me that I could say they were different. I think in order for somebody to be different, they would have to be in a completely different category like animals and stuff like that.
(13, *Black, suburban*)

These same girls who saw people as equal understood that there were individual differences and enjoyed them.

I think everybody is different from me, everybody is different in their own way. I think they're fantastic. If you have two people and you put them in a room and they're both exactly the same . . . you don't have nothing to talk about; but if you have two different people, two completely entirely different people, you never shut up, you just talk and talk, about your way of life, and they're talking about theirs, things they do and the things you do.
(15, *Chicana, urban*)

But girls of minority background had often suffered and therefore stressed differences based on their life experiences. Even those who basically wanted "one world" were painfully aware of the barriers.

. . . It's really strange because you don't run into that up north. People do discriminate but they don't show it that much. It's subtle . . . but two or three years ago I was down south. I guess I never encountered really open prejudice until that time. Here we were and people were stopping and looking at us, just looking at us. . . . I just wanted to crawl in a hole and ignore the whole thing, you know. (16, *Oriental, urban*)

The clubs I do know of, they're racist clubs, and I don't feel racist against any color. But there are some against the Black and some against the White, and I feel that everybody was made the same color on the inside; it's just a different color on the outside. Like the Black Panthers, they have a school going and all they talk about is the Black this and the Black that and you could get to think that Black is everything; and when they see different color, they're ready to fight.

I don't have any grudge against white people. But some are going to have some against me. But then, I wouldn't act violent about it. I'm not really a violent person. Nobody is really; it's all a bluff. People will claim to be bad, just with their mouth; their mouth does all the talking. And people get scared off and don't want to get involved with that person because they've heard so much about them that they don't want to mess with them.   (15, *Black, urban*)

I feel strongly about the race problem. Some of the things they have done to the Black people just wasn't right. I read books about our . . . the Blacks and Whites in slavery times and I have very strong feelings about that.

(14, *Black, urban*)

There were girls of all races who struggled seriously with their feelings. A girl from a southern state said:

Everybody is an individual; everybody's human. Black people should have the same rights as White people, and White people should have the same rights as Black people.

White people believe all the deep dark details and secrets they've heard about Black people, I guess, that they carry knives and they're mean, cut your head off, they'll shoot you in the back. White people believe things like that now because it's been preached, but it's not the truth.   (16, *White, urban*)

And a girl from another ethnic background and another geographic area struggled just as hard.

This dorm, honestly, I don't like it here. These Indians up here are sort of snotty to whites, you know, stuck up and always trying to put them down. When I take up for the white kids, they get mad at me. When I'm in the city, I always take up for the whites and I'll take up for the Indians and white Indians and the Black Indians, and I'm not Black, but Indians, they think of me as if I did. But I feel everybody is equal and nobody is for better than the other. I just can't wait until I leave.   (13, *American Indian, urban*)

I used to be very prejudiced. I mean I wouldn't, I just . . . the only race was the Indian race. And that was it. I was a very stereotyped person. But now, I am able to accept the fact that people aren't any different.

There was a person that talked to me once and he goes, "People are people, no matter what color and what race they are, they're just like you. When you feel bad, you hurt, right? And if you're cut, you bleed, right? And when you feel happy, you laugh, OK? No matter what color you are, they all have the same things, they are like you. They feel the same way. But most of all, they have a heart just like you. And it depends on where their heart is at. If they're true at heart, they're good people. It don't matter if they're green or yellow or whatever color they are, they all have a heart." And I didn't realize that, you know, and he goes, "True, you know, you are an Indian and you do have a lot of pride. It's only natural that you're proud of your own race. But the good thing about it, is to accept people as people and not as a color."

It got to the point where they were so prejudiced towards me, I was going to quit school my freshman year, because I couldn't stand the hassle of being different. There weren't many Indians in the school I went to which made it worse. Students would put feathers in our lockers and tell us to go back to the reservation. They'd cuss at us and spit at us and throw bricks at us. I didn't know what prejudice meant until I went into a school. And they go, "Well, in school you're taught not to be prejudiced." That's where I learned about it! At home I was taught that Indian people love people and accept them into your home, because if they come as a friend, then you give 'em anything that you have. But when I went to school, that's where I learned the prejudice.

(15, *American Indian, small town*)

A very few girls, only twenty-eight out of the whole group, expressed strong, negative attitudes toward members of other races.

I have this whole thing about hating white people. I'll be honest. I read a lot of books about slavery times and stuff like that . . . [Blacks] had to do something different from white folks to get a job, like some white parents leave their money down from way back, and Black folks when they started they just didn't have the money. If you want to survive you have to deal dope or hustle, or something; it's just the way that Black people have to make their money, 'cuz there is no other way of making it unless they're going to work seven days a week. . . .

I have hate for (the whites) inside, but on outside it doesn't show that much because I don't feel that they should really know how much hate is inside. I think white folks look at Black folks like dogs or something, I do. I think that you all think we're supposed to be raised as servants.   (17, *Black, urban*)

I don't really like Black people. All the other people are OK; just Black people, I don't really get along with. I don't know why. Usually they think they know everything, they're always right, and if you get in a fight with them, they have to bring all their friends, all of 'em, all the Black people, have to bring all of 'em up to one white person.   (17, *White, urban*)

I'm afraid of [Blacks], scared to death. It's always the Black people that's always on the news; they commit the crimes and they're always killing people and I'm afraid of death. . . . and I guess I associate the two, you know?

(15, *White, small town*)

Blacks are not too nice . . . you say hello to 'em and they won't say nothing; they just walk on down the street . . . if a Black person does something to a white teacher at school, the teacher couldn't do anything about it.

(15, *American Indian, rural*)

There was yearning for friendship across racial and ethnic lines but distances are still great, not only in the South, but also in Minnesota or Massachusetts or California.

I think it's already been said why they do things and why we do things to them, because they have ideas about us and we have ideas about them and that's why we do it to them and they do it to us. But I don't think there is anything that is going to change it because we are set in our ways and they are set in theirs, but I wish we could!

A lot of my friends say I wish they would send them back to their schools. And that really bothers me, because I would like to try and get along and have better relationships with them.   (14, *White, urban*)

You can't be close to a person; some white people are kind of cold, like they'll be your friend and stuff and they'll fool around with you but they won't confide in you and tell you stuff. They're kind of cold, when it comes to things like that. They'll play ball with you, but they'll run off and have another friend. They won't let it get that close.   (15, *Black, urban*)

The colored people, they are a lot different from us, cause they have a lot of different things in their mind going, I think. They just don't think the same way. Everything they take serious. Well, I like them; I'm not prejudiced.

                    (16, *Chicana, urban*)

Those who had friends across racial or ethnic lines often talked about the disapproval of the adult community. Their strength to withstand this disapproval was often remarkable.

I've gone with a Black guy. My mom knows it. My mom and dad get unhappy with me everytime that a colored guy brings me home.

                    (16, *White, urban*)

I have some really good friends who are Black in a redneck town, and I got put down a lot for having Black friends but that worked out all right because they had a riot and all the Black people protected me; that worked out great.

So, anyway, the thing was, when I got here I didn't really know how much of an influence Black people had on me because my mom always brought me up not to be prejudiced but I think she's a little bit more prejudiced than she would like to admit.   (17, *White, urban*)

There are Black people around here. They are pretty good friends, but my mom doesn't like them. I think she would jump all over us if we ever went out with one.   (18, *American Indian, small town*)

My parents say they aren't prejudiced, but they are. "Oh you can't date Black men 'cause you might marry them and have kids." So what if I was? We used to argue about that point.   (16, *White, rural*)

Minority girls also had to face censure from their own friends when they crossed racial lines; and at the same time they fought the prejudice of the white community. Many developed a quiet, well-thought-through assurance.

The people at the school are kind of narrow-minded. They don't respect Black guys going out with white girls. Both my cousins go out with white girls; it just doesn't bother me. I like to see it, I like it . . . ever since I've been walking, some of my best friends have always been white. Really, it's not that much of a difference. But some of the people that you go out with, they'll be scared to touch me, cause their parents have told them stuff . . . or they look at you so crazy. I don't know what it is. A lot of times they'll come into your house and say "We didn't know Blacks had homes like this." My friends always tell me "You dress too good to be Black". . . . a lot of my Black friends I lost because I associate with whites. (16, *Black, rural*)

She [this white girl] was my friend, really. And they used to call me "whitey" because I used to play with her. (12, *Black, urban*)

The one thing the teachers . . . well Fran and I are Black and Mary is white, and that's one thing they can't see . . . they just think we are brainwashing Mary. But we just don't pay any attention. Mary is a good student and so am I and so is Fran, and I'm not bragging, but they always try and turn us against each other. (14, *Black, urban*)

The honesty in dealing with these problems has vastly increased in recent years. An American Indian girl said:

Somebody calls a Black person names, I do it all the time, but I'm not prejudiced, they know that. I mean, shit, if names are gonna hurt you, you shouldn't be around anyways. You're gonna get called names sooner or later. (15, *American Indian, suburb*)

A Black girl remarked with regret but very openly:

I know for a fact that I am prejudiced; I am very prejudiced around some people. As long as my skin is Black, or there's white or the accent is different, or if you got slant eyes, or something about you looks different, there's always going to be that prejudice there. I think that's the only thing, the only thing that holds the world back, is that right there. (17, *Black, urban*)

A white girl described changes in her attitudes:

I used to be really prejudiced, just because my parents want me to marry Greek and the view of the Black man was someone really low. Our view is a lot different now, because I have come away from what my parents believe in and have developed my own ideas. (18, *White, urban*)

There were those who thought that things would change through their own generation's efforts.

There's only one thing I'm prejudiced against and that's prejudice itself. Because I don't like to see people fight among each other.
(16, *White, small town*)

In general, the intent of the majority of the girls was to overcome racial prejudice. They were not always realistic about the actual situation and very few knew of movements or belonged to movements that were working toward change. They believed more in increasing individual understanding and developing friendship. There certainly are still girls among all races who have racial prejudices as harsh as have existed in other generations. Girls of minority background, especially Black girls, seem to be more realistic about the actual situation, sometimes more wary of advances made to them. But with a pervasive inner pride in their own being grows a capacity to reach out and interact with others.

Besides the general political issues that are of concern to anyone in the country, it was interesting to hear some girls put their finger on *issues directly related to youth.* Some very thoughtfully discussed the problems of young men dishonorably discharged from the army. They believed that it would mark them for life and wondered how young people could help to change a law that affected the lives of many of their contemporaries.

Another example of concern for such issues was the recurring discussion of the legalization of marijuana, and the issue of the curfew that exists in some communities.

> One should vote on how late you are out for curfew, what you are arrested for and everything. I don't think you should get arrested for curfew and all. And how long people are locked up in juvenile hall and things like that.
>
> (14, *White, suburban*)

In the interviews we conducted late in 1974, we heard about concern for jobs for young people, probably influenced by the economic situation. But, in general, the economy was rarely mentioned, unlike in a survey conducted by the National YWCA[1] in which this problem was considered one of the most urgent. It is possible that the girls did not feel that the issue was political, but rather more a personal one.

There were numerous expressions of disappointment in government, directly related to Watergate. It is dangerous for a democracy to have young people grow up to think that their government consists of:

> . . . a bunch of swindlers and they are not doing what the people want them to do.   (15, *White, suburban*)

This same girl cried out:

> I *am* powerless! One vote! Even when I can vote, big deal!

There was no recognition that this one vote could be reinforced by others. Or:

> I don't think I will vote. I mean, I don't really care. I mean, it doesn't involve me, vote whatever they want to vote for; it ain't helping but it ain't hurting me. I like voting if you're really involved in it.
>
> (15, *American Indian, small town*)

> I don't like, you know, the way it is. I don't know. Otherwise, I, I really like it [the USA] it's a nice country. I don't think it will be for very long. One thing I think about a lot: If I had to change the world, I think this a fantasy trip, one thing I'd do is get rid of half the people on the earth. It's overloaded.
>
> (16, *Inuit, rural*)

> 'Cause by me telling somebody to change, don't mean they're gonna change. They tell me, yeah, they're gonna change—they turn right back around and do the same thing. You can't change anybody. I never really think about changing the world; it's not my duty.   (16, *Black, urban*)

[1] National YWCA Resources Center on Women, *Teen Women Tell About Their Needs.* New York: Young Women's Christian Association, National Board, 1974.

Girls from poverty backgrounds worried about their futures and often felt hopeless about them.

Well like right now, you know, the energy crisis, that really bothers me 'cause you know, we're young and we have a whole life to live for. If we have no T.V., no nothing, it's gonna be a boring life. Nothing, well there's nothing I can do, except turn off the lights, but if one house turns off the lights and everybody else does not, one house won't help it. (16, *Chicana, urban*)

I'd like to get something across, you know, how people who sit high and have a lot of authority and stuff, they seem to have, a one-track mind on stuff. They don't ever really listen to where a person's really at. Like drug abuse or stuff like that, they just judge, project and hang you out without even letting you say anything. That's what I would like to change, because I feel that people don't even have a chance, and I mean, if you have any type of record, they don't take you anywhere. They don't want you. (17, *Chicana, urban*)

The girl who had had more opportunities often was intellectually very curious about the world and somewhat more optimistic. She could at least think of getting involved and finding alternatives if she was not satisfied.

Well, I'm interested in how we're getting along with other countries. It's really a mess now. I'm concerned about that, and more funding for colleges. Urban renewal and stuff like that. I'm concerned with getting into another war. It's really—it kind of scares me.

Well, I'd like our system of government changed so you don't have one guy head of it all. It's really stupid. I mean, how could he possibly do it, all that stuff that he's supposed to? And maybe, I mean, like one four-year term, and that's it. Lots of 'em have been in before; they just don't do anything.

And, I don't know, foreign relations to be improved. I think that's really important because just one slip and we could be blown up, and it wouldn't be anybody's fault. It's so stupid to have that danger and have to live with it. What's the point in having all that, because the minute one of us blows up, the other's going to countercheck. And we both lose, so I don't see why we have all that. It's really dumb. (16, *White, suburban*)

If society would quit alienating old people, quit alienating everybody, then there might be a chance that people could just enjoy life, just love each other and just work together.

She spoke of prison reform.

Well, he's in too deep, he's in over his head. That's why I get so pissed off at prison reform. Now that makes me mad because at sixteen they're still young enough, I mean, it's just not right. Give them hell, but don't send them someplace they're going to be exposed to more criminals and just be hardened.

I have a friend that I went to school with in junior high that went to prison. He got out of prison, two months later was back in prison and has not gotten out yet. He probably has had no help. He will probably stay in prison. That's his only life now. When I saw him, when he was out, he could not relate anymore; he was just lost. He didn't even know where to begin living; and so he robbed a bank, tried to rob a bank. He knew exactly what he was doing, that he would be sent back. That's all he could see. That's too bad. (17, *White, urban*)

She was angry and unhappy, but she wanted to be active.

The most impressive indication of deep concern for what the world is, came from a girl who was interviewed in a lonely mountainous area. She had been described to the interviewer as a shy person. Yet she spoke in this interview with animation. She lived in a house that looked out on the abandoned mines. She had quit school early, because she felt that school did not allow her to read and think enough. Her dream was to be a lawyer. To the outside, she was a "drop-out" but this is what she wrote, calling out into the world:

> You talk about the problems of the world
> And I'm not allowed to speak cause I'm just a little girl.
> But there's something I'd like to say to you,
> You know,
> It's my world too.
>
> You think that you can understand more than anyone at all
> But, mister you're really short when you think you're tall!
> And I'm not allowed to give my opinions cause I'm not as big
>   as you.
> Try not to forget,
> It's my world too.
>
> They talk about the young people all the time
> But they don't think about others who are out of line
> And some problems mean nothing to you
> But while I'm living here,
> It's my world too.
>
> What I want is for the best for everyone
> 'Cause thinking of yourself is not good in the long run
> So think about, what do you want for me and you
> And while you're thinking, remember,
> It's my world too!

BOBBIE PREWITT (18, White, rural)

A public issue we singled out was the girls' attitudes toward the *women's movement*. Without question, the woman's role was a very important subject to them. It directly and indirectly affected much of their thinking and feeling. They often talked spontaneously about it. But they were comparatively uninterested in the women's movement. If we had discussed the movement with young college or middle-class or professional women we probably would have gotten a much greater response than we received from our girls, aged 12 to 18. Only half the girls whom we interviewed have anything to say about the women's movement, and usually only when they were asked about it. In general, it had very little personal meaning to them.

As with some other political issues that were mentioned earlier, one must make a distinction between the girls' attitudes toward the movement as a political *activity* and some of the *issues* that are related to this movement. The movement itself, which was, if the girl knew anything about it, frequently referred to as "women's lib," was negatively perceived by about a third of the girls and this perception was augmented by those who had never heard of it. (Remember also that this means only one-third of one-half of *all* the girls.) We heard comments like "this is just a bunch of silly women trying to draw attention to themselves" or "I think they have some good points but they go too far on some things like burning their bras." Few girls had any intention of joining the movement; they did not consider the movement valuable or an obligation.

> I think women's liberation is kind of stupid. Some women just want to get publicity or something like that. They would have to go to the army and all that. If they want to go to the army, let them go; I don't want to go.
>
> (17, *White, rural*)

> Well, what they're going to end up doing by all this complaining and everything is . . . there won't be women as such anymore, but it'll be more or less a name tag just for the sex instead of the idea of being a woman. You know, like some old forty-year-old broad is out there pounding away on a railroad tie; she isn't really what I would call being a woman—she's just a female out there trying to be equal. And they're going to destroy what they've got going for them. (14, *White, suburban*)

> I think women's liberation is dumb anyway. Women were put on this earth for two different reasons, not for one. Women are trying to be too much like men. Men are supposed to be the domineering, male figure or whatever you want; I believe in it to a certain extent. (17, *White, urban*)

> A lot of us think that the women now that are fighting for all this junk might just get everything they want but they are not going to have to pay for the consequences. Like if they pass this women's rights bill, where women are equal to men, then you will have to go to war. There's a lot of girls in the army but are not at the front. And if they get equal rights, I don't think these people that are yelling about this now, are going to have to do that, but it's an upcoming generation. Sometimes I agree with it, like pay things and like that. But what I can't understand is, if a single girl is running against a man that has a family with seven or eight kids—and because of this equal rights, the man is out of a job, he doesn't have any way to support his family, and this woman is just single, then I can't see that. But if they are both single and are trying for the same job, I can't see why a woman can't get it. Some things I agree with and some things I don't. (14, *White, rural*)

The girl who actively wanted to be a part of the movement seldom surfaced in our interviews. Here was a rare exception.

> I just realized while washing my hair that I really have changed. I've become more aware about the women's movement. And I have *changed,* I am *really* different from last year . . . last year I was kind of outside of the movement. Some things I thought were good and others I thought were stupid. I was so ignorant in the eighth grade. . . . (From a diary, 17, *White, urban*)

But the picture is totally different when we move away from the movement and look at the *issues* related to the women's movement. We can say with confidence that the majority of girls thought that there should be equal job opportunity, equal pay for equal work. There was less support for equal social status, although some strong feelings were stressed, especially in the area of marriage and the opportunity to participate in sports. "Equal pay for equal work" and "equal job opportunity," as mentioned, had entered into the consciousness of the girls. They had been accepted—with very few exceptions—without question. But there were differences of opinion in relation to specifics—as, for instance, whether women should do hard physical labor, whether women should be drafted, and whether they should lose some of the courtesies extended to them by men.

Girls want to be *persons*. At times the issue of equal rights became a very personal one because they themselves felt discriminated against within their families or saw their mothers being pushed around. One girl said:

> I don't believe in burning bras and all that, but I believe in women having equal rights . . . that I won't have to be run over by no man. That I won't have to put up with anybody else's bull.   (18, *White, urban*)

And others:

> I'd rather be a boy. I have always wanted to be a boy. Because like, they can do more things than a woman can. Like, when I was little, it seemed like the little boys can stay out late; but the girls have to come in early. And they can do more things than women.   (17, *Black, urban*)

> Sometimes I wish I was a boy, though. I mean, oh, I guess that's when mommy and daddy won't let me do something. You're a girl, you know. My little brother, he's almost allowed to do everything I'm allowed to do. Just 'cause he's a little boy and I'm a girl.   (15, *White, rural*)

> At home, boys are treated a lot different than me; they have a lot more freedom than I do. Like, my brother—well, my big brother can do a lot more stuff than I can. He doesn't even have to check with my mom; he has no deadlines to be home. And my little brother, he's only twelve years old, and he goes to all these places; he's always spending the night at somebody's house, you know, 'cause he's a boy. My mom says, "Boys are just like that. They're real active." Except I'm active, and my mom says "Uh, no, I don't think you better go out tonight; just stay home, be with your family." And my brothers are all gone, you know. It's just—she gives 'em a lot more freedom 'cause they're boys. She's afraid something's going to happen to me.   (16, *White, urban*)

In spite of their strong belief in equal pay for equal work, for many the principle did not apply to physical labor.

> Some of the things they were doing were pretty good, you know. Equal rights for work and pay and all that. I thought that was pretty good. Some of

the stuff, you know. Like working construction and all that. I didn't think too much of that. (13, *American Indian, rural*)

I think, if a woman is doing the same job as a guy, she should get the same pay. But I think a lot of jobs women aren't capable of doing because we're built differently—physical strength. I think a lot of women are really dumb in going out for it, because we are brought up, we are much more emotional than guys and can't take it.

I don't particularly want to go out and fight in wars. If you took 100 women and 100 guys and they were put on the front in the war, the women are probably more likely to crack and couldn't shoot, and that type of thing. I don't know if that's the way we are brought up—or our body chemistry.

(17, *White, suburban*)

Over and over we find this reference to a given weaker biological capacity. It was questioned by only a handful of girls, though recent experiments have shown that nutrition and exercises have a great deal to do with these male/female differences. History has known women warriors who were physically very capable, and the experience of men and women in the concentration camps of Europe under the Nazi regime bear testimony to the extraordinary physical and emotional stamina of women.

The resistance to physical labor is partially related to misinformation and partially to a personal fear of being left with it, especially for the girl who has experienced in her own family the drudgery of such work.

Well, I can see equal rights and equal pay, but some of the extremes, they are going too far. Like some of 'em are working, you know, these hard machines that men do, like they pour concrete and do all this other stuff, and I don't think that's right. Because I'd like to have equal pay, sure, but I mean I wouldn't go to that extreme. Cause in Russia . . . like the women have to do jobs like that; they have to operate cranes, because, there's more women than men in Russia. They've always been faced with that kind of work. But some of these women over here, I don't think will ever take it. (18, *White, rural*)

When one first listened, it seemed that the frequent resentment expressed at the loss of social prerogatives (having doors opened for them) to explain their opposition to the women's movement was very superficial. But as one listened more closely, the reasoning became more profound. Girls who expressed opposition did not necessarily want a totally traditional role for women nor were they just spoiled "little women." Only one of them talked about always wanting to "be babied." What they expressed was a wish to be cherished, to experience gentleness in human relations.

I think we should get equal job opportunities and equal pay for equal work, but a man is definitely different from a woman and I like the differences. I enjoy having them hold my coat, opening doors and things like that. It's a way of making me feel special.

If a woman wants a career, the husband should share the responsibilities for the home. I don't think the woman's place should necessarily be in the home full time unless she wants it that way. (14, *White, urban*)

I'm for it to some extent. Then, I'm not for it. I think a woman should be a woman and a man should be a man in a way. I would still like a man to open a car door for me, or treat me like a lady. I don't want to be treated like a man, 'cause I guess, 'cause I am a lady.

Seems like boys are freer than girls, and a lot of times seems like a boy could do something and he wouldn't get put down for it. If a woman did something she would be put down for it. It's a man's world, I can tell you that.

(18, *Black, urban*)

The way I feel about women's lib is I agree with some of it and I disagree with some of it. I agree that women should have the same pay for the same jobs if they are qualified for it, without saying, "Well, this is a man's job." When guys open doors, it's nice, and I like guys to still be courteous. (15, *White, urban*)

Besides work and pay and equality in the home, girls talked about equal opportunity for education.

I don't know if it's true but I feel that if you can put me next to a male, I can do just as good as he can as far as studies go. I might not be able to lift a thousand pounds like he can, but if you tell me how much there is, six times two, or whatsoever, I surely can tell you. . . . Equal job opportunity and so forth, I am all for it. (17, *Black, urban*)

I think the fact that if a woman has a college degree and if they both apply for the same job, she may be just as qualified or more. I think then she should get the job. There is no questions. (15, *White, urban*)

Girls did not think it desirable to serve in the army but then many objected to the draft for boys, too.

I don't feel women should be drafted. I don't want to go into the army. But I do think if a woman wanted to go out and work in ditches, I don't see why she couldn't, for the same pay. I think they should get the same pay because women are just as smart. (16, *White, small town*)

Women's equality is a good idea but some people can go way too far on it. Like going to war and stuff. I don't think anybody should go to war. I don't think that's right. (17, *White, urban*)

Equality in sports was apt to be mentioned separately because it was something tangible to succeed in for the individual girl and the discrimination against girls in this area was so obvious in school.

Number one, do you know football? Why can't there be a girls' football team? Why can't there be a girls' baseball team? Why should they [the boys] be allowed to have it and not us? It's not fair. (13, *White, urban*)

Women do not have as many recreation facilities as do men. Everywhere we go men got everything, you know. All we see is men; I get sick and tired of looking at men like that. I like to see some women get out there and do something, you know. (13, *Black, urban*)

Like a girl I know, she's only little, she tried out for Little League and they wouldn't let her join because she was a girl. I think it's pretty rotten. They wouldn't let me race in the Patriots' Day road race because I was a girl. I wrote a letter to the editor. I went to the director of the Boys Club and gave them a copy of the letter and sent it in to the paper and the next year they let girls in. (14, *White, suburban*)

Like in sports, we think girls should have an equal opportunity, like in girls' basketball and girls' tennis. We think we should compete against boys in some things and in some things not. (15, *White, rural*)

In general, with a few exceptions, concern for women's rights was not a "cause." We found no burning anger or deep emotions related to the women's movement. Not a single poem was written about it. Clearly, women in the United States are not so subjugated as women in some other countries[2] and also the present older generation has opened many doors for women. No blood has been shed in the fight for women's rights; no jails have been filled in recent years. The progress in women's rights in the 1960s and 70s was and is more a struggle of women in the upper economic levels for self-fulfillment, for equal opportunity for participation in the nation's life; but it is not a drama of brutal suppression nor has it the urgency of basic deprivation. Other kinds of discrimination, especially the one based on race, are still so much harder to fight against—hurt so much more! If, for example, any girl could experience what Katherine J. Kennedy, a Black *Globe* staff member, experienced when she rode a bus carrying Black children from Roxbury to South Boston, she would know that the horror of discrimination and prejudice against being Black is so much greater and unyielding than anything she could experience from being discriminated against as a woman. Katherine Kennedy wrote:

If you're Black and were on a school bus in South Boston last week, it didn't matter whether you were a bus driver, monitor, student or reporter. To the hostile crowds, you were just a busload of "niggers." [3]

She, along with children in the busses, saw people standing along curbs and in the streets making faces and jeering.

"Niggers," "animals," "Niggers aren't human," they shouted. Old and young were sticking out their tongues.

This experience is certainly nowhere duplicated in relation to being a woman. It is understandable, therefore that, especially for girls from the minority groups, the women's movement is significant in terms of equal

[2] Judith Blake, "The Changing Status of Women in Developed Countries," *Scientific American*, September 1974, pp. 137–147.

[3] Katherine J. Kennedy, "View from a School Bus in South Boston: An Angry Crowd Screaming 'Nigger.' " *Boston Sunday Globe*, September 22, 1974.

pay for equal work, but has no great emotional meaning. At times they rejected identification with it.

> Women's lib is fine for white people but not for Black. No. I'm not for women's lib. (16, *Black, urban*)

Yet the position of women was part of a general concern to be treated as equals. An American Indian girl said:

> I'd like to be a politician. I'd like to be something that a lady never was, you know, and what a man does and all that. That's what I'd like to be; I don't want to do just everything a woman does and be the way a woman is now. I think things ought to change, really. It can't be like it was a long time ago where women stayed in the house and had kids and all that. I think it's rotten what they do now. (15, *American Indian, small town*)

Some girls who felt strongly about discrimination also took the women's movement seriously, but they saw it as part of a general liberation of subjugated groups. A girl from a blue-collar background summarized the feeling.

> . . . most of the girls who were taking the class [about the women's movement] were saying, "Men and women are equal, the women are better." I don't like that either. So, I'm not a feminist and I think they waste too much time thinking about liberating separate groups. There should just be a human liberation. It has to be everybody pulling together, men and women, Blacks, Whites, Chicanos and everybody else. When you become a feminist, then you are labeled again and that's ishy. (17, *White, urban*)

We can say, then, that the girls who were at all interested in or acquainted with the women's movement agreed in general with the principle of equality of the sexes, and that most girls wanted equal opportunity. Many thought that there is an anatomical difference between men and women in regard to their strength in performing certain jobs and wanted some protection for women from heavy physical labor.

It is significant that out of the entire group of girls interviewed, not even a quarter of them (192 out of 920 girls) were in favor of the women's movement as a *movement*. This can be interpreted in many different ways. I think it relates partially to what we see in all political issues—namely, that people do not know enough about how to work actively on behalf of issues, but are nevertheless interested in them. Also, this generation of girls seems to be not given to extremes and seems to be rather sober in its thinking through of issues in general and this one in particular. Symbolic acts and rhetoric of the women's movement seemed to have little appeal for them. Their concern was with equality of education, of employment, of training, of equality in the marriage situation, and of equality with boys at home and in school.

SUMMARY

1. The girls were concerned with major issues of the day but thought in terms of simplistic solutions.
2. Politics was frequently considered "dirty."
3. There was very strong individualism in relation to political issues and very little knowledge of how to translate ideals into reality.
4. Girls were politically active primarily because of intellectual interest, only occasionally because of a sense of social responsibility.
5. Active involvement in political movements was approximately equal among white girls and girls of minority backgrounds.
6. Major concerns of social importance were prejudice, war, and corruption in government.
7. The vast majority of the girls, regardless of racial or ethnic background, were against prejudice.
8. There were girls who resented others of various backgrounds, partially out of fear and partially out of limited personal experience. Most of them wanted to overcome this feeling.
9. Actual friendships across racial and ethnic lines were often desired, but were resisted by the adult population, and some young people as well.
10. Girls expressed concern with issues relating specifically to young people— e.g., curfews and juvenile justice.
11. Comparatively few knew much about or identified positively with the women's movement.
12. Issues fought for in the women's movement, especially equal pay and opening of job opportunities, were favored by most of the girls, but they did not approve of the movement as a political device.
13. In spite of comparatively little interest in political organization, many girls wanted to participate in public affairs but did not know how to go about it.
14. Adjudicated girls were most alienated. There seems to be no effort to make them feel a responsible part of the wider community.

BIBLIOGRAPHY

ADELSON, J. and R. P. O'NEIL," Growth of Political Ideas in Adolescence: The Sense of Community," *Journal of Personality and Social Psychology*, Vol. IV, No. 3, 1966, pp. 295–306.

JOHNSON, N. R., "Political Climates and Party-Choice of High School Youth," *Public Opinion Quarterly*, Vol. XXXVI, No. 1, 1972, pp. 48–55.

KENNEDY, KATHERINE J., "View from a School Bus in South Boston: An Angry Crowd Screaming 'Nigger,' " *Boston Sunday Globe*, September 22, 1974.

"Student Survey," *Playboy*, Vol. XVII, No. 9, 1970.

"Student Survey," *Playboy*, Vol. XVIII, No. 9, 1971.

The Mood of American Youth, 1974, Reston, Va.: National Association of Secondary School Principals, 1974.

THOMAS, L. E., "Family Correlates of Student Political Activism," *Developmental Psychology*, Vol. IV, No. 2, 1971, pp. 206–214.

THOMPSON, JANE E., "Political Awareness Among High School and College Women," *Journal of the National Association of Women Deans and Counselors*, Vol. XXXVI, No. 2, Winter 1973, pp. 74–75.

NINE

WHAT IS AND WHAT SHOULD BE

We must try, for trying helps us succeed.
We must care for caring is wanting.
We must want for wanting helps us out.
We must build up for we don't break down.
We must help for help is always needed.
We must always speak truth for we block out lies.
We must speak our piece for we know what to say.
We must live, for we know we will die.
We must think for our brain is desired.
We must have peace for we want no wars.
We must not fight for we all have and need friends.
We must love for loving is to be loved.
We must do right and just things for we need no wrong.
We must cry out for we need to be heard.
We must not turn off for we need communication
        ANONYMOUS (14, *American Indian, urban*)

This value list made by a girl in a delinquency institution represents the same values that most people, whether young or old, would agree upon. Those who decry present-day youth are constantly worried about the loss of such values. We did not find evidence of a loss of values, but the way the girls translated values into reality and *stressed* particular values is significant for the young women of our time and needs to be understood. What are these values?

1. There was a strong and almost pervasive emphasis on *autonomy*. The young women wanted a say in their own destiny, and at an earlier age than this society is accustomed to. They insisted on the right to be an individual. "I am human; I am equal to adults as well as to man" was an accepted value. We saw and heard that comment from girls from so-called "modern" as well as from very traditional families, for example, from ethnic groups in which the male was overpoweringly dominant. Those girls had an especially hard struggle. They knew that "equality" was a value in the larger culture, but they did not always know how to impart it to persons in their own immediate environment. They felt guilty because of this conflict with their families. And in a period such as ours, when "ethnic tradition" is regarded as almost holy, they were in great conflict with themselves. Yet, the majority of girls we talked to accepted the value

of personal autonomy in a rather matter-of-fact way. It was something "given," not to be fought for. Those who saw personal autonomy as an issue were those who had suffered from serious personal discrimination either because of their minority status, status as women, or status as young people. To some of the older young people, the college group who helped to analyze our material, this generation of high school girls seemed too conservative, too "tame." In my opinion, they reflected the typical attitude of people who have profited from the fight of others. There is a similar phenomenon, for instance, in the economic struggle that labor unions waged in this country.

The "they" that is used here is especially dangerous since there are large groups of young people who have not profited from the struggle for equality during the 1960s, and therefore either despair or rebel against the discrepancy between what they consider their right and what is actually accorded to them.

2. Value was attached to *family life*, but in a particular sense: *family life should be based on mutual trust and respect between men and women.* Family harmony was especially valued, with a high expectation that it is based on honest and open communication and not on submission of the woman to the man.

Cooperation on an equal footing between husband and wife was valued by almost all the girls. There was a range of opinion from those who wanted to maintain a rather clear role differentiation—the husband working outside the home and the wife inside the home—and those who did not. Yet they want their contribution to the family, whatever it is, to be valued highly.

Having children and raising children was highly valued by the majority of the girls. Yet having children was not regarded as a "duty" nor was it accepted as something that fate had imposed on them. *Having children was part of the freedom and responsibility of having choices about the matter.* And again, to have such choice was highly valued. In the minority were girls who did not know that they had such a choice or considered it wrong to place this decision into the realm of reality.

Raising of children in its entire consequence frequently was not grasped. The view of child rearing was "taking care of babies."

3. *Material goods* were valued. It is not true, as it seemed during the sixties, that young people totally reject possession of material goods. We frequently heard expressed wishes for comfortable housing, for opportunity to travel, for good clothes, cars, and bicycles. Significantly, these wishes were expressed more often by those who came from poverty backgrounds. It was also expressed by those who were older and had had to struggle to find work or remain in school. Total rejection of material goods occasionally was found among upper-income girls who were turned off by what they considered a far too materialistic and non-caring outlook on the part of their parents. Yet, some among this same group took comfort and

luxury for granted. We found only a few. The stereotype of a totally non-materialistic youth versus a materialistic adult generation is just as ridiculous as that touted just preceding the 1960s, when many adult preachers brought fire and brimstone down on the "materialistic" young people. Obviously there is a wide range of opinion among young people not only regarding the value of money, but also concerning what they want to do with it.

4. Also contrary to some popular thinking, most of the girls we talked to, who addressed themselves to this subject, saw education as an important part of their lives, as a means of fulfilling life goals, vocationally or professionally. This concept has not really changed much down through the ages. Education or wish for education for the sake of knowledge is rare and, if it comes, it comes usually much later in life. But there has been a change in what is considered positive in education. A *creative component* of it appears as a value. A fulfillment of individual capacities is valued more now than in the periods when even the young often were satisfied with learning by rote, with mechanical repetition without thinking through problems. Education was most valued if it included a form of participation and actual involvement instead of forcing young people to be exclusively listeners and receivers of information.

5. *Honesty*, which is directly related to *trust*, was especially highly regarded. Trust was the cornerstone of human relations, something that should rule a person's dealings with others as well as in the relationships between nations and races. Phoniness was spotted very quickly and rejected with scorn. The girls cried for receiving trust and most of them were willing to return trust. In fact we were overwhelmed by the fact that interviewers, who were total strangers, were trusted even by those girls who had not had good relationships or experiences with adults and who had felt that their trust had been frequently betrayed. The demand for honesty was markedly stronger among the girls than in the wider fabric of society. The "games people generally play" with one another, including many of the so-called "treatment" therapies, totally contradict this ethos of honesty.

6. The girls valued *justice*, and especially *equal treatment of all people regardless of race, sex, national, or ethnic origin.* We found this value in the majority of girls, but not in all of them. There were bigots among them, as in the total population, some outspoken, some unaware of their prejudice. Their frequent and earnest concern for social justice leads at times to conflicts with elders. On the other hand, it also makes them, under other circumstances, close allies with those of the older generation who are active in such movements.

7. *Cooperation* was stressed. The value of competition, strong in our society, was hardly acknowledged. I do not know whether this means that we have really entered a period of less competitive and more cooperative

relationships among people, but most of the young women in our group seemed to adhere closely to Kipling's[1] idea.

And no one shall work for money, and no one shall work for fame,
But each for the joy of the working, and each, in his separate star,
Shall draw the thing as he sees It for the God of Things as They are!

8. Related to this more cooperative value system was the high value accorded honest, open, and gentle *intimacy*. The picture of the United States as a prudish, puritanical country in which people constantly suppress their true feelings, is a totally misleading one even for the past decades. It is exclusively related to one part of the population, predominantly middle-class Anglo-Saxon, but even here it does not represent the completely true picture. The United States never has been as puritanical as present-day China or as Russia after the revolution. The lusty custom of "bundling" in early Pennsylvania,[2] the open necking on the shores of the Atlantic on Coney Island in the early 1940s, the affectionate warm embraces among family members or friends certainly do not indicate a very puritanical general culture. For many people in the United States, intimacy is not a new phenomenon. It was missing in families in the past twenty or thirty years when parents pursued competitive goals that took all their attention. This lack of intimacy occurred more often in the upper income strata. But the unfair generalizations prompted by the television portrayal of a family like the Louds[3] in California, to the stereotyped paper doll people as drawn in *The War Between the Tates* by Alison Lurie,[4] has led adults and young people alike to assume that these figures are representative of the American family. They surely are not, and never were.

Yet this generalization about American puritanism may have produced one positive result: the pervasive antipathy of most young people to superficial and cold relationships. The essential loneliness of all human beings continues to exist—and I do think that this is a basic human trait—but high value is placed on overcoming it, moving out of it. Sex is discussed openly and premarital sex is not considered a sin. But most girls hoped that sex would be part of a genuine and responsible relationship.

9. *There was no particular stress on involvement in political and social issues.* A few felt a sense of social obligation; many hoped for specific social and

---

[1] Rudyard Kipling, "When Earth's Last Picture," *The Oxford Dictionary of Quotations*, 2nd ed. London: Oxford University Press, 1955, p. 303.

[2] "Lovers or engaged couples, partly dressed, lay or slept together on or in the same bed." *Britannica World Language Dictionary*, Vol. 1. New York: Funk and Wagnall's, 1956, p. 180.

[3] *An American Family*, 12-week series, begun January 11, 1973, KTCA, Channel 2, Educational Television, Minnesota.

[4] Lurie, Alison, *The War Between the Tates*. New York: Random House, 1974.

political improvements, such as peace and better human relations, especially among races.

10. There was a serious struggle to find *meaning in life*, a struggle common to all adolescents. This is a search that never ends, and the most alive adults are those who always continue the quest. Still, adolescence is the time of life when doubts are especially strong because one cannot follow totally in the footsteps of the adult. We found that this generation of young women struggled with particular confusions. They had been taught that they should think for themselves, but frequently they were punished for doing so. They found an enormous amount of conflicting expectations placed upon them. Some parts of the society wanted them to continue the traditional role of a pliable woman subjugated to the male, while others pushed them into extremes of independence. We found that many were quite able to find a reasonable definition of themselves as individuals and part of an interdependent society full of a variety of people. Some of the girls cope well, struggle, defy, work things through alone or with their peers or some adults. There are also many who are strangled by the conflicting goals. They become angry, at times violent; they withdraw into drugs, even suicide—they hurt very much.

This generation of young women also grows up in a period in which many myths are defunct, in which history for instance is being rewritten. They wonder what they should believe in and reject. In general, we did not encounter a totally "turned off," cynical attitude, but we did find a desperate searching for some answers to the question: "What is the meaning of life?" This search rarely surfaces in long, philosophical discussions. It is often expressed in mute desperate behavior, in a hopeless shrug of the shoulder, a drowning in alcohol, or in angry outbursts. These young women felt the complexity of their time. Some expressed it to themselves.

> *The earth in all its glory*
> *Suspended with no limits*
> *A peculiar pattern it traces;*
> *That we may rise each morn.*
>
> *A new day comes with wonder,*
> *Causing creature, a man, to ponder—*
> *As droplets envelop within*
> *Melt beneath the soil, then*
> *To only find the sun.*
>
> *Pressure, tension, agony, strain*
> *Striving toward an equal goal.*
> *After what one can gain.*
> *Can't you? Will you?*
> *Haven't you? Did you?*
> *Different—seeming the same.*
>
> VIDA BANHAM   (15, *Black, suburban*)

With their value system as a base, what were our findings concerning the girls' views *towards the major institutions* in which they were growing up?

1. *Family* had a deep meaning to them; they wanted a loving, open, stable family in which they were respected as human beings and accorded the same dignity as everyone else. They did not want a totally "permissive" atmosphere, but they definitely could not accept an authoritarian one. They wanted to create ideal families, in which they themselves, as adults, were respected human beings. This ideal applied to the girls who wanted to combine marriage with a career (the majority) as well as to those who wanted to make family life their total career.

The girls' family situations frequently were satisfactory, but we found serious hangovers of dictatorial behavior by parents as well as evidence of brutality, mental and physical. The victims themselves, "battered" adolescent girls, usually were blamed for such conditions by the wider community.

2. *School* was seen as offering the wonderful opportunity to be with their contemporaries, which the girls need very much. Schools also give stimulation and opportunity to learn which most girls want. But schools, too, labor under a tradition of autocracy and rigidity, of too little individualization and of frequent denial of respect to those who belong to a minority. There certainly are exceptions and the capacity of the American school system to develop various forms of schools, not based on economic or intellectual differences, has enormous potential.

3. *Youth-serving agencies* have the potential of fulfilling the girls' expressed needs for intimacy with their peers, of providing informal contact with understanding adults, and an outlet for their adventure spirits, and for giving the opportunity to discuss their problems and find life's meaning in interaction with both young and older people. Yet most youth serving organizations are not perceived as fulfilling this potential. Girls' organizations seemed to have lost their original momentum as "movements" and have become purely recreational organizations. Programs often were not individualized and leaders frequently were autocratic and did not know how to inspire imagination and creativity. We found girls not especially interested in a high degree of organizational structure, but wishing for informal contacts which voluntary agencies could provide. And, with exceptions, girls with difficulties felt alienated from those organizations.

4. Those organizations that were created *to help* the girl who has been *in difficulties* fell especially short of what they should be, in the eyes of the girls. The *juvenile justice system* most frequently exposed girls who already had been damaged by violence in the family, by failure in school, by isolation in the community, to exactly the same withering experiences.

> Being locked up, being made to do something (it's the worst thing). Locked up you can't get out some place; you can't say what you want, do what you

want. Bothered by the law and every one in the law, like they bust teenagers for just anything. Well, there's nothing you can do; they're over you. [Solution]: Blow everybody up. And get people to know what they're doing instead of just shooting down and hitting you on the head.   (15, *Chicana, urban*)

Got in a bunch of trouble for it, got put in the hole, that's what we call it, you know. It's like a padded cell, and there are no windows, nothing. And you know, in there they can beat you; but man, they threatened you a lot, too. And one time they did, they threw me in a cell; they just went and threw me up like that against the cell and I hit the back . . . hit the window with the bars, and I hit my head. There was a big lump on my head. So they were really mean. . . . I never knew people could be that mean.   (15, *White, small town*)

Usually when you are really upset and you are really raising up a storm, they put you in there and lock you up and what it does to me, it makes me even worse, 'cuz I sit there, and they move everything out, you don't have nothing to throw around or hit, so you end up pounding, kicking, and banging yourself up against the wall, and that's hurting you more than anything else. So I don't think a large place like this is any good at all. 'Cuz that's what us kids were trying to get away from in the first place, was the restrictions, and here we got even more.   (15, *Inuit, small town*)

What is that like? Something like jail. But just being here is jail, you know. You don't go nowhere. You stay in one big room; you get an hour out in the rec room every day, one hour! Here I'm just going crazy in that one room looking at four walls. If you do something they tell you not to do, you get three days strict in your room. You can't get to smoke; you don't get no snacks. But you buy your own snacks. If you don't have money, you don't get none no way.

(16, *Black, small town*)

This same girl described what happened to her after she delivered her baby.

They took it the second day after I was in the hospital . . . the third . . . the third day. The morning I was getting ready to leave and they took it. I didn't know nothing about that, but they took it, you know, the third day. I had no idea, nothing about it. I was ready to go home, and my mother and them went to go get the baby and they told her that the welfare lady had come and took it. And I didn't know nothing about it. I had so much planned, you know, for what we was going to do and everything. That's what really hurt me. Maybe if they would have given me a warning or something, I wouldn't be so hurt. When the welfare lady came to my house and my mother told me we didn't want to have anything to do with . . . we'd try to survive without them. Cause we had never been on welfare, you know. Fourteen kids in our family; we hadn't never asked them for nothing. That's why I felt bad about it, you know, because we hadn't never asked them for nothing. I had my mother and she was working, and my father was working and my boyfriend was working. He was willing to take care of the baby. And I figured we could make it. Go to court about that? I went to court, got a lawyer and went to court. But we didn't have that much money; we didn't have a very good lawyer, see.

These are not the policies nor the practices that are followed in good adoption agencies, but they do occur in delinquency institutions. The girls could not help one another.

> And my mother told me whenever I see anybody crying just try to talk to em, you know, and cheer em up or something. And, you know, really, up here you can't do it cause they'll start yelling at you. "You shut your mouth or else you're getting three days strict, you know." And you can't say nothing without getting them three days strict.
>
> And the girls in Cottage X, they're like confined, you know? Locked behind a door almost twenty-four hours. When you shut your door you cannot open it until they pop this button. So everytime we come up . . . they only give us about five or ten minutes to smoke and do this, you know. And it's really boring. It really upsets you. And you really get too much on your chest. And then, after so much, you're going to get mad and flare up and cut your arm like I did.   (17, *White, small town*)

This led to suicide or increased hate.

> And I looked in the housemother's face and I said, "You're going to keep it up until one of these days," I said, "You're getting paid back." I said "It might not be now, and it might not be soon," I said, "but I'll pay you back." And I'll pay her back.   (17, *White, small town*)

They learned to pretend "improvement" because they had to get out some way.

> You got to be on their schedule, you know. If you don't do what they want you to do, they'll lock the door on you—just like that. And I can't stand that. So I play along with it, you know. I get ready to go home and it'll be another long, long time before I come back here again. Shit.   (16, *Black, urban*)

So-called "therapy" consisted of forcing girls into more pretense.

> They always want to talk about it; they are always on the case to talk about it. "Let's talk, let's talk." I don't like that.   (16, *White, rural*)
>
> I been trying to keep a smile on my face while I'm here 'cause that's the only way to get out. I seem to get involved in a group and have a smile on my face. So I do it. I'm sad when I'm locked up. I don't want to be locked up, or in the room back there in security.   (16, *Black, urban*)

Perhaps the worst outcome of all this was that the girl herself began to resign herself to brutality and humiliation and stopped fighting. A very young girl responded to the question of what she would change for the better with a pitiful suggestion for "reform."

> I would make . . . I would have more than one supervisor on at once. Like I'd have two or three, maybe. And I wouldn't make them all women. There'd be some of 'em men. And I'd make them . . . not be able to hit you and stuff like that, like beat on you.
>
> Because a woman, if . . . like there's a fight or something, she'll just get in there and start beating on you. Beating both of you to make you stop. The man, all he has to do is grab your hands.   (14, *White, suburban*)

Substitutes for the girl's own home could be different if they offered an opportunity for girls to help one another, if they were staffed by understanding adults, and if there were room for individual decision-making by the girls. We found a few such places and listened to the girls' opinions about them.

> All the girls here try to help you out with your problems. Our counselor here, if you have a problem, go to her and she'll try to help you out. And if you don't want to go to her, talk to one of the girls cause she's your own age, and they'll try to help you out in all ways. It's a wonderful place . . . they're all here to help and to talk to you about it and to decide. These people here are like . . . almost like sisters and brothers if you don't have any. And so they really become closer to you.   (16, *White, urban*)

> I like it. It's not home; you're not around friends and your family and stuff, but I have visitors all the time so I don't get lonely and I made a couple of good friends since I came here.

> It was really good because it's the kind of a place where you can come to make a decision of your own. No decision, either way, is forced upon you. You can find all sides of anything, and they do give you all sides, like the good and the bad of adoption . . . it really opens your mind. I wasn't here two weeks when my knowledge must have increased 100 percent. I really love it here in a sense. Then there's the other sense of . . . that you still aren't living at home. In a way, those lonely nights you still feel kind of packed away. (14, *White, urban*)

In discussing societal institutions, I have already made value judgments and not confined myself exclusively to what the girls' opinions were about them. If our ideal were an authoritarian society and the production of subjects who obey the orders of one ruler, we would approve of places and manners and mores that force people into one mold. Obviously we have to clarify what kind of a society we are and want to be, to consider what services to provide for our young people, how we want to bring them up. From Jacques Maritain[5] on to many other recent observers of the North American scene, people have tried to describe this country. It is so varied, physically and culturally, that describing it is a complex task. To move towards any kind of system that suggests our relationships and our tasks in regard to our youth, we have to look at the goals of our society. Its basic value document is the Bill of Rights. Ideologically, then, this society should be

1. Open and free, based on the proposition that the purpose of government is to advance and protect basic human rights.
2. A representative democracy which means that citizens should have a say in their own destiny as well as that of the nation.
3. Ruled by law. Even though the law is made and administered by people, it should not be based on the arbitrary decisions of an autocrat.
4. Egalitarian and non-discriminatory, with equal opportunity for everybody.

[5] Jacques Maritain, *Reflections on America*. New York: Scribners, 1958.

5. Pluralistic, with opportunity for groups to follow a variety of life styles.

Those are the ideals. Programs and suggestions regarding work with young women must be congruent with the goals of a society. We therefore must combine the reality of what we heard about the needs and concerns and aspirations of the girls with the goals we think important and ethical. Such combination requires that *all* adolescents in our time be given opportunities:

To participate as citizens, as members of a household, as workers, as responsible members of society;

to gain experience in decision-making;

to interact with peers and acquire a sense of belonging;

to reflect on self in relation to others and to discover self by looking outward as well as inward;

to discuss conflicting values and formulate their own value system;

to experiment with their own identity, with relationships to other people, with ideas; to try out various roles without having to commit themselves irrevocably;

to develop a feeling of accountability in the context of a relationship among equals;

to cultivate a capacity to enjoy life.[6]

If they have these opportunities, then we can expect them to participate in their own society as healthy, comparatively satisfied, and responsible human beings.

Girls, even more than boys, have not been given enough of these opportunities. Creative thinking needs to be done *with* them to develop practical ways of translating these demands into reality. I would like to make a few suggestions, which grow out of what we heard during our interviews.

1. We should do away with the neat separation of family-school-youth organizations based on assumptions that are now obsolete: home is for support; school is for learning; youth organizations are for fun and character building. This separation does not work; it is illogical and damaging. The human being is a social and a complex one. All the various institutions in our society can and do choose major goals. But those that work with adolescents work with an age group in which DEVELOP-MENT is the critical issue. The people and the institutions that are privileged to work with the young must learn to say yes to the young, to recognize their potential, to sympathize with their difficult tasks. *They must learn to cooperate with young people, to meet them on common and equal ground.*

2. All societal institutions must place *priority on the kind of adult they choose or help develop to work with the young.* Essential qualities of such adults are:

a. capacity to listen and to empathize;

[6] See also Gisela Konopka, "Requirements for Healthy Development of Adolescent Youth," *Adolescence*, Vol. 8, No. 31, Fall 1973, pp. 291–316.

b. accepting young people as equals in society and understanding the great variety of their capacities and aspirations;

c. capacity to show their deep respect, regardless of race, ethnic background, economic status, etc.;

d. letting young people play a significant part in program and planning; programs run only by adults should be totally avoided;

e. accepting sex as a healthy part of a young person's total being;

f. understanding the impact of drugs and alcohol.

Such adults should themselves learn to be alive and interesting personalities. This means provision of good *parent education* and *education of staff and volunteers.* It is inconceivable that we continue to place the life and thinking and feeling of our youth in the hands of people who know less about them than a carpenter knows of wood. Such training should not be purely intellectual nor purely emotional and it must be gimmick free. It must include as a minimum:

a. knowledge of adolescence, with emphasis on the particular position of girls;

b. knowledge and appreciation of various cultures and economic groups and their value systems;

c. knowledge of our political system;

d. insight into oneself and one's philosophy about working with people;

e. skill in creating an atmosphere conducive to human growth, which includes honesty with young people, without being offensive.

Teachers, youth workers, social workers, and correctional workers can become significant to young people only if they are sensitive toward them, honest with them, and can offer in their work with them more than the raised finger, the moralistic talk, harsh confrontation, or information without allowing them to raise questions.

3. *Girls who have been subjected to severe violence, rape, or other harsh treatment should not be segregated.* For far too long they have been pushed into the correctional system, which has further diminished their sense of dignity. It is obvious that degrading and inhuman practices in mass institutions must cease. In these places, where the girl is supposed to be helped, more often the unbelievable degradation that started at home, in school, and in the neighborhood is continued. An entire separate inquiry must be made into these practices and it must be considered a priority item in relation to our girl population. This system has driven them often deeper into despair, into prostitution, and self-destruction. If it continues, we not only will add to it, but also will drive the girls more into violence directed towards other people because of their increased anger and frustration.

Schools and informal educational organizations such as the youth-serving ones (Camp Fire Girls, Big Sisters, Girl Scouts, 4-H, YWCA, etc.) should not see themselves serving only those girls who have a great deal of parental support and who do not question prevailing standards. They not only have to serve the girls in poverty areas, but they must also understand them as young people and consciously learn to find and develop their strengths. Youth-serving agencies should actively recruit girls who seem "difficult."

4. *Informal organizations* for girls must be accorded more recognition. Our work with young people, especially girls, has led me to believe that interest in the informal youth-serving organizations is decreasing. Most of them started around the middle of the twentieth century as very meaningful movements, but they have increasingly lapsed into purely recreational organizations. Their financial support has dwindled, and with it their own sense of significance. A leading representative of one of these organizations once remarked in a meeting that her move from college teaching into one of these organizations meant almost complete loss of status for her in the eyes of other professionals. There is hidden gold in the potential of these organizations, but it has to be mined and the organizations themselves have to make their programs relevant to girls today. I am convinced that they themselves, with the help of their constituency, will find and develop programs that will make them as important as formal educational institutions. I will name a few projects that come into my mind.

A. Youth organizations and schools should include early, honest and informed *sex education* programs in their offerings that enable girls (all young people) to express their feelings and not let them feel that they are merely attending a biology lecture. Every youth worker must be able to discuss sex openly and competently with girls, and at an early age. Youth organizations should provide "listening" posts, drop-in services, or whatever one wants to call them—a place where the girls can talk to an adult confidentially without, as one girl put it, "always making an appointment."

B. Programs of youth-serving agencies should encourage *active participation* in public life—not "social studies classes" but actual learning how one can become effective in one's community. The inclusion of young lawyers as resource people and development of a youth force that is knowledgable about laws that concern young people can be valuable and an exciting project to develop. What Ralph Nader has done for consumers, young people should be stimulated and helped to do for themselves about the laws that directly concern them.

C. Youth-serving agencies should help girls find *real work*, not only traditional work, and should become a force to encourage economists, management, and labor to develop work opportunities for young women instead of bemoaning that they are an addition to the labor market. These agencies, together with higher education, must develop *work studies* which allow the girl from low income areas to gain an education and therefore hope for the future. And they must become active in legislation to develop scholarships for college education and vocational education.

D. High priority should be given to real outlets for the spirit of adventure. Co-ed organizations can equip themselves better for these outlets. There should be youth hostels all over the country, including "swimming hostels," that would enable young people to get to know the land without having to expose themselves to the dangers of the road. Boys and girls can learn to cooperate on such voyages.

E. It is most important to help girls develop *individual or group projects* and to diminish "canned programs." These projects must bring tangible success to individual girls or to a small group of girls who want to work together. They may prove especially exciting to girls if they allow them to *experience new non-traditional roles*, as, for instance:

the development of a youth lobby in the legislature;

the actual physical building of a youth center in which girls themselves lay the bricks, do the carpentry work, etc.

taking responsibility for young people in institutions for delinquents, and staying with them when they return to their homes;

taking on this kind of responsibility with a girl who has serious problems in her own home;

designing comprehensive services for single mothers and their children;

monitoring units that serve girls outside their homes. Even small community-based units could develop into traps and need monitoring.

F. All organizations and individuals who work with young people must realize that they must make the young *active participants* and not program *for* them. Often adults should be present as resources and as consultants and at times as sensitive listeners. But they are not there constantly to impose their own ideas on the young. The rigid club, for instance, is as distasteful to many of our young girls as a rigid forty-five-minute class period in which the teacher lectures and the students quietly take notes. Those forms occasionally may be appropriate.

Certainly basic to all those efforts is a society that genuinely loves and respects its young people. The movement for "youth rights" has raised almost as much storm as the movement for racial equality. There appears to be deep fear of—and some real hostility toward—youth. The movement toward more equal rights for women is regarded with even more anger because it violates the traditional picture of girls as being "sugar and spice and everything nice" and deprives the total population of a large number of rather submissive people. Often such opposition is rationalized or disguised by the argument that too much freedom means too much license. Too many rights will enable young people who have "no judgment" to do whatever they please. This is a faulty argument. Having rights never means complete and unlimited freedom, either for young or old. Rights are always limited by the rights of others. It includes the responsibility to regard the rights of others. People who are subjugated do not learn this responsibility. They learn to "obey" only as long as they are watched by those who have power over them. Unquestionably, a society that allows its citizens to make choices places a high responsibility on them. It is easier to follow orders—or to reject them angrily, blaming those who gave them, than to take on the responsibility for one's own decisions. And it is unfair to expect adults—or teenagers—to learn to make decisions without letting them try out their wings early, letting them make simple and then more and more complicated decisions, letting them make mistakes and thereby learn from them. Our main task is to let young people learn to make decisions on their own and trust them, without expecting that they will always make the right decisions, or the decisions we consider right. We must let them try. One girl described this best:

> *I used to be the cocoon—*
> *all wrapped up in what I then thought was safety—*
> *insulating myself from all the hurts and the joys of life.*
> *Afraid of so much—*
> *of love, strangers, of trying new things,*
> *of being rejected, of being wrong,*
> *of being laughed at or of just being. . . .*
> *Swaddled in my security blanket,*
> *I missed so much. . . .*
> *Now I am the worm—*
> *just breaking the cocoon, crawling slowly.*
> *Inching my way toward the light,*
> *Crawling a little each day (I hope)*
> *Trying not to slip back a foot for every inch I gain. . . .*
> *Someday I will be that butterfly,*
> *Free and glorious, not afraid of everything I do.*
> JOANNE RHIGER (16, *White, urban*)

Will we help or will we—as we have done too often—stamp out the larva and never let the butterfly live? Or will we prepare our young to be more than butterflies? Help them to enjoy life, yes, but also help them find a meaning in life that makes them feel fulfilled, respected, part of a humanity that they can cherish and that cherishes them.

> *I've been lost for so long and,*
> *like the night fading into day,*
> *my hopes slowly passed away.*
> *I lose touch with the stars in my imaginary space*
> *and when the sun shows,*
> *it melts away gladness.*
> *I hide tears when I am weakest*
> *to show I am strongest.*
> *Time has overpowered me*
> *and I am lost in minutes.*
> *I need to be needed!*

And so, you see my friend,
I am yours to listen
But I have no answers
So you must seek for what is lost—
I can only be there clearing the path of obstacles.

ROBIN WHITE (16, *Black, urban*)

They are not all exciting, beautiful, idealistic, but they are an amazing struggling generation with an overwhelming potential—we can and we must work *with* them to open the doors to life—with its sorrow, unhappiness, meanness, but also possible joy and meaningful fulfillment.

BIBLIOGRAPHY

ALEXANDER, THERON, *Human development in an Urban Age.* Englewood Cliffs, N.J.: Prentice-Hall, 1973.

An American Family, 12-week series, begun January 11, 1973. KTCA, Channel 2. Educational Television, Minnesota.

Center for Youth Development and Research, *Youth Responds to Social Systems*, Seminar Series No. 2. University of Minnesota, Minneapolis: Center for Youth Development and Research, 1971.

HEALEY, GARY W. and RICHARD R. DeBLASSIE, "A Comparison of Negro, Anglo, and Spanish-American Adolescents' Self-Concepts," *Adolescence*, Vol. IX, No. 33, Spring 1974, pp. 15–24.

KONOPKA, GISELA, "Corrections and Human Dignity," *Georgia Journal of Corrections*, Vol. 3, No. 1, Winter 1974, pp. 49–57.

———, "Formation of Values in the Developing Person," *American Journal of Orthopsychiatry*, Vol. XLIII, No. 1, January 1973, pp. 86–96.

———, "Requirements for Healthy Development of Adolescent Youth," *Adolescence*, Vol. VIII, No. 31, Fall 1973, pp. 291–316.

LURIE, ALISON, *The War Between the Tates.* New York: Random House, 1974.

MARITAIN, JACQUES, *Reflections on America.* New York: Scribners, 1958.

INDEX